The Penitential Psalms

The Penitential Psalms

The Rise, Fall, and Future of the Seven Psalms

EDITED BY MARK J. WHITING

Foreword by Susan Gillingham
Epilogue by Ian Stackhouse

WIPF & STOCK · Eugene, Oregon

THE PENITENTIAL PSALMS
The Rise, Fall, and Future of the Seven Psalms

Copyright © 2025 Wipf and Stock Publishers. All rights reserved. Except for brief quotations in critical publications or reviews, no part of this book may be reproduced in any manner without prior written permission from the publisher. Write: Permissions, Wipf and Stock Publishers, 199 W. 8th Ave., Suite 3, Eugene, OR 97401.

Wipf & Stock
An Imprint of Wipf and Stock Publishers
199 W. 8th Ave., Suite 3
Eugene, OR 97401

www.wipfandstock.com

PAPERBACK ISBN: 979-8-3852-1489-1
HARDCOVER ISBN: 979-8-3852-1490-7
EBOOK ISBN: 979-8-3852-1491-4

VERSION NUMBER 12/16/25

Permissions

The cover photograph of Roger Wagner's *The Flowering Tree*, a stained-glass window installed in St. Mary's Church, Iffley (Oxfordshire, UK), is used with kind permission of the artist.

Excerpts from *A Book of Psalms* by Edward Clarke
Copyright 2020 Edward Clarke
Used by permission of Paraclete Press

Bible verses denoted as KJV are taken from the KING JAMES VERSION, public domain.

Bible verses denoted as NIV are Scripture quotations taken from The Holy Bible, New International Version®, NIV®. Copyright © 1973, 1978, 1984, 2011 by Biblica, Inc. Used with permission of Zondervan. All rights reserved worldwide. www.zondervan.com

Bible verses denoted as NRSV are from the New Revised Standard Version Bible, copyright © 1989 National Council of the Churches of Christ in the United States of America. Used by permission. All rights reserved worldwide.

For Anne and Richard
For Mum and Dad

Contents

List of Contributors | ix
Foreword | xiii
    Susan Gillingham
Acknowledgments | xvii
    Mark J. Whiting
Abbreviations | xix
Introduction | xxi
    Mark J. Whiting

Part 1: Setting the Scene

1   The Uniqueness of the Penitential Psalms | 3
    Mark J. Whiting

2   Opening Up the Penitential Psalms | 20
    Richard S. Briggs

Part 2: The Rise and Fall

3   The Seven Penitential Psalms in the Hands of the Allegorist | 41
    Jason Byassee

4   From the Sixth Century to the Thirteenth Century | 53
    Mark J. Whiting

5   From the Fourteenth Century to the Sixteenth Century | 69
    Mark J. Whiting

6   Fear and Hope in the Life of the Justified:
    Luther's Reading of the Penitential Psalms | 87
    Channing L. Crisler

7   "A Limited and Restrained Form": John Donne
    Reads the Penitential Psalms | 104
    EMMA RHATIGAN

8   C. H. Spurgeon: Treasuring David's Penitential Psalms | 122
    PETER J. MORDEN

9   Bonhoeffer and the Penitential Psalms | 137
    TIM JUDSON

Part 3: The Penitential Psalms Today

10 The Musical Legacy of the Seven Psalms | 157
    JONATHAN ARNOLD

11 Preaching the Penitential Psalms | 172
    STEPHEN I. WRIGHT

12 The Beauty of Penitence | 187
    KAREN CASE-GREEN

13 The Seven: A *Prosimetrum* | 203
    EDWARD CLARKE

Epilogue | 219
    IAN STACKHOUSE

Index | 225

List of Contributors

Jonathan Arnold is executive director of the Social Justice Network, Canterbury Diocese, and an honorary research fellow, University of Kent. Formerly he was dean of Divinity and fellow of Magdalen and Chaplain of Worcester Colleges, Oxford. Publications include *Sacred Music in Secular Society* (2014); *Music and Faith: Conversations in a Post-Secular Age* (2019); *The Everyday God* (2024).

Richard S. Briggs is principal of Lindisfarne College of Theology and an honorary fellow in Old Testament at Durham University's Department of Theology and Religion. He has taught Old Testament in the North East for over twenty years, and worked in a range of church and mission roles. He has written several books at both popular and academic levels, including *The Lord Is My Shepherd: Psalm 23 for the Life of the Church* (2021), and is currently writing a "theology of the book of Psalms."

Jason Byassee is the senior minister of Timothy Eaton Memorial Church in Toronto, Ontario. He previously held the Butler Chair in Homiletics at the Vancouver School of Theology. He is a contributing editor to *Christian Century* and a trustee of Wycliffe College at the University of Toronto. His previous work on Augustine and Scripture includes *Praise Seeking Understanding* (2007) and *Surprised by Jesus Again* (2019).

Karen Case-Green is associate minister at Guildford Baptist Church (Millmead) where she enjoys preaching, pastoring, and community outreach. She lectured in the English language department at the University of Surrey for many years before training for Baptist ministry at Spurgeon's College. Karen is coauthor of *Imaging the Story*, a course which puts the arts in conversation with the salvation story.

Edward Clarke is a fellow of Kellogg College, Oxford, and a departmental lecturer in lifelong learning (English literature) at the Department for Continuing Education, Oxford University. Publications include his poetry collections, *Cherubims* (2022), *The Voice Inside Our Home* (2022), and *A Book of Psalms* (2020), as well as the critical works, *The Secret Mind of Art* (2023), *The Vagabond Spirit of Poetry* (2014), and *The Later Affluence of W. B. Yeats and Wallace Stevens* (2012).

Channing L. Crisler is professor of New Testament, Anderson University, South Carolina. His publications include *Reading Romans as Lament: Paul's Use of Lament in His Most Famous Letter* (2014), *Always Reforming: Reflections on Martin Luther and Biblical Studies* (2021), and the four-volume *An Intertextual Commentary on Romans* (2021, 2021, 2022, and forthcoming).

Susan Gillingham is emeritus professor of the Hebrew Bible at the University of Oxford and emeritus fellow in theology at Worcester College, Oxford. Her *Psalms Through the Centuries* (2008, 2018, 2022) has taken up twenty-five years of her life. It is a reception history commentary on the entire Psalter, from Qumran to the present day, looking at Jewish and Christian representations of the psalms through translation and the commentary tradition, and through art, music, literature, liturgy, and film. Soon to be published is another Psalms commentary in the Penguin World Classics Series, arguing that the book of Psalms is of universal value in what it says about God and humankind.

Tim Judson is research fellow at Las Casas Institute for Social Justice, Blackfriars Hall, Oxford. He is a Baptist minister and pastor at Broadway Baptist Church, Chesham, UK. Recent publications include *Awake in Gethsemane: Bonhoeffer and the Witness of Christian Lament* (2023), *The White Bonhoeffer: A Postcolonial Pilgrimage* (2025), and *Bonhoeffer and the Voice of the Other: Critical Essays on Bonhoeffer's Theology in a World of Struggle*, edited with Anthony G. Reddie and Alison Walker (2025).

Peter J. Morden is a Baptist minister and principal of Bristol Baptist College. He has served in church-based pastoral ministry in Leeds, Solihull, and Eastbourne, and was formerly on the staff of Spurgeon's College, London. Publications include *Communion with Christ and His People: The Spirituality of C. H. Spurgeon* (2013); *The Life and Thought of Andrew Fuller* (2015); *The Message of Discipleship* (2018).

List of Contributors

Emma Rhatigan is senior lecturer in English in the School of English at the University of Sheffield. Her research and publications focus on the genre of the early modern sermon. She is coeditor of *The Oxford Handbook of the Early Modern Sermon* (Oxford University Press, 2011) and *Mapping the Early Modern Inns of Court: Reading Community* (Palgrave, 2025). She is currently editing a volume of John Donne's Inns of Court sermons for *The Oxford Edition of the Sermons of John Donne*.

Ian Stackhouse has been senior minister of Millmead (Guildford Baptist Church) since 2004 and in pastoral ministry for nearly thirty years. He ministers in churches, seminaries, conferences, and retreats in the UK and overseas. Publications include *The Gospel-Driven Church: Retrieving Classical Ministries for Contemporary Revivalism* (2004), *The Day Is Yours: Slow Spirituality in a Fast-Moving World* (2014) and *Praying Psalms: A Personal Journey Through the Psalter* (2018).

Mark J. Whiting is professor of materials aging at the University of Surrey. For many years he was a lay member of the leadership team of QE Park Baptist Church, Guildford, UK, where he continues to preach and teach. His publications include the Grove booklet *The Penitential Psalms Today: A Journey with Psalms 6, 32, 38, 51, 102, 130 and 143* (2022) and the paper "Rebaptising the Psalter" (2023).

Stephen I. Wright is an Anglican priest in Southwark diocese. He was formerly director of the College of Preachers and a tutor and vice principal of Spurgeon's College, London. Publications include *Preaching with Humanity: A Guide for Today's Church* (with Geoffrey Stevenson, 2008), *Alive to the Word: A Practical Theology of Preaching for the Whole Church* (2010), and *Jesus the Storyteller* (2014).

Foreword

SUSAN GILLINGHAM

AS MARK WHITING ACKNOWLEDGES, it is unclear who chose this odd collection of seven "penitential psalms," or why they did it. What is clear is that the "seven" did not form a coherent group at the time of the Psalter's compilation—unlike the Kingship Psalms (95–100) and the Psalms of Ascent (120–34), they are scattered throughout the Psalter. Some attribute a separate commentary on them to Pope Gregory (590–604), and this would have offered more information, but even if this attribution is correct, the commentary has been lost. Clearly by the time of Cassiodorus (c. 490–590) who divides up the psalms into twelve separate categories in the preface to his commentary, the seven "penitential psalms"—i.e., 6, 32, 38, 51, 102, 130, and 143—form the sixth category, and the number of references here to Augustine (354–430) suggest that his *Expositions on the Psalms* might be the source.

The identical opening lines in Pss 6 and 38, and again in 102 and 143, offer some unifying features, but as a whole the "seven" have little internal coherence: only Ps 6, with its sense of human frailty, and 51, with its prayers of profound guilt, and 102, with its expressions of remorse, and finally 130, with its deep despair, are really penitential in tone. Psalm 32 is about penitence as a past experience, being a thanksgiving for forgiveness of sins; 38 has a brief confession of sin in verse 18, but there is no request for pardon; and 143 has more to say about God's righteousness than human sin. Conversely, Ps 25 would have been an excellent candidate among the "seven"; and in Jewish tradition, Pss 78 and 85, for example, are frequently used as penitential psalms.

Both public and private liturgical practices were fundamental in promoting the "seven." The Benedictine, Augustinian, and Carmelite monastic traditions each adapted them as a collection, and just as the Psalms of Ascent were used at Easter, the Psalms of Penitence became part of Advent discipline. Indeed, several illuminated psalters from abbeys and priories in Northern France and Southern England testify to their significance in the formation of monastic devotion. Furthermore, in later cathedral liturgy, the "seven," especially Pss 51 and 130, were frequently sung: Renaissance composers such as Josquin (c. 1450–521), and later English and Italian composers such as Tallis and Byrd, and Palestrina, Giovanni, and Allegri, all testify to this. And because the "seven" were also incorporated into the Office of the Dead, they appear as separate collections in fourteenth-century handwritten Prymers ("first prayers," used for personal devotion and for teaching the laity to read) and illuminated books of hours.

As with all aids for piety, the psalms of penitence were open to abuse. The promotion of Penance (and with this, the use of the "seven") by the Fourth Lateran Council (1215) led to the exploitation of the laity through indulgences, a practice which in Langland's *Piers Plowman* (1360–380) and Chaucer's *Canterbury Tales* (1387–400) receives criticism; the same abuse later aroused Luther's wrath and this in part initiated his *Ninety-five Theses* (whilst at the same time influencing Luther's own more positive commentaries on these "seven" in 1517 and 1525).

This publication also redeems the "seven," advocating, despite their enigmatic quality, their potential as psalm-prayers. From Augustine to Cassiodorus, from Bede to Alcuin, from Richard Rolle to Dame Eleanor Hull, from Luther to Calvin, from the Sidneys to John Donne, and from Spurgeon to Bonhoeffer, reflections on the "seven" have usually been a single-author project. Mark Whiting himself authored a Grove booklet entitled *The Penitential Psalms Today: A Journey with Psalms 6, 32, 38, 51, 102, 130 and 143* in 2022; in so doing he recognized that to look at the psalms "then" as well as "today" requires more than one mind alone. Hence this publication, edited by Mark: it incorporates the studies of experts in the Old Testament, New Testament, and early modern English literature alongside scholars of Augustine, Luther, Spurgeon, and Bonhoeffer, as well as skilled preachers, musicians, artists, and contemporary poets. Mark fills several gaps, writing three chapters himself: the first defends the uniqueness of the "seven," whilst the second and third explain their use between the sixth and thirteenth centuries and fourteenth and sixteenth centuries respectively.

This does not claim to be a comprehensive work: it is necessarily selective, with a bias in the later reception history towards examples primarily (but not exclusively) from the Protestant tradition. The result is nevertheless a unique, rich, and multivalent publication, which deserves much commendation.

Professor Sue Gillingham
Emeritus Professor of the Hebrew Bible, University of Oxford
Emeritus Fellow in Theology, Worcester College, Oxford

Acknowledgments

MARK J. WHITING

I AM GRATEFUL TO so many people who over the years have engaged in dialogue with me on the psalms. Some have even encouraged me to teach and preach on these captivating ancient poems—thank you Steve Godfrey, Peter Hancock, Kirsten Rosslyn-Smith, Chris Scupham, Ian Stackhouse, Rob Stevens, and John Valentine. The bravest encouragers are those who offered constructive critical feedback on my writing, which I can only hope has improved over the last two decades. Deryck Sheriffs and Richard Briggs deserve special recognition in this regard as they patiently read and reread drafts of my work in 2011 and 2021 respectively. I am of course delighted that Jonathan Arnold, Richard Briggs, Jason Byassee, Karen Case-Green, Edward Clarke, Channing Crisler, Tim Judson, Emma Rhatigan, Peter Morden, and Stephen Wright agreed to write chapters on various aspects of the Penitential Psalms, encouraged by an editor whose day job centers on engineering materials.

On the way I had delightful conversations with others about this book or specific matters connected with the Seven Psalms, including Alexandra Barrett (Dame Eleanor Hull and Middle English), Peter Clarke (preaching the psalms), Malcolm Guite (poetry and the psalms), Clare Costley King'oo (the Penitential Psalms in the Middle Ages), Mary Ann Lund (John Donne and the Seven Psalms), Denis Ngien (Luther), Derek A. Olsen (Cassiodorus and monasticism), David O. Taylor (psalms for penitence), Roger Wagner (Ps 51) and Diane Watt (Dame Eleanor Hull). Thank you, one and all, for your contagious enthusiasm for the psalms and/or passion for medieval English literature.

I am also grateful to John W. Rogerson (1935–2018) who led a weeklong introduction to the psalms at Sarum College c. 2009. He graciously challenged some of my many dubious presuppositions in his lectures and lengthy, patient dialogue that week. I am also indebted to another giant of psalms scholarship, Sue Gillingham. When I first asked her a few questions some years ago now, she patiently and enthusiastically gave me some helpful pointers as if I was a peer rather than a distracted materials scientist. It is an ongoing encouragement that she was willing to write the foreword to this volume.

Speaking of encouragement, Kathryn Harkup has provided a lot, along with even more tea. We made a vague plan to each write an A–Z book, me on the psalms and Kathryn on the poisons of Agatha Christie. She published her book in 2015 and its sequel in 2025; mine remains only 75 percent written.[1]

Finally, thank you to my patient family—Kate, Jonathan, James, Rachel, and Jess—who've put up with a lot of prattling about "the book I'm editing." This is especially true of my wife, Revd. Kate Whiting, who for some time seemed suspicious that I was simply inventing an excuse to avoid DIY and decorating. As Sam puts it at the close of *The Lord of the Rings*: "Well, I'm back."

Mark J. Whiting

---

1. Harkup, *A Is for Arsenic*, and Harkup, *V Is for Venom*.

Abbreviations

ESV English Standard Version translation of the Bible
KJV King James Version, or Authorized Version, translation of the Bible
LXX Septuagint text of the Hebrew Bible
MT Masoretic text of the Hebrew Bible
NIV New International Version translation of the Bible
NJPS New Jewish Publication Society translation of the Hebrew Bible
NKJV New King James Version translation of the Bible
NRSV New Revised Standard Version of the Bible

Introduction

MARK J. WHITING

DISCOVERING THE SEVEN

THE VOLUME IN YOUR hands—or on the screen of your e-reader of choice—is part of a long-term personal project concerning interpretation of the biblical psalms. Its earliest visible fruit was a paper on reading the Psalter using Pss 1 and 2 as a hermeneutical lens.[1] At that point I must confess that the Penitential Psalms, which are our concern here, were a curiosity that I had all but dismissed as an irrelevance. It was quite some time later, on reading *Miserere Mei*, a remarkable volume by Clare Costley King'oo, that I first grasped the magnitude of the cultural, devotional and liturgical impact of these Seven Psalms and especially Ps 51, King'oo's titular *miserere*.[2] Since then the Penitential Psalms have eclipsed the rest of the biblical psalms in my thinking and reading. My early exploration gave rise to a Grove booklet in 2022 which was an attempt to write a short introduction to the Seven Psalms of the sort I wished for at the outset of my inquiry to understand them and their wider impact.[3] That short booklet was meant to mark the cessation of my exploration of Pss 6, 32, 38, 51, 102, 130, and 143 as a group. I soon realized, however, that I had arrived back at the beginning, feeling I knew these psalms for the first time. And yet I now had new and more acute questions. Indeed, so many questions that a year after starting the impossible—to single-handedly write a monograph accounting for the rise and fall of the Penitential Psalms—it became all too evident I needed some help. In the absence of a therapist, I decided that this help might

1. Whiting, "Psalms 1 and 2."
2. King'oo, *Miserere Mei*.
3. Whiting, *Penitential Psalms Today*.

come in the form of authorities on specific aspects of the psalms, and of course the Penitential Psalms themselves.

This book is the culmination of reaching out. It soon became apparent that there were others who shared my passion for the Seven Psalms from a variety of perspectives. Against the odds my help came in the form of a team, who have never all met, but who proved to be more generous and more illustrious than I could have imagined. The goal, which I hope has been achieved to some measure, was to provide an inviting, even tantalizing, encounter with the Penitential Psalms. At the same time, I hope that despite each contributor being given free rein in terms of tone, direction, and presuppositions, that the whole is greater than the sum of its parts. My delight certainly grew throughout the project as each contribution was penned. For it seemed that each of the ten authors that joined me in contributing the book's chapters exceeded the short brief I gave them in ways I had not imagined.

GROUNDING THE SEVEN

One of the issues that lies behind this book is the fact that the Penitential Psalms are a closed group only within Western Christianity. Though these psalms are individually read penitentially to some extent in Judaism and orthodox Christianity, in neither of these religious arenas did these Seven Psalms become a fixed mini corpus. The opening pair of chapters of this book consider this matter in two distinct ways—these complementary encounters with the Penitential Psalms lay a foundation. In the first chapter I consider the "origin story" of the Seven as a united and unified whole. This chapter enables some questions to be framed which underpin the whole book. In the second chapter Richard Briggs provides a reading of each of these psalms in their original milieu. He argues that despite their diversity they can collectively, meaningfully, and helpfully be read through a penitential lens. He also notes that there are other fruitful lenses through which these Seven Psalms can each be read.

RECEIVING THE SEVEN

The next seven chapters examine the rise and fall of the Seven Psalms—from their origin, through their heyday, to their gradual loss of traction in church and culture. Jason Byassee initiates this account as he considers

Augustine's part in the story of the Penitential Psalms. His essay is a playful examination which displays its origin as a delightful online lecture, a contribution to the Oxford Interfaith Forum's "Psalms in Interfaith Contexts" series.[4] This lecture was delivered on November 7, 2024, and the chapter here has some additional material, but it remains stylistically and provocatively close to the original. The chapter is something of a tour de force of perspectives on Augustine and suggests that the "arch-allegorist," on his terms, reads the Penitential Psalms literally. For the ancient bishop this, of course, means through Christ.

Chapter 4 considers the early centuries of the medieval period, from the time of Cassiodorus in the sixth century when the Penitential Psalms were an established group. Their complex synergy with the doctrine of penance is outlined and we will be left wondering as to "cause and effect" in this complex relationship between dogma and biblical text. The chapter concludes with the pastoral implications of the Fourth Lateran Council and the prominence, both direct and indirect, that it gave to the Seven Psalms. Chapter 5 continues the medieval journey of the Penitential Psalms. As their prominence in medieval culture is examined through the work of four people, it will become apparent that our Seven Psalms are a canon within the canon of medieval liturgy, piety, and doctrine.

In chapter 6 Martin Luther arrives on the scene, and it will come as little surprise that he is a disruptor. He gave great prominence to the Penitential Psalms in his writing, teaching, and preaching. Crisler helps us read these psalms through Luther's eyes. He argues that Luther sees them through the paradoxical twin lenses of "hope" and "fear." This reading is compelling, and indeed coherent with Luther's wider agenda as Reformer. Despite Luther's commitment to the Penitential Psalms, the Reformation marked the beginning of the slow fall of the Seven from prominence. This might owe something to the initial lack of clarity over the reform of Penance, followed by its marginalization as a doctrine in the various Protestant streams. And yet, the demise of the Penitential Psalms was both uneven and slow. Some key figures, John Donne, Charles Haddon Spurgeon, and Dietrich Bonhoeffer, for example, valued them enormously. But for every celebrant of these psalms there were many other prominent figures who gave them scant, if any, attention.

Emma Rhatigan, in chapter 7, provides an insightful exploration of how John Donne's preaching of the Penitential Psalms was shaped by

4. The home page is https://oxfordinterfaithforum.org where the rationale of this forum is explained and a link to Byassee's original lecture hosted on YouTube is found.

these texts. A compelling case is made for the transposition of the Psalter's redolent use of metaphor and prosopopoeia from psalm to sermon. The readiness with which the Seven Psalms can be voiced by preacher, David, Christ, congregation, etc., provides for a level of sublime rhetoric that made Donne so compelling as an orator. In chapter 8 Peter Morden examines another preacher who, like Donne, was widely recognized as the homiletic exemplar of his day. Spurgeon, more than two centuries after Donne, was just as captivated by the Seven Psalms. His penitential hermeneutic is explored by Morden, and we see the Victorian preacher's practice of unpacking each of the Seven so as to address, with evangelical zeal, the plight of the sinner and the remedy found in Christ. In this way, Spurgeon adapts the Penitential Psalms that had served the doctrine of penance so well in the medieval period to mainstream Protestant evangelicalism.

Despite Spurgeon's work as preacher and biblical commentator, the Penitential Psalms continued to fall from the limelight; we might even say out of favor. Modern biblical criticism played its part, with its emphasis on literary and form critical categories that tended to fragment the psalms—much of the twentieth century's biblical criticism eclipsed traditional readings by seeing each psalm as an isolated text. In contrast, Augustine, Cassiodorus, Rolle, Maidstone, Hull, Fisher, Luther, Donne, and Spurgeon, as seen in chapters 3 to 8, read the Penitential Psalms collectively. Whether in the form of a paraphrase, commentary, book, or sermon series, they proceed dogmatically using variations on Augustine's *totus Christus*.

Tim Judson, in chapter 9, shows that Bonhoeffer also reads the Penitential Psalms through a christological lens. Bonhoeffer recovers Augustine's "total Christ" reading whereby a sinner praying the psalms of guilt, as Bonhoeffer designates them, is identifying with Christ who is the true prayer of these psalms. For Bonhoeffer, as the church prays these Penitential Psalms like its Savior, it petitions vicariously. By the mid-twentieth century the Penitential Psalms were solidly preserved in Catholic liturgy, but somewhat obscure in most Protestant churches. If the quantity of publications on the Penitential Psalms reflects their devotional usage and cultural significance, then the meager two texts of the sixties, by Baggott[5] and Snaith,[6] might indicate their near demise from the heights of the late

---

5. Baggott, *Seven Penitential Psalms*.
6. Snaith, *Seven Psalms*.

medieval hegemony. Since the sixties there have been few new treatments or celebrations of the Penitential Psalms as a whole.

RETRIEVING THE SEVEN

This is not the end of the Seven, of course, and the final four chapters of this book celebrate the living legacy of these psalms in music, preaching, worship, and poetry. Jonathan Arnold provides a detailed tour de force of how the Seven have given rise to collective and individual works. As noted in earlier chapters Ps 51 occupies a pivotal place. This is evident in both the quantity of pieces, as well as the singular cultural impact of Allegri's *Miserere*. To my ear MacMillan's 2009 setting of Ps 51 is just as perfect a distillation of penitential purity, enabling the chief Penitential Psalm to reach modern ears.

Stephen Wright's chapter 11 is a call to preach the Penitential Psalms today. Wright is a sure guide on how we might take the Seven seriously as Scripture with an authentic contemporary approach that enables us to preach them penitentially by doing justice to their language and imagery, whilst not attempting an unobtainable rhetorical artistry to match that of Donne or Spurgeon.

In the penultimate chapter, Karen Case-Green examines the profound question as to the beauty of penitence and asks, if it is beautiful, "to whom is its beauty visible?" For the reader of faith, this chapter also offers ways to recover the Seven Psalms. Case-Green offers an array of creative and imaginative ways in which this might be achieved in collective worship and personal devotion.

From early in this project, I hoped the final chapter would focus on the Penitential Psalms as poems. Edward Clarke fulfills this hope as he reflects on his journey with the Seven, which enabled him to pen his own Seven Psalms, which formed a coherent thread of his larger project to write 150 fresh psalms.[7] The experience he recounts with the Seven is unique to him, and yet his testimony points to how the Penitential Psalms are as alive today as they have always been, especially when read through the lens of our human frailty before a holy God, and the merciful resolution of this brokenness in Christ.

Throughout all the chapters here, these psalms cannot be decoupled in an abstract manner from study of the Bible. In celebrating their

---

7. Clarke, *Book of Psalms*.

recognition and reception as Christian penitential psalms, this is not to take away the possibility of Jewish, secular, or critical readings of these psalms. Quite rightly there are cultural, linguistic, and religious stories here which are of interest to diverse audiences. Nevertheless, I imagine many who read this volume will do so from a stance of Christian faith. Such a stance provides much, but not all, of my motivation for editing this book. The fall of the Penitential Psalms from their position of grace was arrested by two of the greatest post-Reformation preachers. Similarly, a notable martyr of the twentieth century claimed them as Jesus' prayers. For these reasons alone, we surely must consider what we might lose if we jettison the Penitential Psalms, and the penitential hermeneutics and practice with which they work hand in glove. For all the travails and travesties that went with Indulgences and the worst excesses of penitential angst inspired by purgatory, are we not missing something without the Seven in our worship, devotion, and praxis? Ian Stackhouse certainly thinks so, as we see in his epilogue to this book. I hope that readers of this book will not only ask questions of the Penitential Psalms but will allow them to ask questions of us.

SOME CONVENTIONS

The numbering of the Psalms differs between Hebrew (Masoretic) and Greek/Latin (Septuagint and Vulgate) traditions, which affects how they are presented in different Bible translations. Rather than rehearse the full details of this here,[8] this book uses the former numbering, but where a person under discussion or the literature associated with that person favors the latter, the Latin/Greek tradition's numbering is appended in square brackets. So, for example, Ps 51 would have been counted as Ps 50 by Cassiodorus (c. 485–c. 585), who even provides commentary on the significance of it being the Fiftieth Psalm. In this context we would denote this psalm as Ps 51 [50]. On some occasions verse numbers differ too, and so, for example, Ps 51:4 [50:6] might be discussed in a similar manner.

Capitalization is a vexed problem, and the modern preference is for minimizing capitalization of technical terms. When discussing the Penitential Psalms in this volume I have decided that there is some value in using this capitalized designation for the definitive Seven Psalms that

---

8. Gillingham, *Psalms*, 454–58.

have been known as the Penitential Psalms for well over a millennium. The term "penitential psalms" will be used to refer to psalms that have a penitential content or could be readily read penitentially but are not coterminous with the Seven. The designation "the Seven Psalms," or just "the Seven," will also be used from time to time to refer to the Penitential Psalms for variety. Where psalm types which are recognized closed groups are referred to, capital letters are used in a similar way. So, for example, we will meet the Psalms of Ascents and psalms of lament.

Mark J. Whiting
The Feast Day of Augustine of Hippo 2025

BIBLIOGRAPHY

Baggott, L. J. *The Seven Penitential Psalms*. London: Mowbrays, 1963.
Clarke, Edward. *A Book of Psalms*. Brewster, MA: Paraclete, 2020.
Gillingham, Susan. *Psalms Through the Centuries, Volume 3: A Reception History Commentary on Psalms 73–151*. Oxford: Wiley Blackwell, 2022.
Harkup, Kathryn. *A Is for Arsenic: The Poisons of Agatha Christie*. London: Bloomsbury Sigma, 2015.
———. *V Is for Venom: Agatha Christie's Chemicals of Death*. London: Bloomsbury Sigma, 2025.
King'oo, Clare Costley. *Miserere Mei: The Penitential Psalms in Late Medieval and Early Modern England*. Notre Dame, IN: University of Notre Dame Press, 2012.
Snaith, Norman. *The Seven Psalms*. London: Epworth, 1964.
Whiting, Mark J. *The Penitential Psalms Today: A Journey with Psalms 6, 32, 38, 51, 102, 130 and 143*. Cambridge: Grove, 2022.
———. "Psalms 1 and 2 as a Hermeneutical Lens for Reading the Psalter." *Evangelical Quarterly* 85 (2013) 242–62.

Part 1

Setting the Scene

1

The Uniqueness of the Penitential Psalms

Mark J. Whiting

INTRODUCTION

THIS CHAPTER EXAMINES THE origin of the Penitential Psalms—Pss 6, 32, 38, 51, 102, 130, and 143 [6, 31, 37, 50, 101, 129, and 142][1]—as a closed group of seven psalms. We first consider two distinct ways of classifying psalms and show that the Penitential Psalms do not owe their collective identity to either approach. Understanding their uniqueness enables the framing of a series of questions which provides much of the motivation for this book. Exploring the answers to these questions in subsequent chapters is a journey on which we will be able to appreciate the past importance and contemporary significance of the Penitential Psalms.

PSALM GROUPS AND INTERNAL EVIDENCE WITHIN THE PSALTER

The text of the Psalter, or book of Psalms, bears direct evidence of the grouping of psalms. It is highly likely that these groups predate the final

---

1. As explained in the introduction, psalms are referred to primarily by their numbering in the Hebrew (MT) textual tradition. In some contexts their number in the Greek (LXX) and Latin (Vulgate) tradition is added in square brackets where this is judged useful.

editing of the Psalter.² Modern scholarship has concluded that the grouping of the psalms reflects the intent of the final editors.³ The clearest evidence of psalm groups are the titles, or superscripts, which head well over half of the psalms. When multiple psalms, whether adjacent to each other or close neighbors, bear a common heading, they have unsurprisingly been understood to be a group. Whether we can go beyond this initial evidence to understand the nature of these groups with certainty has been the subject of much debate. Some early twentieth-century scholarship ascribed limited value to the psalm titles because they were understood to be late additions to earlier psalms. This lateness is supported by the inconsistencies in psalm titles between textual traditions. The source normally given priority by scholars critically assessing the biblical text for the church is the Masoretic Text (MT), named after the Masoretes, who preserved this Hebrew textual tradition. The MT forms the backbone of modern Bible translations because the broad consensus is that this is the best-preserved textual tradition. The Greek textual tradition, known as the Septuagint (LXX), differs with regard to some psalm titles to the MT. Examples include:

a. The LXX text of Ps 27 [26] has an extra Davidic biographical element in the superscript meaning "before his anointing."[4]

b. The MT of Ps 71 [70] has no heading but in the LXX is denoted as "David's. Of the sons of Jonadab and the first exiles."[5]

c. Similarly, the LXX has a heading for Ps 97 [96]: "Composition. David's. When his land was established," whilst it has no superscription in the MT.[6]

d. The MT superscription identifies Ps 143 [142] as Davidic; the LXX adds "when his son is pursuing him."[7]

e. The MT denotes Ps 144 [143] as Davidic, and the LXX adds "concerning Goliath."[8]

---

2. See, for example, Holladay, *Three Thousand Years*, 26–36, for an engaging exploration of the role of headings for the psalms with Korahite and Asaphite superscriptions.

3. See Wilson, *Editing of the Hebrew Psalter*, 139–97, for such a proposal. His work has been variously championed, challenged, and evolved in numerous studies over the last four decades. Such editorial intent is now close to being the consensus view.

4. Goldingay, *Psalms Volume 1*, 389.

5. Goldingay, *Psalms Volume 2*, 363.

6. Goldingay, *Psalms Volume 3*, 109.

7. Goldingay, *Psalms Volume 3*, 671.

8. Goldingay, *Psalms Volume 3*, 681.

This sort of evidence is enough for some critical scholars to be skeptical of the hermeneutical value of any headings. They argue that the antiquity of all headings is cast into doubt. Consequently little, or no, attention is given to a heading in interpreting a psalm. This marginalization of psalm headings is in marked contrast to the precritical period, where headings were often central to interpreting a psalm. The value placed on psalm headings as evidence of a psalm's origin reached a low point in the 1960s and 1970s, at the height of cult critical approaches to the psalms. Following Wilson's work in the mid-1980s, however, increased attention has been given to superscriptions.[9] This renewed interest is relevant to our discussion as the headings are understood to offer evidence of purposeful grouping of psalms by the editors of psalm groups and/or the final editors of the Psalter. A brief consideration of two psalm groups, identified as such by their headings, will help clarify what we mean by this type of group.

Examination of the majority of modern English Bible translations reveals that eleven psalms have a heading which includes the phrase "of the Korahites" (or similar). These eleven psalms are Pss 42, 44, 45, 46, 47, 48, 49, 84, 85, 87, and 88 [41, 43, 44, 45, 46, 47, 48, 83, 84, 86, and 87]. Chapters 9 and 26 of 1 Chronicles mention the Korahites as a group of temple gatekeepers. The modern Australian worship band, Sons of Korah, who celebrate the psalms by creating contemporary reworkings, give a nod to this possible Korahite legacy. Contrary to those who see psalm headings as late accretions and of little hermeneutical value, Gillingham points to a broad consensus of scholars who agree that, "even if the Jerusalem Temple was not the focus at the time of composition," it is likely that editing was "undertaken by the Korahites of Levitical descent."[10] Later in the same essay, Gillingham argues that it "would not be surprising if this group of editors and compilers belonged to the same Levitical circles as those who compiled and edited the books of Chronicles."[11] In this way critical scholarship has gone full circle, now recognizing the superscriptions as indicators of psalm groups—thus echoing, with some added nuance, the precritical affirmation of the ancient psalm groups. In this way, even if the titles are later additions, they still provide a legitimate lens through which a psalm can be read.

9. Wilson, *Editing of the Hebrew Psalter*, 155–81.
10. Gillingham, "Zion Tradition and Editing," 322.
11. Gillingham, "Zion Tradition and Editing," 334.

A more overtly unified group are the fifteen psalms—Pss 120 to 134 [119–33]—that have the phrase "A Song of Ascents" (NRSV) or similar, as either their heading or part of their heading. Unlike the Korahite psalms, this group is all placed consecutively. They are generally understood to have a narrative concerning a pilgrimage to Jerusalem. So, for example, near the beginning of the collection, we read:

> I was glad when they said to me,
> "Let us go to the house of the Lord!"
> Ps 122:1 (NRSV)

In the closing psalm of the sequence, the pilgrims are in the Holy City:

> Come, bless the Lord, all you servants of the Lord,
> who stand by night in the house of the Lord!
> Lift up your hands to the holy place,
> and bless the Lord.
> Ps 134:1–2 (NRSV)

That there are fifteen Psalms of Ascents has been suggested as an intentional allusion to the fifteen temple steps.[12] There are also frequent literary markers that are more commonly found here than in the rest of the Psalter.[13] This includes their remarkable brevity whereby they are all between three and nine verses in length, apart from Ps 132 with its eighteen verses. They often exhibit what is termed "step parallelism." The psalms are, of course, well known for their use of parallelism where two generally terse statements correspond to one another in a variety of ways that pair them semantically. Modern scholarship has established the richness of this poetic device beyond the rather crude threefold form that vitiates older psalm introductions.[14] A common form of parallelism is where a second line is reinforced by a statement that is semantically close, or parallel, to the first. This is evident, for example, in the fourth Penitential Psalm:

---

12. There are several works that explore the Psalms of Ascents as a group and their function as pilgrim psalms. For example, Mitchell, *Songs of Ascents*, provides a scholarly examination of these fifteen psalms and Peterson, *Long Obedience*, a more devotional appropriation of them.

13. See, for example, Mitchell, *Songs of Ascents*, 3–11.

14. See Berlin, "Parallelism," 155–62, for a concise introduction, or Berlin, *Biblical Parallelism*, for what might be regarded as the definitive exploration of parallelism in biblical Hebrew.

> Purge me with hyssop, and I shall be clean;
> wash me, and I shall be whiter than snow.
> Ps 51:7 (NRSV)

Here the second statement makes a semantically similar statement to the first. From a poetic point of view their subtle difference and concurrent nature enable a richness otherwise absent from a single propositional statement. In the Psalms of Ascents whole phrases are echoed verbatim and, on a few occasions, whole half verses repeat. For example, in Ps 130 [129], the sixth Penitential Psalm, there is an especially obvious example:

> My soul waits for the Lord
> more than those who watch for the morning,
> more than those who watch for the morning.
> Ps 130:6 (NRSV)

Here the second line furthers, rather than semantically parallels, what has been said in the first. The third line simply repeats the second. Any reader interested in examining the distinctiveness of the Psalms of Ascents as a group further would do well to read Mitchell's *The Songs of Ascents*.[15]

Other psalm groupings that are made explicit in the text via the use of superscripts include:

1. The Asaph Psalms which comprise twelve psalms, Pss 50 and 73–83 [49 and 72–82].
2. Some 73 Psalms of David scattered throughout the Psalter but found in distinct clusters or subgroups. For example, Pss 3–9 [3—9:1–21], 11–32 [10–31], 34–41 [33–40] are known as the first Davidic group. Pss 10 [9:22–39] and 33 [32] are usually included in the groups by association despite their lack of a Davidic heading. Indeed, as explained in the introduction, in the LXX manuscript tradition, MT Pss 9 and 10 are a single psalm: Ps 9.
3. Two psalms are designated "of Solomon." These are Pss 72 [71] and 127 [126], which complicates matters as the latter is also one of the Psalms of Ascents.

We will see in subsequent chapters that precritical interpretive practices often assumed Davidic authorship of the 73 psalms that bear his name in their titles, and this played a significant role in understanding

---

15. Mitchell, *Songs of Ascents*, 3–26.

the Psalter as thoroughly Davidic in nature.[16] This is an important aspect of the rise of the Penitential Psalms. Although only five of them have a Davidic heading all seven were generally read as Davidic after their recognition as a group.

Additional psalm groupings might be said to be implicit in the text. For example, Pss 113–18 [112–17] and 146–50 [145–50][17] are often designated as Hallel Psalms because of their use of the Hebrew word *hallelujah*, meaning "praise *Yah*" or "praise the Lord" (NRSV), at the opening and/or the close of these psalms. The former group is known as the Egyptian Hallel because of the Jewish liturgical practice of using them as part of the celebration of Passover. This is a rare example of Jewish liturgical use of a psalm grouping identified in the text. Another group of psalms implicitly grouped in the Psalter are the *Yahweh Malak* Psalms. Psalms 92 to 100 [91–99] are given this designation because they contain frequent statements about Yahweh as king. In addition, they include what we might term "kingly" and "kingdom" language as they speak about God.

Readers interested in the internal evidence for psalm groups within the Psalter will find the work of Wilson instructive.[18] At this point we note that the seven Penitential Psalms are not demarcated as a group in the text by the use of headings. Nor are these seven psalms collected in a group or groups in the text. On the contrary they are scattered throughout the Psalter. We must conclude that during the formation of the Psalter in the exilic period, there is no internal textual evidence that suggests these seven psalms were understood as a group. Before we attempt to identify the origin of these psalms as a group, we will first consider more recent attempts at grouping psalms.

PSALM GROUPS IN MODERN SCHOLARSHIP

In the nineteenth century German critical scholars initiated a method which became known as form criticism.[19] Gillingham helpfully traces the

---

16. Many ancient interpreters went a step further and saw the whole Psalter as authored by David.

17. Noting that Ps 147 in the MT is two psalms—146 and 147—in the LXX.

18. Wilson in his *Editing of the Hebrew Psalter* was the first modern scholar to pay extensive critical attention to what might be gained from examining psalm superscriptions. See Ho, *Design of the Psalter*, 82–133, for a more recent account of headings and their role in the Psalter.

19. See, for example, Gillingham, *Centuries* 1:199–203.

rapid development of psalm classification in this movement from W. M. L. de Wette's 1807 proposal that there were four main types of psalm through to the thoroughgoing maturity of Hermann Gunkel's work in the early twentieth century.[20] Gunkel went beyond solely literary types by proposing groups, or *Gattungen*, defined by both their literary form and hypothetical life setting.

Gunkel's work has been the subject of significant criticism since the 1970s. It has been argued by many that his focus on individual psalms eclipsed an appreciation of the Psalter as a literary whole.[21] In addition to classifying the psalms by genre, he proposed hypothetical pure forms of the psalms said to lie behind the extant biblical psalms. This view has since been thoroughly discredited as it depends on a developmental view of Jewish religion which has no basis in evidence and demonstrably has elements of antisemitism at its core. Despite such criticism, the actual *Gattungen*, or groups, proposed by Gunkel have largely stood the test of time, and his terminology still provides the vocabulary for discussing the literary form of psalms, their ancient origin, and how they might be used today.

Gunkel identified various categories which have become part of the consensus for discussing psalm groups. Although the terminology for these groups has been widely adopted there is considerable debate regarding the specific classification of many individual psalms. The following four groups are among the largest of Gunkel's *Gattungen*:

1. The largest group are the individual complaint (lament) songs, and thirty-nine are identified by Gunkel.[22]
2. Some eight psalms are judged to be songs of communal complaint (laments).[23]
3. Gunkel identified twenty-five psalms as hymns, rising to thirty-seven if his subcategories of Zion songs, enthronement songs, and thanksgiving songs of Israel are included.[24]
4. There are thirteen psalms which are said to take the form of individual thanksgiving songs, according to Gunkel.[25]

20. Gillingham, *Centuries* 1:200–2.
21. For example, Muilenburg, "Form Criticism," 1–18; Wilson, "Shaping the Psalter," 72–82; and Wenham, *Psalter Reclaimed*, 57.
22. Gunkel and Begrich, *Introduction to the Psalms*, 121.
23. Gunkel and Begrich, *Introduction to the Psalms*, 82.
24. Gunkel and Begrich, *Introduction to the Psalms*, 22.
25. Gunkel and Begrich, *Introduction to the Psalms*, 199.

These four groups account for well over 60 percent of the content of the Psalter. Two of the above categories are directly relevant to our interest in the Penitential Psalms, as we shall see below.

THE PENITENTIAL PSALMS AND FORM CRITICAL CATEGORIES

We saw above that the Penitential Psalms are not demarcated as a group in terms of textual evidence such as psalm headings, nor based on biblical Jewish practice or that of the early church. It is therefore natural to ask whether the Penitential Psalms can be identified as a group by form-critical methods. Nasuti summarizes Gunkel's categorization of the Penitential Psalms thus:[26]

Ps 6 [6]	A mixture of individual lament and penitential elements
Ps 32 [31]	An individual thanksgiving with wisdom elements
Ps 38 [37]	A mixture of an individual lament and a penitential psalm[27]
Ps 51 [50]	A penitential psalm
Ps 102 [101]	An individual lament with hymnic and prophetic elements
Ps 130 [129]	A penitential psalm (but with some reservations)
Ps 143 [142]	An individual lament

We can see that these seven psalms traverse several form-critical categories. In this way, the Penitential Psalms do not cohere as a modern group, and even in the most generous of form-critical efforts, only four of seven can be said to be penitential to some extent. In addition, it could be argued that Ps 25 is a penitential psalm, but traditionally it is not considered as part of the group.

The seven Penitential Psalms are, therefore, a group of psalms identified neither explicitly within the Psalter nor as a group according to critical scholarship. This makes them truly *sui generis*. All other recognized psalm groups are identified in one of these two ways. To add to the puzzle, these seven psalms came to exhibit an interpretive hegemony, and

---

26. Nasuti, *Defining the Sacred Songs*, 31–32.

27. Gunkel uses the term "penitential psalm" in a form-critical sense with no intention of aligning his modern reading with the seven Penitential Psalms.

indeed a devotional and liturgical canon-within-the-canon of medieval spirituality. This uniqueness and the associated puzzle over their origin as a group provides the context of this book. At this point it is helpful to frame some questions that will be addressed within this book:

1. Why are Pss 6, 32, 38, 51, 102, 130, and 143 [6, 31, 37, 50, 101, 129, and 142] designated as *the* Penitential Psalms?
2. What rationale was there for their grouping?
3. Why did these seven become a closed group?
4. When were they grouped in this way?
5. Who identified these seven as belonging together?
6. For what purpose were they gathered?
7. Why were they so influential for around a millennium?

The rest of this chapter will outline some provisional answers to the earlier questions in this list. We will do this by firstly considering a proposed link between Paul's Letter to the Romans and the Penitential Psalms, and secondly by noting some subtle textual symmetry that seems to underlie the placement of the Seven Psalms within the Psalter. This book aims to celebrate these psalms as a remarkable, and sometimes puzzling, entity rather than providing a definitive overview. As we journey with these psalms, answers to the above questions will be considered with varying degrees of detail and certainty.

PAUL'S LETTER TO THE ROMANS AND THE PENITENTIAL PSALMS

This section owes much to the work of Nasuti, who appears to be the first scholar to propose that the Seven Psalms and Paul's Letter to the Romans might both be understood as something of loci for divine anger and that this is the basis for strong intertextual links.[28] He notes that three of the seven refer directly to divine anger and wrath, so:

---

28. Nasuti, *Defining the Sacred Songs*, 37.

> O LORD, do not rebuke me in your anger,
> or discipline me in your wrath.
> Ps 6:1 (NRSV)

> O LORD, do not rebuke me in your anger,
> or discipline me in your wrath.
> Ps 38:1 (NRSV)

> For I eat ashes like bread,
> and mingle tears with my drink,
> because of your indignation and anger;
> for you have lifted me up and thrown me aside.
> Ps 102:9–10 (NRSV)

In addition to noting this threefold pairing of God's anger and wrath, we note the very close parallel between the openings of Ps 6:1 [6:2][29] and Ps 38:1 [37:2], which we will explore below. The other four Penitential Psalms make no explicit reference to divine wrath and/or anger, although in Ps 32:4 the psalmist speaks of experiencing God's "heavy hand":

> For day and night your hand was heavy upon me;
> my strength was dried up as by the heat of summer. *Selah*
> Ps 32:4 (NRSV)

Turning to Paul's epistle to the church in Rome we note, with Nasuti, that it is widely recognized as the key place in the New Testament where God's wrath is a central concern. Nasuti unpacks how the early chapters of Romans make reference to the Penitential Psalms; perhaps surprisingly these are the four that make no explicit mention of God's anger and/or wrath.[30] Psalm 51:4 [50:6] is quoted by Paul in Rom 3:4, although he uses the LXX which accounts for the differences seen here:[31]

> Against you, you alone, have I sinned,
> and done what is evil in your sight,
> so that you are justified in your sentence
> and blameless when you pass judgment.
> Ps 51:4 (NRSV)

---

29. Verse numbers in square brackets, like the psalm numbering, refer to the LXX verification. This sometimes differs to that of the numbering of the Vulgate.

30. Nasuti, *Defining the Sacred Songs*, 37. Crisler, *Intertextual Commentary on Romans*, provides extensive additional insight into additional echoes of all seven Penitential Psalms in the first four chapters of Romans.

31. See, for example, Fitzmyer, *Romans*, 328.

By no means! Although everyone is a liar, let God be proved true, as it is written,
"So that you may be justified in your words,
and prevail in your judging."
Rom 3:4 (NRSV)

Psalm 143:2 [142:2] is alluded to in Rom 3:20:

Do not enter into judgment with your servant,
for no one living is righteous before you.
Ps 143:2 (NRSV)

For "no human being will be justified in his sight" by deeds prescribed by the law, for through the law comes the knowledge of sin.
Rom 3:20 (NRSV)

According to Nasuti, Ps 130:7 is alluded to in Rom 3:24:

O Israel, hope in the LORD!
For with the LORD there is steadfast love,
and with him is great power to redeem.
Ps 130:7 (NRSV)

They are now justified by his grace as a gift, through the redemption that is in Christ Jesus.
Rom 3:24 (NRSV)

There is some difficulty in perceiving the alleged allusion in translation, and this is not confined to the NRSV quoted above. The question is whether Paul's concern with the redemption made possible by Christ was a conscious nod to the Lord's power to redeem in Ps 130 [129]. The most developed analysis of this possible intertextuality is that of Crisler.[32] He makes a compelling case that whilst this is neither a quotation nor an allusion, it can rightly be claimed to be an echo.[33] Crisler's analysis goes further in arguing that Ps 130 [129], as a whole, has further echoes in Romans: "Paul develops several of the motifs of the psalm throughout the letter."[34] Finally, we note, with Nasuti, that Rom 4:7–8 quotes Ps 32:1–2:[35]

---

32. Crisler, *Intertextual Commentary on Romans*, 222–27.

33. See Hays, *Echoes of Scripture*, 29–32, for a now widely adopted approach for assessing the echoes of the Old Testament found in the Pauline corpus and beyond.

34. Crisler, *Intertextual Commentary on Romans* 1:227.

35. Nasuti, *Defining the Sacred Songs*, 37.

> Happy are those whose transgression is forgiven,
> whose sin is covered.
> Happy are those to whom the LORD imputes no iniquity,
> and in whose spirit there is no deceit.
> Ps 32:1–2 (NRSV)
>
> So also David speaks of the blessedness of those to whom God
> reckons righteous apart from works:
> "Blessed are those whose iniquities are forgiven,
> and whose sins are covered;
> blessed is the one against whom the Lord will not reckon sin."
> Rom 4:6–8 (NRSV)

This relationship between these seven otherwise scattered psalms and Paul's Letter to the Romans is a complex theological nexus.[36] Whilst Nasuti appears to be the first to trace this relationship in print, it seems entirely plausible that similar observations lie behind Martin Luther's reference to four of the Penitential Psalms—Pss 32, 51, 130, and 143 [31, 50, 129, and 142]—as the "Pauline Psalms."[37] In the light of our earlier discussion, it is interesting that Luther presumably finds a clear link between Rom 3:24 and Ps 130 [129]. It seems plausible that, in a similar way, whoever was responsible for understanding the Seven as a group drew theological motivation from observations about Paul's use of four of these psalms and the Pauline concern with God's wrath captured explicitly in the other three.

THE SYMMETRY OF THE PENITENTIAL PSALMS

In addition to the argument above, there is further textual evidence within the Seven that is suggestive of an interpreter making the most of serendipitous textual symmetry. Before examining this, it is worth pointing out the obvious fact that there are seven Penitential Psalms. It is well known that in the ancient world the number seven was understood as capturing a sense of completeness and perfection. This is demonstrably the case in both Old and New Testaments. Early interpreters paid close attention to the role of numbers within the biblical canon. Modern interpretive practice rightly tempers the excesses of numerology. It seems highly likely,

---

36. Ballentine, "'I Was Ready,'" 2.

37. This reference to four of the penitential psalms by Luther is repeated frequently in both scholarly and popular literature but usually lacks a clear citation. This is Luther, *Tischreden*, 375. See chapter 6 of this book for a full treatment of Luther and the Penitential Psalms.

however, that an ancient interpreter would have been receptive to seven being a fitting number for psalms focused on such a core aspect of the gospel as penitence. The book of Revelation is infamous for celebrating the symbolism of the number seven—almost everything seems to come along in sevens including churches, angels, spirits, lampstands, stars, trumpets, plagues, and so on. It seems highly plausible that the identification of seven, rather than six or eight, penitential psalms might owe more to numerology than any systematic interpretive process. Certainly, much has been made of the number seven in subsequent reception of the seven psalms. The following is just one, albeit rather extreme, example from the mid-nineteenth century where the seven are said to be

> the seven weapons wherewith to oppose the seven deadly sins: the seven prayers inspired by the sevenfold Spirit to the repenting sinner: the seven guardians for the seven days of the week: the seven companions for the seven Canonical Hours of the day.[38]

Now that we are alert to the potential significance assigned to the number seven, we note that the fourth, or central, penitential has some special characteristics that make it especially appropriate for occupying center stage. We have already noted that it is the most purely penitential of the seven. Whilst this designation is anachronistic in terms of the ancient interpreter, it is plausible that such an interpreter would have perceived its highly singular nature, albeit in different terms. When we note the heading of Ps 51 [50] and its reference to the account of the twin sins of David in 2 Sam 11–12, this might also be part of the process of selection of the seven. It will be seen frequently in this book that David's sins became a key interpretive aspect of the Penitential Psalms.

If, for a moment, we accept the possibility that Ps 51 [50] neatly occupies the prominent center ground of our collection, we might well ask whether there are any formal links within the two parts created either side of Ps 51 [50]. The most obvious place to look is to the headings and opening text, as we have already seen how ancient interpreters often saw these as instructive. When we do this, we find some interesting symmetry. Firstly, as already noted above, the first and third are paired by their opening. Secondly, a similar pattern emerges for the fifth and seventh penitential psalms:

---

38. Neale and Littledale, *Primitive and Mediaeval Writers* 1:124.

> Hear my prayer, O LORD;
> let my cry come to you.
> Ps 102:1 (NRSV)

> Hear my prayer, O LORD;
> give ear to my supplications in your faithfulness;
> answer me in your righteousness.
> Ps 143:1 (NRSV)

Thirdly, we can note that this pairing of Ps 6 [6] with Ps 38 [37] and the pairing of Ps 102 [101] with Ps 143 [142] is symmetrical either side of the fourth Penitential Psalm. This is illustrated below with the Latin text of the opening words of the psalms which has a long tradition in the reception of the psalms, here from Coverdale's Psalter as presented in the 1662 *Book of Common Prayer*:

> Ps 6   *Domine, ne in furore*
> Ps 32 *Beati, quorum*
> Ps 8   *Domine, ne in furore*
> Ps 51 *Miserere mei, Deus*
> Ps 102 *Domine, exaudi*
> Ps 130 *De profundis*
> Ps 143 *Domine, exaudi*

Whilst this symmetry is evident, it is more difficult to ascribe with certainty how much it might have informed the establishment of the Penitential Psalms and how much it is what we might term "a happy coincidence." Some caution is needed here as it is a well-known phenomenon that chiasmus patterns like this are often in the eye of the beholder but have little, if any, bearing on the motivations that guided the author, or editors, of a text. In this case, of course, the claimed symmetry is observed within the final text. There is no basis for its origin with the editors of the Psalter.

EARLY RECEPTION OF THE PSALMS THAT BECAME THE PENITENTIAL PSALMS

Once the Penitential Psalms were framed as a fixed group of seven psalms, ancient interpreters rarely questioned that they were usefully understood as mutually reinforcing. Even before their formal recognition as the Seven—see chapters 3 and 4 which explore their origin somewhere between the lives of Augustine (354–430) and Cassiodorus

(c. 490–c. 483)—interpreters frequently read them intertextually. Augustine recognized some psalms as penitential in nature and is said by his biographer to have

> commanded that the shortest penitential Psalms of David should be copied for him, and during the days of his sickness as he lay in bed he would look at these sheets as they hung upon the wall and read them; and he wept freely and constantly.[39]

Theodoret of Cyrus in his Psalms commentary, dating between 441 and 448, interprets the first four Penitential Psalms as having a strong focus on repentance, and he makes some intertextual references that links them to David's twin sins of murder and adultery, captured explicitly only in the heading of Ps 51 [50].[40] The commentary on the last three Penitential Psalms—Pss 102, 130, and 143 [101, 129, and 142], however, shows little interest in the topic of repentance or penitence.[41]

Intertextuality was a given in the centuries which saw the establishment of the Hebrew Bible and the writing of the New Testament. Early Christian interpreters expected to find such organic connectivity. In the ancient world it seemed natural that inspired texts, whose human authors shared a common worldview and who had the same divine author, would be mutually interdependent and useful for interpreting one another. It is hardly surprising that allegorical approaches arose as interpretive strategies in early Christianity. Such methods have sometimes been understood by modern interpreters as eisegesis. This is, however, an ill-founded oversimplification of such readings, as we shall see in chapter 3.[42]

CONCLUSION

This opening chapter has shown that the Penitential Psalms are a unique group. They are not identified as a group by any textual evidence such as the use of superscriptions. There is therefore no reason to think the

---

39. Possidius, *Life of St. Augustine*, 142. This has been taken as evidence that Augustine either knew of the Seven or even grouped them himself. Nevertheless, there is scant additional evidence to support either claim. Even this biographical text might be better understood as identifying four Davidic psalms "of penance" as in Brown, *Augustine*, 436. Byassee considers this matter at length in chapter 3 of this book.

40. Theodoret, *Psalms 1–72*, 73–76, 198–201, 229–32, 294–303.

41. Theodoret, *Psalms 73–150*, 149–54, 302–3, 343–45.

42. Young, *Biblical Exegesis*, 119–39, and her exploration of interpretive methods, with special attention to Origen.

editors of the psalms understood these seven scattered psalms to be a whole in any sense. The Seven Psalms have not been judged by modern scholarship to be a form-critical genre, although we saw that a number are laments or contain elements of petition. This uniqueness gave rise to seven questions, and some preliminary answers were proposed. The rest of this book will provide further answers, both directly in chapters 2 to 6 and less directly in chapters 7 to 13.

In chapter 2 it will become apparent that there are words and motifs that further unite the Seven Psalms. These associations are not unique to these seven texts, but they do cohere with a fruitful way of reading these psalms penitentially. Chapter 3 examines the intertextual and theological association among the Seven, and beyond, in the works of Augustine. Chapter 4 explores the medieval readings of the seven psalms that crystallize the intertextual relationship between them into nothing less than a canon-within-the-canon.

BIBLIOGRAPHY

Ballentine, Samuel E. "'I Was Ready to Be Sought Out by Those Who Do not Ask.'" In *Seeking the Favor of God Volume 1: The Origins of Penitential Prayer in Second Temple Judaism*, edited by Mark J. Boda et al., 1–20. Atlanta: Society of Biblical Literature, 2006.

Berlin, Adele. *The Dynamics of Biblical Parallelism*. Rev. and expan. ed. Grand Rapids: Eerdmans, 2008.

———. "Parallelism." In *The Anchor Bible Dictionary*, edited by David Noel Freedman, 5:155–62. New York: Doubleday, 1992.

Brown, Peter. *Augustine of Hippo: A Biography*. 45th ann. ed. Berkeley: University of California Press, 2000.

Crisler, Channing L. *An Intertextual Commentary on Romans, Volume 1: Romans 1:1—4:25*. Eugene, OR: Pickwick, 2021.

Dunn, James D. G. *Romans 1–8*. Dallas: Word, 1988.

Fitzmyer, Joseph A. *Romans*. New York: Doubleday, 1992.

Gillingham, Susan. *Psalms Through the Centuries: Volume 1*. Oxford: Blackwell, 2008.

———. "The Zion Tradition and the Editing of the Hebrew Psalter." In *Temple and Worship in Biblical Israel*, edited by John Day, 308–41. London: T. & T. Clark, 2007.

Goldingay, John. *Psalms Volume 1: Psalms 1–41*. Baker Commentary on the Old Testament Wisdom and Psalms. Grand Rapids: Baker Academic, 2006.

———. *Psalms Volume 2: Psalms 42–89*. Baker Commentary on the Old Testament Wisdom and Psalms. Grand Rapids: Baker Academic, 2007.

———. *Psalms Volume 3: Psalms 90–150*. Baker Commentary on the Old Testament Wisdom and Psalms. Grand Rapids: Baker Academic, 2008.

Goulder, Michael D. *The Psalms of the Sons of Korah*. Sheffield: JSOT Press, 1982.

Gunkel, H., and Joachim Begrich. *Introduction to the Psalms: The Genres of the Religious Lyric of Israel*. Translated by James D. Nogalski. Macon, GA: Mercer University Press, 1998.

Hays, Richard B. *Echoes of Scripture in the Letters of Paul*. New Haven, CT: Yale University Press, 1989.

Ho, Peter C. W. *The Design of the Psalter: A Macrostructural Analysis*. Eugene, OR: Pickwick, 2019.

Holladay, William L. *The Psalms Through Three Thousand Years: Prayerbook of a Cloud of Witnesses*. Minneapolis: Fortress, 1993.

Leithart, Peter J. *1 and 2 Chronicles*. Grand Rapids: Brazos, 2019.

Luther, Martin. *Werke, Tischreden 1531–46*. Weimar: Hermann Böhlaus Nachfolger, 1912.

Mitchell, David C. *The Songs of Ascents: Psalms 120 to 134 in the Worship of Jerusalem's Temples*. Newton Mearns, UK: Campbell, 2015.

Muilenburg, James. "Form Criticism and Beyond." *Journal of Biblical Literature* 88 (1969) 1–18.

Nasuti, Harry P. *Defining the Sacred Songs: Genre, Tradition, and the Post-Critical Interpretation of the Psalms*. Sheffield: Sheffield Academic, 1999.

Neale, John Mason, and Richard Frederick Littledale. *A Commentary on the Psalms: From Primitive and Mediaeval Writers* 1. 2nd ed. London: Joseph Masters, 1869.

Peterson, Eugene H. *A Long Obedience in the Same Direction: Discipleship in an Instant Society*. 20th ann. ed. Downers Grove, IL: InterVarsity, 2000.

Possidius. *Life of St. Augustine*. Translated by Herbert Theberath Weiskotten. London: Oxford University Press, 1919.

Theodoret. *Commentary on the Psalms, 1–72*. Translated by Robert C. Hill. Vol. 101/136 of *The Fathers of the Church: A New Translation*. Washington: Catholic University of America Press, 2000.

———. *Commentary on the Psalms, 73–150*. Translated by Robert C. Hill. Vol. 102/136 of *The Fathers of the Church: A New Translation*. Washington: Catholic University of America Press, 2001.

Wenham, Gordon. *The Psalter Reclaimed: Praying and Praising with the Psalms*. Wheaton, IL: Crossway, 2013.

Wilson, Gerald H. *The Editing of the Hebrew Psalter*. Chico: Scholars, 1985.

———. "Shaping the Psalter: A Consideration of Editorial Linkage in the Book of Psalms." In *Shape and Shaping of the Psalter*, edited by J. Clinton McCann Jr., 72–82. Sheffield: Sheffield Academic, 1993.

Young, Frances M. *Biblical Exegesis and the Formation of Christian Culture*. Cambridge: Cambridge University Press, 1997.

2

Opening Up the Penitential Psalms

RICHARD S. BRIGGS

INTRODUCTION

THIS CHAPTER INTRODUCES THE content, themes, and nature of the seven Penitential Psalms. While the rest of the volume explores their rich interpretive history and resonance, here the emphasis is on how they work in their original context(s), including historical, literary, and canonical matters. Modern commentators often give the impression that the postcanonical categorization of Penitential Psalms superimposes a rather alien grid on these texts.[1] In contrast, I seek to show that there is good reason to see each text as leaning into the heart of penitence in a variety of ways. Of course, each of these Psalms is also doing a range of other things, but it is still a valuable orientation to think of them as Penitential Psalms.

I begin the discussion of each Psalm with a brief reflection on its classification, taking as a convenient benchmark the 1906–7 International Critical Commentary of Briggs and Briggs because it predates Gunkel's form-critical classifications, but is still immersed in full critical and analytical mode.[2] As is now generally understood, Psalm titles are seen as relevant points of entry to a psalm without implying that they were originally

---

1. For a lucid study of this issue see Nasuti, *Defining the Sacred Songs*, 30–56.
2. Briggs and Briggs, *Psalms*. Gunkel's work is mainly in his 1933 *Introduction*. Form-critical classifications of several scholars are conveniently tabulated in Johnston, "Index."

present. I mainly then focus on elements of sin, forgiveness, and penitence in each psalm, alongside other matters relevant in each case.[3]

PSALM 6

Briggs and Briggs call Ps 6 "a penitential prayer," arguably in light of its reception as one of the Penitential Psalms.[4] In Jewish tradition the Psalm has become part of daily liturgy: recited every morning in preparation for the day ahead.[5] From Gunkel onwards, commentators classify it as an individual lament, but commonly note that what is lamented is not straightforwardly identified as sin. In fact, Ps 6 is a good example of how an elegant and terse poem can set running so many interpretive possibilities that the tradition is able to pick up multiple angles on life with God that are illuminated by this one short text.

The title of the Psalm is not overly informative. It is one of five of the Penitential Psalms ascribed to David (all except 102 and 130), which is now generally understood to mean that the Psalm is "Davidic" in association without likely having been written by David. Taking a more traditional line, Waltke et al. read the Psalm as directly royal—i.e., about Israel's king—since their whole project is governed by reading the heading *ledawid* as meaning "by David."[6] They also alert readers to Gregory of Nyssa's reading of *sheminith* ("the eighth") as a reference to the eighth day, or resurrection day, which leads towards interpretations stressing the eighth-day forgiveness of sin pronounced in Sunday praise and worship.[7] Such a reading plays into penitence as part of the matter in hand.

Three imperatives punctuate the text:

v. 1 "do not rebuke me . . ."—addressed to Yнwн

v. 4 "turn, save my life . . ."—addressed to Yнwн

v.8 "depart from me . . ."—addressed to "evildoers" (or "troublemakers," *po'alê 'āven*)

---

3. In this chapter I follow the English verse numbering, which compared to the Hebrew makes no difference in Pss 32, 130, 143; a difference of one in Pss 6, 38, 102; and of two in Ps 51 with its long title. Very occasionally I have altered references within quotes (or to NJPS) to fit this approach.

4. Briggs and Briggs, *Psalms* 1:45.

5. Berlin and Brettler, "Psalms," 1273.

6. Waltke et al., *Psalms as Christian Lament*, 43–70. For the governing supposition see their *Psalms as Christian Worship*, 89–91.

7. Waltke et al., *Psalms as Christian Lament*, 45.

One option is to take these as structuring the Psalm, which thus moves through attention to God's "wrath" (or "anger," *chēmâ*, v. 1), to the need for deliverance, to a turn to vindication. The plea for deliverance (vv. 4–7) is grounded in a range of reasons varying from God's lovingkindness (*chesed*), to the silence of death, to the ongoing experience of weeping and grief that incapacitates the psalmist. While v. 5 does include a sense that it is the tragedy of death that motivates the psalmist's plea, there are also echoes of that most robust of Old Testament prayers: what will it profit God if one of God's potential worshipers is silenced?

The final section, on this approach, brings resolution: those who have been causing trouble are sent away on the basis that Yhwh has heard the psalmist's plea. This leads to obvious speculation regarding what may have happened between vv. 7 and 8. Candidates include a priestly word (e.g., a declaration of forgiveness in a worship context); a prophetic word regarding the fate of the evildoers; or any experience that underlines to the psalmist that the existential night has passed and the trouble is gone. Of course, the simplest observation is that the Psalm does not say, and no marker in the text requires anything specific to have happened (as per the similarly unmarked transition around Ps 22:21–22). One can read vv. 8–10 equally as celebrating the experience of new life beyond the suffering, or as celebrating the conviction that there *will be* new life beyond. There is the assurance of being heard (v. 8) and the sense of vindication (v. 10), but whether this is still or no longer perceived through a vale of tears is less clear. Finally, it is worth noting that the address switches from prayer (to Yhwh) to interaction with some other unnamed interlocutors. Now the psalmist testifies *about* Yhwh. In the context of the finished Psalm as received in the Psalter, the psalmist is thus testifying to us as readers, or to those hearing it recited.

The question that relates most directly to the role of Ps 6 as a Penitential Psalm concerns the nature of the initial despair and anguish from which the psalmist goes on to celebrate being heard and vindicated. The language, typically, is earthy and physical: the psalmist is "weak" (KJV), "faint" (NIV); "languishing" (NRSV; ESV; NJPS) (*'umlal*, "feeble," as an adjective deriving from the root *'ml*, "to be faint")—their bones shake and, in v. 3, their whole body/soul/person (*nephesh*) is "stricken with terror" (NJPS). Verse 3 ends startlingly: rightly translated "But you, Yhwh, how long. . .?," this reads as an incomplete question, a half-formed cry for help in which the pain being endured makes it hard even to know what to ask for.

Modern interpreters scrupulously observe that there is no mention of sin, which is true, but this cascade of physical symptoms is attributed by the logic of the psalm to God's "anger" (v. 1).[8] So the question is: would this combination of divine anger and the psalmist's groaning, tear-filled, physical anguish most naturally have called to mind the consequences of sin, or would it have been more generally heard as "trouble (unspecified)"? The latter reading allows the "troublemakers" of v. 8 to be, literally, troublemakers, and Ps 6 becomes a resource for the maligned and/or traumatized. The former reading, which is the more traditional "penitential" one, leaves the "troublemakers" vague, while placing greater weight on the holistic sense of sin causing distress.

Readers aware of their own sin and distress could doubtless read this psalm either way: about sin or general trouble. It is no surprise that this poem can sustain both lines of interpretation.

PSALM 32

Briggs and Briggs see a built-up Psalm here from a base of "proclaiming the blessedness of the one whose sins are forgiven" in vv. 1–5, but their simple classification is that this "was a penitential Ps" (though they are not clear on when it was so classified—originally or in the tradition?).[9] Gunkel thought it a psalm of (individual) thanksgiving, and this classification has carried the day in the form-critical era. According to Gillingham, this can be the psalm for the day on Yom Kippur—the Day of Atonement.[10]

While the emphasis of the Psalm is clear, its somewhat unusual composition does raise questions about how the Psalm might have been used. Nevertheless, regarding penitence, we will find a core move in vv. 1–5 that makes this text a key pillar of one scriptural view regarding the nexus of sin, suffering, and forgiveness.

Readers of Ps 6 will immediately note here a familiar catalog of physical symptoms in vv. 3–4: the psalmist's body wastes away; they groan all day long; and (despite obscurities in the Hebrew) there is a sense of the loss of all physical strength. The vocabulary is not all the same as Ps 6

---

8. Jacobson offers a thoughtful reading of God's anger as being in the service here of God's love, in DeClaissé-Walford et al., *Psalms*, 107–8.

9. Briggs and Briggs, *Psalms* 1:276.

10. Gillingham, *Psalms* 2:198. But for multiple variations and exceptions see Sommer, "Introduction," xxxv–xl.

(in fact some terms are echoes of the description of physical despair in Ps 22[11]), but the portrait is similar, except here it is being viewed clearly in retrospect, with v. 5 boldly proceeding to the acknowledging/confessing of sin. All three major OT words for sin appear here: "sin" (*chatā't*); "iniquity" (*'âwon*); and "transgression" (*pesha'*). Everything was wrong, but all is now forgiven.

This was exactly where the Psalm started: "Happy are those whose *pesha'* is forgiven, whose *chatā't* is covered . . . to whom YHWH imputes no *'âwon*" (32:1). So vv. 1–5 make a concise statement of the release to be found in confession and forgiveness, and by being repeated by the psalmist to their audience (and in the end to us as readers or hearers) the importance, and "happy" result, of forgiveness is affirmed. Verse 1 begins with a dual "Happy . . .," *'ashrê–*, which is the Hebrew term used in describing a person who is favored, or doing well, or in a desirable circumstance. Translations vary between "blessed" (KJV, ESV, NIV) and "happy" (NRSV, JPS), and while it can indicate the result of a blessing it is not as strong as an actual act of blessing.[12]

In short: Ps 32:1–5 is a straightforward expression of how good it is to be forgiven for confessed sin, releasing the penitent one from the groaning and travails of suffering. Note that anyone reading Ps 32 and then turning to Ps 6 could more easily read Ps 6 as penitential.

There is a careful balance to strike here: the Old Testament frequently contests the idea that suffering (or physical anguish) is the result of sin, but at times it draws the link too. After all, if there were no link ever, then it is not an idea one would need to contest much. It is because there is sometimes a link that the caveats have to be entered.[13]

All this said, two further observations are worth making. First, 32:1–5 is effectively silent on what it means to confess sin, or how forgiveness is received. It is a report of a done deal, from a position of "happiness." The use of Ps 32 as a Penitential Psalm is therefore an affirmation of what would be believed already about sin and forgiveness and their workings. Or in other words: the reader (or supplicant) would have to supply the penitence: the awareness of sin, and the access to means of forgiveness.

---

11. The "body" (*'etsem*) of v. 3 is "bone"—as per Ps 6:3 and Ps 22:14, 17; and the "groaning" (or "roaring," *she'āgâ*) in the same verse is in Ps 22:1.

12. *'Ashrê–* is translated as *makarios* in LXX, which is the word used in Matt 5:3–11 (the Beatitudes). This is in contrast to *bārak/eulogeō*, "to bless," which is not used in any of the seven Penitential Psalms.

13. Goldingay, *Psalms Volume 1*, 460–61, is helpful on the balance involved here. He titles his discussion of Ps 32 "When Suffering Issues from Sin."

Secondly, and only in mild tension with this, the remainder of the Psalm proceeds in slightly awkward stages to a range of exhortation and wisdom-like discourse.[14] Psalm 32:6 does encourage readers (or supplicants) to "offer prayer to you [Yhwh]," but that is as specific as the Psalm gets. Indeed it switches to a first-person address in v. 8, which some take as moving to the voice of Yhwh, while others see the psalmist now addressing those who can learn from his own experience. Attempts to deduce what the psalmist had been doing wrong, from this further text, are speculative at best, since all we learn is that he did not follow the right path, and was "wicked."

PSALM 38

"Ps. 38 is a lamentation," say Briggs and Briggs, reading it interestingly as *Israel's* lament, which could work if read in David's voice, following the Davidic title.[15] The Targum takes this direction, as does Jewish worship.[16] From Gunkel onwards it is normally classified as an individual lament. Its core elements will be familiar to readers of Pss 6 and 32, but with a striking lack that creates a different tone here.

In most English translations Ps 38 indeed begins the same as Ps 6: "O Lord, do not rebuke me in your anger" (NRSV). The word for "anger" here, though, is *qetseph*, a much less common word, sometimes translated "wrath" (as here KJV), compared to Ps 6:1's use of *'aph* for "anger." The distinction is maintained by the NJPS: "in anger" (6:1)/"in wrath" (38:1) and then using "fury" to contrast in the second half. Most translations save "wrath" for that second term, *chēmâ* (which is the same in 6:1/38:1). The Hebrew is phrased mildly differently even here, but the result is close enough that most translations have identical opening verses.

What follows also begins familiarly: a catalogue of physical travails and mental anguish—unsound "flesh" and "bones" in v. 3 (with "bones" being the same as in Pss 6 and 32), and burdens "over their head," as it were, in v. 4. The difference, this time, is that the rehearsal of the suffering will effectively continue unabated all the way through the Psalm's

---

14. Christians of a certain age may recognize v. 7, whose NIV translation ("You are my hiding-place, you . . . surround me with songs of deliverance") formed the basis of a 1981 praise chorus written by Michael Ledner ("You Are My Hiding Place").

15. Briggs and Briggs, *Psalms* 1:335.

16. Gillingham, *Psalms* 2:232, 234.

twenty-two verses.[17] Psalm 38 will end with the psalmist still imploring, "Do not forsake me…" (v. 21). Along the way the severity of the suffering approximates to mourning (v. 6, using the idiom "to walk in darkness"—as per NJPS's "I walk about in gloom"). It may be actual mourning. Houston helpfully clarifies the difficulty of rightly situating the language: "In cultures prior to the modern discoveries of medical science, mortal sickness was experienced as a mixed confusion of diverse agencies" (including sin, the devil, illness, and emotional affliction).[18] It includes a mixture of what sounds like physical sickness (vv. 5, 7), social isolation (v. 11), and undefined enemies (vv. 12, 16, 19).[19] Some commentators wonder if the overall picture is hyperbolic, though arguably it makes sense as the articulation of overwhelming despair regardless of whether every element is actually being experienced.

The psalmist is aware, though, that for all this, it is their own sin that is (also?) a cause of their trouble. Verses 3–4 repeat some of Ps 32's claims: the suffering is "because of my sin (*chatā't*)," and the psalmist is overwhelmed by their "iniquities" (using *'āwon*), with both terms also being used in v. 18. The same tensions thus arise as with Ps 32: the attribution of trouble to sin is real, without being intended as a full explanation of all suffering. The despairing mood of Ps 38 might even leave a reader wondering if the use of sin language in vv. 3–4, 18 is something of an inchoate response to overwhelming pain, physical and mental, rather than the calling to mind of anything specific. The Psalm's title may indicate, though, a more deliberative moment: *lehazkîr*, "for remembering(?)," often translated "for the memorial offering."[20]

Interestingly, Goldingay wonders whether Ps 38 is particularly relevant in cases of ongoing/chronic illness.[21] It is also not difficult to see how the suffering psalmist paying the ongoing price for sin would feed into medieval readings connecting the Psalm to purgatory.[22]

---

17. Despite the number of verses, this is not in fact an acrostic psalm. Arguably its unresolved lament echoes the structure of an acrostic but in a deliberately disordered way—as per Lam 5.

18. Waltke et al., *Psalms as Christian Lament*, 122.

19. Enemies are usually undefined in the Psalms, which allows them to function in endlessly re-applicable terms for today's readers.

20. The reference may be to the grain offering of Lev 2. Note that the NJPS leaves this term untranslated, and footnotes "meaning of Heb uncertain." The LXX takes it in a different direction: remembrance concerning the Sabbath.

21. Goldingay, *Psalms Volume 1*, 552.

22. Waltke et al., *Psalms as Christian Lament*, 128–30, 136.

In short, Ps 38 adds emotional and psychological intensity to the portraits already painted in Pss 6 and 32, and omits either the potentially anticipated vindication of the former or the joyous embrace of forgiveness of the latter. God is trusted to act (see especially vv. 9, 13, 21–22, some of which use "Yhwh" and some do not), but there is no actual divine action after the setup of Yhwh's "discipline" in vv. 1–2. This is a Penitential Psalm of considerable "gloom" (see, for example, NJPS v. 6). The expectation is surely that a regular worshiper availing themselves of the Psalter will encounter moments in life when this unresolved context for penitence is what is needed.

PSALM 51

With characteristic higher-critical certainty, Briggs and Briggs write, "Ps. 51 is a penitential prayer of the congregation in the time of Nehemiah," explicitly dismissing the title as "impossible," and asserting that "the author was one of the companions of Nehemiah in the great effort to give the city walls."[23] This has the merit of taking vv. 18–19 seriously, indeed literally, and reckons with the Psalm as a (royal) expression of national failure, which is plausible.[24] Most helpfully, after Aquinas: "The walls of Zion, a synecdoche and symbol of the kingdom of God, can only be built by penitent sinners."[25]

Yet the title should not be so summarily dismissed, and the resonance of Ps 51 with personal sin and penitence remains profound, with some "twenty images of forgiveness and cleansing in this psalm."[26] From Gunkel onwards, the Psalm is seen as an individual lament. As its reception amply attests, Ps 51 has been a focus of penitence in Jewish and Christian spirituality for centuries: "No other psalm has been so central to the complex history of Christian penitential devotion."[27] Without a doubt, it is the Penitential Psalm that most naturally and readily lends itself to the "penitential" classification. As Ellen Davis expresses it: "Psalm 51 is the

---

23. Briggs and Briggs, *Psalms 2*, 3–4.

24. Hossfeld and Zenger, *Psalms 2*, 16, see vv. 18–19 as "a secondary liturgical appendix," but are rightly nervous about Christian attempts to sideline them as early Jewish "legalism."

25. This is Waltke et al.'s summary of Aquinas' reading; *Psalms as Christian Worship*, 467 (see also 457).

26. Waltke et al., *Psalms as Christian Worship*, 475.

27. Waltke et al., *Psalms as Christian Worship*, 446.

Lenten psalm *par excellence*, for it is the only psalm—and perhaps the only passage in the Bible—that offers in-depth guidance for the particular work of that season, the work of contrition."[28] This hint regarding liturgical seasons offers a helpful way to understand the Psalm's persistent focus on perpetual sinfulness and forgiveness: it is always true, and sometimes needing to be expressed (as indeed Ps 51 is one among many Psalms). When the time is right, all Jews and Christians will need Ps 51.

There is only space to select highlights of the Psalm's focus on penitence. The title locates the Psalm's lament in the context of the well-known story of David's adultery with Bathsheba in 2 Sam 11–12. After Nathan the prophet has relayed Yhwh's condemnation to David (12:7–12), 2 Sam 12:13 has David saying to Nathan, "I have sinned against Yhwh." This is the settled perspective of Ps 51 too: "Against you, you alone, have I sinned" (v. 4). We would more naturally say in English today that David has also sinned against Bathsheba, Uriah, and others, but while it is not unknown to speak of sin against another human being in the Old Testament, it is relatively uncommon (and often spoken by non-Israelites).[29] There is no need to deny that broken human relationships were culpably caused, but the language of sin tended to be reserved mainly for the offense against God, i.e., even when the offense against God was the interpersonal transgression.

The opening verses of Ps 51 include multiple instances of the same language of transgression/iniquity/sin that we have encountered in Pss 32 and 38, with a strong new element of specific confession and requesting of cleansing (vv. 2, 7, 10 . . .). Some of the same language that we have met in the earlier laments is reproduced here in the midst of hope for a forgiven future: "Let the bones [plural of *'etsem*, from 6:3; 32:3; 38:3] that you have crushed rejoice" (v. 8). I highlight here four points of the transformative journey envisaged by Ps 51 as the penitent sinner seeks and receives forgiveness.

First, vv. 4–5 emphasize the completeness of the sin of which the penitent psalmist (or reader) is aware. It is a fundamental barrier between the sinner and Yhwh—as noted above this is the core issue being

---

28. Davis, *Getting Involved with God*, 168.

29. See for example Abimelech of Gerar (Gen 20:9) or Pharaoh (Exod 10:16). For an Israelite view, see the people in Num 21:7 confessing sin (against Yhwh) as a result of *speaking against* Yhwh and Moses. All these examples use *chatta'*. By Hossfeld and Zenger's reckoning (*Psalms 2*, 12), fewer than 10 percent of 181 uses of the verb in the Qal refer to interpersonal sin.

addressed, not interpersonal sin. What is less clear is what prompts the psalmist to make this plea for mercy. On the one hand, the title points to David, convicted by Nathan's parable, as an example of a guilty man seeking forgiveness. But more generally, is it the awareness of God's steadfast love (*chesed*) and "abundant mercy" (in v. 1) that draws the petitioner then to reflect on their sinfulness? The Psalm does not say. Then in v. 5, the psalmist reckons with having been born "guilty," or, more traditionally, "in iniquity" (*'āwon*; so KJV, ESV). Further, they were conceived, by their mother, "in sin" (from the same root as *chatā't*), which may or may not be the same nuance as the NIV and NRSV's "sinful." This verse chimed with (and partly generated) the traditional doctrine of original sin: it is fallen human nature to be "in sin," unavoidably and universally (until the incarnation, as Christians would affirm), rather than because each individual has willfully gone astray—even if that comes later. It is interesting to consider whether this claim may be colored by the context of David having fathered a child with Bathsheba, but whether or not that is relevant, it is important to note that this verse is not implying sinfulness in the sexual act of procreation as such, or indeed pinpointing sex in particular as sinful, despite various such claims in the history of (Christian) theology.

Secondly, vv. 10–12 articulate the transformation of forgiveness in terms of a clean (or pure) heart (*leb tāhor*), and the renewing within the penitent one of a right (or firm) spirit, which suggests that there was still some restorable sense of spirit in the one praying. Verse 11 then offers the striking wording: "Do not take your holy spirit from me" (NRSV), which along with Isa 63:10–11 gives us the only use of "Holy Spirit" language in the Old Testament. As John Levison has shown, the point here refers to the heart and spirit as the core of the psalmist's person, seeking cleanness, rightness, and holiness in heart and spirit.[30] This offers one particularly clear instantiation of Levison's helpful overall thesis that the s/Spirit of God in the Old Testament and beyond is the spirit who sustains life (old life and new life), in regular ways as well as spectacular ways. There are elements of both in the renewal of the penitent sinner in Ps 51: restored to (full) life (see the final point below), in ways that speak of the cleansing work that only God can do.[31]

---

30. Levison, *Filled with the Spirit*, 30.

31. See Levison, *Inspired*, for the dual thesis of the Spirit of life and new life, in the first and in the new creation(s).

Thirdly, v. 13 (and perhaps v. 15 in connection with it) envisage that one result of the forgiveness will be the psalmist's ability to turn to instructing others who are in the same sinful situation in which the psalmist began the Psalm. This highlights that the broken human heart is teachable, and thus that there is at least some degree of continuity between the penitent and the forgiven human heart in this Psalm. In other words, as so often, the "new"-ness of which the psalmist speaks is renewal and reorientation to the right paths.

Finally, a life of renewed sacrificial devotion will follow the restoration of the sinner. Some interpreters are tempted to read v. 16 as suggesting a less significant role for the sacrifices of burnt offerings—especially interpreters predisposed to prefer a cult-free "contrite heart" as the one thing that matters. Such a trajectory of interpretation finds resonance in Luke 18:9–14, for example, where the penitent Pharisee finds justification without attending to matters of cultic obedience. However, it is clear from the closing of Ps 51 that, once restored, the penitent will go on to offer "right sacrifices" (or "sacrifices of righteousness," *zibchê-tsedeq*; v. 19; parsed as none other than burnt offerings in the same verse). Furthermore, YHWH will once more delight in them. Allowing its final verses their full import, Ps 51 is not opposed to burnt offerings, or the importance of sacrifice. The point is rather that the barrier of sin can be forgiven by YHWH's gift of right(eous)ness and holiness, in life and spirit. When forgiveness comes to the penitent sinner, they are then restored to the very practices of sacrifice in which YHWH delights.

Everything in Ps 51 will in due course nourish and inform a New Testament and Christian understanding of the life-giving gift of salvation, indeed the gift of the Holy Spirit no less, in which forgiveness of sin is filtered through the gift of God in the cross of Christ. While the Psalm's own horizons do not go as far as this, the celebration of forgiveness that comes to the penitent is still, on its own terms, powerful and deeply encouraging.

PSALM 102

This complex Psalm is labeled "composite" by Briggs and Briggs: a prayer of afflicted Israel, followed by confidence in the restoration of Zion, amidst various glosses.[32] Gunkel and the modern era classify it as an

---

32. Briggs and Briggs, *Psalms 2*, 316.

individual lament, but recent fuller commentaries still acknowledge the complexity of its structure, and in the end we cannot know whether it is composite.[33]

The keynote of its elusive unity is the alternation between individual lament directed to Yhwh (vv. 1–11; 23–28) and a reflection on Yhwh's future intervention for Zion that is only in part addressed to Yhwh, preferring to speak of Yhwh in the third person while addressing an unidentified "audience" (vv. 12–22). Goldingay pinpoints the thematic contrast as circling around time.[34] The psalmist has suffered long, with multiple references to the passing of time and the extensiveness of suffering, right up to "I wither away like grass" (v. 11). In contrast, v. 12 affirms that Yhwh is "enthroned forever," and on behalf of a generation still to come (v. 18) this section celebrates Yhwh's decisive future intervention (vv. 12–17), and the wondrous impact it will have on those—beyond the psalmist himself—who await vindication (vv. 18–22). Verses 23–24 then return to the individual voice of lament with a renewed reflection on time: but now it is to do with days cut short, and strength "broken . . . in mid-course," in light of which God's own "long-ago" perspective (vv. 25–26) is used as the basis of a final hope, in the last verse, that children yet to come may live secure.

If the poem is taken as a unity (composite or not) then all this might lean in the direction of reading the first-person lament as voiced by a personified Jerusalem, or at least someone speaking on behalf of Jerusalem.[35] The title moves more decisively towards the individual—one who, afflicted and faint, pours out his complaint before Yhwh, but this too could conceivably be spoken for Jerusalem.

If we take it as individual, then some familiar points regarding physical suffering and distress surface once more: a withered heart and bones ('etsem again) that cling to flesh (v. 5); and the reappearance of "enemies" (v. 8, using the same vocabulary as 6:10; 38:19). Absent though is any of the language of sin, iniquity, or transgression. Here the suffering is either illness or the result of enemies, indeed reading a lot like starvation (vv. 4, 9), which would then also fit with the travails of Jerusalem at various points in its history.[36]

---

33. Hossfeld and Zenger suggest composite unity; *Psalms 3*, 20–22.
34. Goldingay, *Psalms 3*, 161–62.
35. Goldingay, *Psalms 3*, 149.
36. On the wonderful allusive language of lonely birds in vv. 6–7, see Byassee, *Psalms*, 9–10.

In verse 10, though, we do have a recurrence of *qetseph* ("anger"; "wrath," as per Ps 38:1).[37] On this slender basis, arguably (but likely what happened in the tradition), we have a way of linking Ps 102 to the themes of sin and forgiveness found in the other Penitential Psalms. But in fact just here Ps 102 seems to turn away from pursuing this line, reckoning Yhwh's anger "opaque and arbitrary," in Hossfeld and Zenger's phrase, regarding v. 10's language of being thrown aside.[38] Furthermore, there is no mention of, or cry for, forgiveness. The restoration of the city, to which the Psalm proceeds, does in a sense imagine the removal of anger, but the language and conceptuality of forgiveness (and indeed anger) remains absent, with the focus instead being that "it is time to favor it" (or "have compassion" on Zion; from *racham*; v. 13).

For a penitent sinner seeking Yhwh, the language of yearning at the beginning of the Psalm would work well, as would the comfort from reminding oneself (and others) of Yhwh's future restoration of Zion. By extension, there is comfort and hope for the praying psalmist and their listeners and readers, if seeking forgiveness, since their future vindication is caught up in this divine victory of "years without end" (v. 27). But in this case, more than with any of the other Seven Psalms, the penitential context and the hope of forgiveness has to be imported from elsewhere.

PSALM 130

The classification of this Psalm repeats features we have seen before: Briggs and Briggs see "a cry of Israel to Yahweh for help in deepest distress," while Gunkel and the form-critical tradition find an individual lament.[39] Hossfeld and Zenger note that there is not any actual lament, though—the tone is trust and assurance, and the result is a psalm of petition.[40] Furthermore, and given the likely (post)exilic context of the final book of the Psalter, the "I" here seems to be the leader of a communal prayer that, explicitly in vv. 7–8, turns its attention to Israel's longing for restoration. Clearly the Psalm (or most of it) could function as an individual lament, and has often done so, but the corporate dimension

---

37. These are the only two uses of this noun in the Psalter.
38. Hossfeld and Zenger, *Psalms 3*, 24.
39. See Briggs and Briggs, *Psalms 2*, 464.
40. Hossfeld and Zenger, *Psalms 3*, 426. They also offer a plausible defense of seeing vv. 7–8 as a redactional addition.

seems integral to it.⁴¹ As so often, form-critical classification (in this case "individual lament") obscures as much as it enlightens.⁴²

The title identifies this as a "song of ascents," a title repeated all the way through Pss 120–34. The thus-indicated subcollection of psalms is a coherent one, focusing on aspects of God's blessing on Israel in a Jerusalem/Zion-centered way. But the meaning of the title remains obscure. Berlin traces various interpretations: musical (sung in ascending voice), literary (referring to poetic structure), historical (ascending out of exile), or liturgical (ascending as "going up" on procession to Jerusalem). She mildly favors seeing it as "liturgy for a stylized procession near or at the Temple Mount," including locals as well as pilgrims.⁴³

The Psalm confidently approaches Yhwh, strong on "hope" (vv. 5, 7; see 131:3 also), and very aware of the psalmist's/Israel's "iniquities" (the plural of *ʾāwon* once more; vv. 3, 8). The note of assurance is clear in the celebration of "forgiveness" (*selîchâ*; v. 4),⁴⁴ and steadfast love (*chesed*; v. 7), which are both said to be "with" Yhwh (or "you"). This builds to the powerful conviction of the final verse: Yhwh "will redeem Israel," which makes sense to a Christian reader as referring to forgiveness partly because of the success of this very metaphor to stand for such a wider significance.⁴⁵ For the psalmist the hope for "redemption from sin" (or iniquity), a unique phrasing in the Old Testament, would probably have been for the restoration of Israel to the land (if the Psalm is exilic), or to fullness of life in the land if a postexilic context is still looking for a fuller "end of exile."⁴⁶

Two comments on the Psalm's penitential echoes. First, v. 3 may be read two ways. Most commonly, it is taken as saying that Yhwh does not in fact keep a record of wrongs, because if that were so, who could stand (i.e., survive it)? Berlin argues, however, that the point is that Yhwh does indeed keep such account, but the divine nature is to forgive—and it is

---

41. Goldingay, *Psalms 3*, 523; Berlin, *Psalms*, 54, sees it as longing for return from exile.

42. For a positive approach to the form-critical ambiguity here, and a helpful history of interpretation of Ps 130, see Nasuti, "Plumbing the Depths."

43. Berlin, *Psalms*, 183–88, on which this paragraph is based.

44. A postexilic term used only here and in Neh 9:17 and Dan 9:9, though the cognate verb (*sālach*) is less uncommon.

45. Goldingay, *Psalms 3*, 530.

46. Berlin, *Psalms*, 53, linking end of exile to forgiveness of (national) sin.

the forgiveness that means the sins "do not count."[47] Therefore we (readers of the Psalm) draw near to the one who forgives, since it is forgiveness we need. The end of v. 4 resists any move to making this the "cheap grace" of automatic forgiveness: forgiveness is found with Yhwh so that Yhwh may "be feared" (KJV, ESV, NIV) (or "revered," NRSV): this is the "fear of God" that points to a whole life oriented to honoring God.

Secondly, not only is there no lament in this Psalm, but nothing actually happens with regard to forgiveness: "Within the internal life of the psalm itself, there is no movement; the depths are as deep at the end as they are at the beginning."[48] What makes the Psalm ripe for appropriation for the voice of the penitent sinner is its striking confidence that God forgives and will redeem. Anyone "crying out from the depths" (as v. 1 almost says) may draw comfort here, even though the way to inhabiting forgiveness is left unexplored.

PSALM 143

"An importunate prayer of the congregation to Yahweh in great peril for speedy deliverance," says Briggs and Briggs, though they excise much supposedly secondary material in so analyzing.[49] Gunkel and those who follow prefer again a classification of individual lament, with an admixture of petition. Some imagine a juridical setting: the psalmist awaits judgment after being pursued and crushed by an "enemy" (v. 3), with hope of a positive verdict come the morning (v. 8).[50]

What is worth taking from such a view is the sense, similar to that in Ps 130, that the psalmist is in a predicament for which the cause is left largely unexplained, and where there is no resolution in the Psalm itself. There is a little more forward motion than in Ps 130—here the psalmist is clearly looking for Yhwh's vindicating judgment to come (as a "quick answer," v. 7 echoing v. 1; and with a longing to hear of Yhwh's steadfast love [*chesed*] in the morning). There is the confidence that God will act (vv. 10b–12), which of course already undergirds the nature of the prayer from v. 1 onwards.

---

47. Berlin, *Psalms*, 51.
48. Goldingay, *Psalms 3*, 531.
49. Briggs and Briggs, *Psalms 2*, 514.
50. This view is surveyed but rejected by Hossfeld and Zenger, *Psalms 3*, 572.

If the context is not actually legal, it is nevertheless painted in terms of spirit-sapping trouble caused by an enemy (vv. 3–4), from which rescue or deliverance is sought (v. 9). The Davidic title is expanded in some LXX versions to read "when his son is pursuing him." The reference is perhaps to Absalom in 2 Sam 15.[51] As such, the Davidic prayer of Ps 143 would address trouble and distress with a confident turning to God for help.

However, a sense of the trouble being brought on by sin or wrongdoing is absent. The reason the Psalm became one of the seven is found in v. 2: "no one living is righteous before you," and hence "the speaker's appeal is based not upon his own merit, but upon God's beneficence."[52] As Waltke et al. note, though, "David makes that assertion as dogma . . . not as a penitential *cri de coeur*."[53] The language of sin or forgiveness is absent, and the strong framing of the Psalm offers a different basis for vindication: the psalmist appeals not to forgiveness, but to God's "faithfulness" ([*'emûnâ*, v. 1] // "steadfast love" [*chesed*, v. 12, as well as v. 8]), and to God's "righteousness" (*tsedāqâ*, vv. 1, 11).

Two comments may be made regarding verse 2 and its significance. First, the apostle Paul quotes it in Rom 3:20 as part of his argument concerning the universal (i.e., Jew and gentile) need for justification, owing to humanity's lack of righteousness, including by way of following the law. Richard Hays has argued that scriptural citations in Paul should be seen as pointing not just to single phrases or verses but to the underlying argument(s) of the quoted passages. In this case: "Ps 143 illuminates the structure of the logic that underlies Rom 3 because the psalm already contains both an affirmation of the unconditional inadequacy of human beings to stand before God (see Rom 3:9–20) and an appeal to God to exercise his own righteousness to rescue the psalmist (see 3:21–26)."[54] By way of Ps 143, in the LXX, Paul is able to draw on this language of the active righteousness (*dikaiosunē*) of God for the purposes of Romans.

Secondly, what of penitence in Ps 143? The psalmist is suffering, as the language of a crushed life/soul (*nephesh*) in v. 3 makes clear, and the images of darkness, faintness, and thirst that pile up in vv. 3–6 could easily connote physical distress as per some of the earlier Penitential Psalms. Combine this with the acknowledgment of v. 2 regarding the lack of righteousness, and the repeated emphasis on turning to prayer, and we have

51. Hossfeld and Zenger, *Psalms 3*, 578.
52. Berlin, *Psalms*, 129. "Beneficence" is Berlin's word for *tsedāqâ* at the end of v. 1.
53. Waltke et al., *Psalms as Christian Lament*, 270.
54. Hays, "Psalm 143," 60.

all the ingredients for a penitent sinner longing for life-giving release from the travails of sin. The Psalm does not put all the pieces together, but readers—perhaps with prompting from Rom 3—have found it easy and appropriate to do so.

CONCLUSION

The tradition of reading these seven psalms as Penitential Psalms picks up on aspects of the subject matter of each Psalm, ranging from sin and forgiveness being core concerns (e.g., 32:1–5) through to being relatively marginal matters (e.g., 102, perhaps in v. 10). But the intersection of each of these texts with the concerns and practice of penitence can still be profound, as the rest of this volume will demonstrate. As is the case with all collections of rich poetry, grouping poems (psalms) into meaningful subcollections can be done in multiple ways. Some approaches with the Psalms predated the canonical collection, resulting in coherent sequences within the finished book, such as the Hallel Psalms (113–18). The focus on penitence postdates the canonical collection, and hence Pss 6, 32, 38, 51, 102, 130, and 143 are scattered across the five books, though interestingly containing no examples from the distress-laden book III (Pss 73–89). But the collection is still coherent, and penitence remains one hermeneutical lens through which readers may read—and pray—with profit.

BIBLIOGRAPHY

Berlin, Adele. *Psalms 120–150*. The JPS Bible Commentary. Philadelphia: Jewish Publication Society, 2023.

Berlin, Adele, and Mark Zvi Brettler. "Psalms." In *The Jewish Study Bible*, edited by Adele Berlin and Mark Zvi Brettler, 1265–435. 2nd ed. Oxford: Oxford University Press, 2014.

Briggs, Charles, and Emilie Briggs. *A Critical and Exegetical Commentary on the Book of Psalms* 1–2. International Critical Commentary. Edinburgh: T. & T. Clark, 1906–7.

Byassee, Jason. *Psalms 101–150*. Brazos Theological Commentary on the Bible. Grand Rapids: Brazos, 2018.

Davis, Ellen F. *Getting Involved with God: Rediscovering the Old Testament*. Cambridge, MA: Cowley, 2001.

DeClaissé-Walford, Nancy L., et al. *The Book of Psalms*. New International Commentary on the Old Testament. Grand Rapids: Eerdmans, 2014.

Gillingham, Susan. *Psalms Through the Centuries, Volume 2: A Reception History Commentary on Psalms 1–72*. Wiley Blackwell Bible Commentaries. Oxford: Wiley Blackwell, 2018.

Goldingay, John. *Psalms Volume 1: Psalms 1–41*. Baker Commentary on the Old Testament Wisdom and Psalms. Grand Rapids: Baker Academic, 2006.

———. *Psalms Volume 3: Psalms 90–150*. Baker Commentary on the Old Testament Wisdom and Psalms. Grand Rapids: Baker Academic, 2008.

Gunkel, Hermann. *Introduction to Psalms: The Genres of the Religious Lyric of Israel*. Completed by Joachim Begrich. Translated by James D. Nogalski. Macon, GA: Mercer University Press, 1998.

Hays, Richard B. "Psalm 143 as Testimony to the Righteousness of God." In *The Conversion of the Imagination: Paul as Interpreter of Israel's Scripture*, by Richard B. Hays, 50–60. Grand Rapids: Eerdmans, 2005.

Hossfeld, Frank-Lothar, and Eric Zenger. *Psalms 2: A Commentary on Psalms 51–100*. Hermeneia. Minneapolis: Fortress, 2005.

Hossfeld, Frank-Lothar, and Eric Zenger. *Psalms 3: A Commentary on Psalms 101–150*. Hermeneia. Minneapolis: Fortress, 2011.

Johnston, Philip S. "Index of Form-Critical Categorizations." In *Interpreting the Psalms: Issues and Approaches*, edited by Philip S. Johnston and David G. Firth, 295–300. Leicester: Apollos, 2005.

Levison, Jack. *Inspired: The Holy Spirit and the Mind of Faith*. Grand Rapids: Eerdmans, 2013.

Levison, John R. *Filled with the Spirit*. Grand Rapids: Eerdmans, 2009.

Nasuti, Harry P. *Defining the Sacred Songs. Genre, Tradition and the Post-Critical Interpretation of the Psalms*. Vol. 218 of *Journal for the Study of the Old Testament Supplement Series*. Sheffield: Sheffield Academic, 1999.

———. "Plumbing the Depths: Genre Ambiguity and Theological Creativity in the Interpretation of Psalm 130." In *The Idea of Biblical Interpretation: Essays in Honor of James L. Kugel*, edited by Hindy Najman and Judith Newman, 95–124. Vol. 83 of *Supplements to the Journal for the Study of Judaism*. Leiden: Brill, 2004.

Sommer, Benjamin D. "Introduction to the Sidebars." In *Psalms 120–150*, by Adele Berlin, xxvii–xl. The JPS Bible Commentary. Philadelphia: Jewish Publication Society, 2023.

Waltke, Bruce K., et al. *The Psalms as Christian Lament: A Historical Commentary*. Grand Rapids: Eerdmans, 2014.

———. *The Psalms as Christian Worship: A Historical Commentary*. Grand Rapids: Eerdmans, 2010.

Part 2

The Rise and Fall

3

The Seven Penitential Psalms in the Hands of the Allegorist

JASON BYASSEE

CHARLES TAYLOR, PERHAPS CANADA's greatest living philosopher, wrote one of several masterpieces on the introspective self in the West, tracing its origins to St. Augustine of Hippo.[1] It's a declension narrative—without the "I" of the *Confessions* we wouldn't have the modern buffered self. I don't know whether Augustine accidentally birthed the modern self or not, but whenever I am in the psalms I see the word "I" a lot. Augustine's *Confessions* is a life drenched in the language of the psalms. Now of course the "I" in the psalms is much more corporate than our modern individual use of the word. And something new does happen with Augustine's *Confessions*. But maybe the self, in all its ragged glory, comes not from Augustine but from David.

My title has at least two question-begging claims: the seven Penitential Psalms in the hands of the allegorist. Augustine does not know the medieval Christian liturgical tradition of the seven psalms of penitence. And Augustine tends to be dismissive of the term "allegory" when it comes up: it seems to him something pagan actors do, and worse, it confuses reality with lies. I therefore use the term advisedly. Robert Wilken taught me to read Augustine on the psalms, and has valiantly dusted off the term "allegory" as a churchly way of reading Scripture over against its detractors.[2]

---

1. Taylor, *Sources of the Self*, 127–43.
2. See Byassee, *Praise Seeking Understanding*, 44–48.

Twentieth-century histories of doctrine tended to distinguish typology from allegory. A biblical typology was taken to be a connection between two historical events in the Bible that each illumine the other. For example, compare Abraham's near sacrifice of Isaac and Jesus' sacrifice on the cross. They differ in their particularity and the traffic flows in one direction: Old Testament to New. An allegory by contrast was taken to be more fanciful, to depart from the historical particulars of the text into more metaphysical speculation or spiritual pablum. If you have been schooled at all in historical criticism, you will know the criticisms of allegory. Better to listen to Scripture "on its own terms" historically, then you can go on and make whatever extraneous connections you want. Or not.

I remember when I first started to question this. The great C. H. Dodd opens his outstanding book on parables with a reading of the good Samaritan, and Augustine as the villain.[3] The man in the parable goes down the road to Jericho, is beaten, stripped, left for dead in the ditch. A priest comes by and ignores him. A Levite does the same. Then a Samaritan stops, tends to the man's wounds, puts him on his animal, takes him to an inn, pays for his care, promises to return and pay any further amount owing. St. Augustine sees here a glimpse of the incarnation. The assaulted man is humanity. The priest and Levite represent Judaism—we'll say more about Augustine's anti-Judaism later. The Samaritan is Christ, who comes down the road into our world, lowers himself to the ditch we are in, tends our wounds, picks us up, and loads us onto the beast of his flesh, leaves us at the church, promises to return to pay anything owing. Dodd dismisses such a reading entirely. But learning of it, in between the lines of Dodd's dismissal, I thought, "OK, that might be bonkers, but it's kind of beautiful. And why is he so anxious to undo it?"

I've unpacked Augustine as a reader of the Psalms in my book *Praise Seeking Understanding*. Michael Cameron is a proper patristics scholar who presents Augustine's hermeneutic without the apologetic in his book *Christ Meets Me Everywhere: Augustine's Early Figurative Exegesis*. What I want to do here is attend to Augustine's readings of what would become the seven Penitential Psalms. Do critics of allegory have a point? Or does Augustine respect the letter of the text such that its straightforward call to repentance is maintained, or even strengthened?

First, take our Ps 38, his 37, "O Lord, do not rebuke me in your anger . . . there is no health in my bones because of my sin" in the NRSV

---

3. Dodd, *Parables of the Kingdom*, 13–14.

translation (Ps 38:1 and 3). Augustine's Latin text, translated into English by Maria Boulding, has "Lord, do not rebuke me in your wrath. . . . There is no peace in my bones in the face of my sins."[4] Augustine's first question is always to ask, "Who is speaking here?" Scholars call this prosopological exegesis: determining the identity of the speaker comes first. The superscription attributes the words to David. Our assumption today is that the words are attributed to David honorifically in later centuries. Jewish and Christian communities pray these words corporately, so that "I" becomes "we." Augustine's mind goes elsewhere: "Some take this to be Christ's voice, on account of all that is said a little later about his passion."[5] The psalm describes suffering, chastisement, betrayal by friends, and desperation for help.

This is precisely where modern exegetes get nervous. Let the psalm speak "on its own terms." A christological move here is ahistorical at best and, we worry, supercessionist or even anti-Jewish at worst. There is enough anti-Judaism in Augustine and in the church after him to lend credence to this charge. But pause with me for a moment. Jews read the psalms, like the rest of the Hebrew Bible, through the rabbis, and don't skip directly to the present. It is not inherently anti-Jewish to steep Scripture in later tradition. Let's see what Augustine's reading yields.

What it yields is a problem. "How can one who was guilty of no sin say, 'There is no peace in my bones in the face of my sins?'" Here Augustine's hermeneutic doesn't smooth over a problem, it intensifies one.[6] If the "I" is Jesus Christ who prays psalms from his cross, how can he claim that sin causes his suffering? It is basic Christian grammar that Christ, being God, has no sin. Augustine's answer powers his entire psalm hermeneutic: the *totus Christus*: the whole Christ. He borrows St. Paul's image of Christ's body into which believers are baptized. In this body, Christ speaks sometimes for himself, the head, as when he speaks words of union and delight. Other times the head speaks on behalf of the members, as when he confesses sins. These aren't his sins, properly speaking. They are the body's, "ours." He graciously makes our sins his when we pray them. In Augustine's words:

> The need to make sense of this forces us to recognize that "Christ" here is the full Christ, the whole Christ; that is, Christ,

---

4. Augustine, *Expositions II*, 147–50.
5. Augustine, *Expositions II*, 150.
6. I am using Rowan Williams' language here.

Head and body. When Christ speaks, he sometimes does so in the person of the Head alone, the Savior who is born of the virgin Mary; but at other times he speaks in the person of his body, holy Church diffused throughout the world. We are within his body . . . we are members of it, and we find ourselves speaking those words.[7]

When Jesus quotes Ps 22 [21] from his cross, he is showing his body, the church, how to read his Bible. Christ our head speaks our desolation. Then he in turn gives us his divine words of blessing. Augustine calls it the *admirabile commercium*, the wonderful exchange, the divine business deal. Christ takes sinners' words and makes them his. In return, we receive his divine words and they are made ours. That's a good trade. And once he has that psalm hermeneutic in place, Augustine can read all the depths of the psalms in a new christological light.

Now that all got very theological very fast, I realize. It also got very specifically Christian. And it is baffling to most Christians, let alone others. While Western churches revere Augustine, this psalm hermeneutic really lives on only in monasteries. In university and seminary settings, it is mostly unknown, or if brought up, disdained. But like C. H. Dodd's interpretation of the good Samaritan, I am not sure that it is ridiculous or dangerous. It is actually sort of beautiful—it has a compelling logic to it. The New Testament metaphor of the body of Christ is omnipresent in Christian liturgy, and has Jewish and other antecedents. Another metaphor is of Christ and his church as bridegroom and bride, drawing on the Song of Songs. "This is a great mystery," Paul says, "but I am referring to Christ and the Church"[8] (Eph 5:32). Other places in the New Testament also suggest a permeability between Christ and human beings, Matt 25 most famously: "Inasmuch as you did it to one of the least of these My brethren, you did it to Me" (Matt 25:40b NKJV). In Acts 9, when the risen and ascended Christ appeals to Paul the murderer he asks, "Why are you persecuting me?" Not "my people," but me. This deep union between Christ and his people—one body, a marriage, where you can't tell where one stops and another starts, powers Augustine's understanding of salvation and so his sermons on the psalms. He preaches elsewhere, "Wherever Scripture does not indicate when the body is speaking, when the Head, we hear them speak with one single voice."[9]

7. Augustine, *Expositions II*, 150.
8. Augustine, *Expositions II*, 151.
9. Augustine, *Expositions II*, 151.

To our ears that is all profoundly nonliteral. Augustine is importing an apparatus from elsewhere and bending the letter to his whims. In one way I agree. My book *Praise Seeking Understanding* tries to unpack this hermeneutic by calling it "allegory." The church, like our elder siblings in Israel, had a place for multivalent interpretations until the Reformation, the Enlightenment, and modernity insisted texts could only have one sense. A more generous and lighter touch would grant that texts can have multiple meanings without these competing with one another. Notice where Augustine is drawing this apparatus from: the New Testament. One portion of the canon is interpreting another. That is what all faith traditions do. As a Christian theologian and preacher, I argue that the church's only access to Israel is by baptism. Gentiles have no natural right to Israel's story. We're grafted in by grace like a branch into a tree we're not naturally part of. It is appropriate for us who come to this text in Christ to read it through the one who incorporates us into it. I have no argument by which Jews or other non-Christians should read this way. I call it allegory, but Augustine does not. He thinks he is reading literally. Those in Christ approach this text and cannot not see him here. This is not allegory, contrary to my title's characterization. It is christological literalism. Augustine cannot not see Christ here in the Bible and everywhere else too. We see one of Augustine's rules for reading in his sermon on our Ps 32, his Ps 31:

> Happy are those to whom the Lord imputes no iniquity
> and in whose spirit there is no deceit.
> Ps 32:2 (NRSV)

Augustine's Latin version translated into Maria Boulding's English says, "Blessed is the one . . . in whose mouth is no guile."[10] No guile. Now, this is where linguistic precision matters, and it is beyond my abilities. Others spend their lifetimes steeped in Hebrew, Latin, Greek. I wish I had extra lifetimes. So let's pretend he and others rightly translated Hebrew to Greek to Latin to English. A New Testament ear hears "in whose mouth is no guile" and thinks of the story of Nathanael, whom Jesus calls "a true Israelite in whom there is no guile."

> "Where did you get to know me?" Jesus answered, "I saw you under the fig tree before Philip called you." Nathanael replied, "Rabbi, you are the Son of God! You are the King of Israel!" Jesus

---

10. Augustine, *Expositions I*, 371.

> answered, "Do you believe because I told you that I saw you under the fig tree? You will see greater things than these."
> John 1:48–50 (NRSV)

In Augustine's Latin the two words are the same, "a true Israelite, in whom there is no guile" and "one in whose mouth there is no guile."[11] Now he has a verbal link between Israel's Scripture and the New Testament that powers his whole reading.[12] That is an aesthetic rule. It is hard and fast, not a rule of thumb: there must be a verbal link to enable the move between Testaments. If there are rules, by definition, this is not an arbitrary exercise. The lines on the field are painted; you cannot go outside them. Within those lines there are infinite possibilities. As every artist knows, the only freedom there is, comes with limits.

But here too we see Augustine in his full horror. Now remember Augustine is better than most of his contemporaries on the Jews, as Paula Frederiksen shows.[13] When Christ says he "saw" Nathanael under the fig tree, that means he had mercy on him. For God to see us without guile is only possible with God's own mercy, Jews and Christians then and now would agree. For Augustine this is a figure of all humanity: Jesus sees us, the whole human race, under that fig tree. Then Augustine says that Christ condemns the Jews for producing rotten fruit. In Augustine's substitutionary logic, Jewish people get guilt so the rest of humanity gets grace. This is substitution gone horribly wrong.

In *Praise Seeking Understanding* I have a chapter on Augustine and the Jews that argues with him: he reads the imprecatory psalms as prayers to turn enemies into friends.[14] If he took this christological insight seriously, he could not have said what he said about our Jewish forebears. Often, we who want to champion ancient Christian thought pass over its anti-Judaism without engaging. But we must also correct it. Augustine shows us another tool with which to do so.

> Happy are those whose transgression is forgiven,
> whose sin is covered.
> Ps 32:1 (NRSV)

---

11. Augustine, *Expositions II*, 371.

12. It is Robert Wilken's point that a verbal link is needed for allegory to work. See, for example, Byassee, *Praise Seeking Understanding*, 45.

13. Frederiksen, *Augustine and the Jews*.

14. Byassee, *Praise Seeking Understanding*, 149–93.

Augustine is worried that sin here is merely "covered." That sounds like sin is left in place, but disguised, maliciously covered over. But forgiveness has to mean sin's removal. So he has to bend the letter.[15] To answer Hans Frei's famous question: the literal sense of Scripture will bend, it will not break; it is not brittle and will not shatter.[16] Whatever "covered" means, it cannot mean sin is still there. In the last of what would become the psalms of penance centuries later, Augustine comments on Ps 143 [142]: "For the glory of your name, O Lord, you will give me life."[17] We have no merits of our own; we deserve only punishment. Grim, but that is him. Then he says this, in language so vivid any preacher of any faith would have to be jealous: "You have torn out my demerits and engrafted your gifts."[18] Sin cannot just be covered. It has to be torn out. Rooted out. Excised. Elsewhere he uses medical language to suggest precision, as in Ps 51 [50] when he says this: "To cut away diseased tissue in David's heart and heal the wound there, Nathan used David's tongue as a knife."[19] Ooh, that's good. But here in Ps 143 [142], Augustine uses more desperate, hurried language, "torn out." Another rule: Scripture is its own interpreter.

Another place where Augustine interprets one Old Testament text via others is our Ps 38:2, "For your arrows have sunk into me." Remarkably, in the game of telephone between translations, these arrows hit their mark:

> Where do they come from, the arrows that have found their mark in him? Perhaps what he calls arrows are the punishment, God's vengeance itself, plus the pains of mind and body which are unavoidable in this life. Holy Job also mentioned arrows of this sort: amid his woes he said that the arrows of the Lord had lodged in him. However, we customarily take arrows as representing God's words, so surely it is impossible for anyone struck by them to suffer in this way? The arrows of God's words inflame love, not pain. Yes, surely that is true, because if we love something and do not possess it, we inevitably feel pain. The only person who loves without experiencing any pain is the one who possesses the beloved object; but, as I have said, anyone who loves but does not yet possess must of necessity groan with pain. This is why Christ's bride in the Song of Songs, speaking for the Church, cries out, "I am wounded with love" (Sg 2:5 LXX). She

---

15. Augustine, *Expositions I*, 376.
16. Frei, "'Literal Reading,'" 117.
17. Augustine, *Expositions VI*, 359.
18. Augustine, *Expositions VI*, 359.
19. Augustine, *Expositions II*, 415.

says that charity has wounded her because something she loves is not yet hers, so she suffers, not yet possessing it. If she is suffering pain, she rightly says she is wounded, but this wound is sweeping her on toward true health.[20]

I'm sorry for the long quote, but I wanted you to have a taste of Augustine as he thinks out loud. Are arrows divine punishment? That's true in Job 6:4. But no, he pivots to say these must be the arrows in the Song of Songs, with which the lover entices the beloved. Old Testament interprets Old Testament here. The only way to be happy is to possess what one loves. But humans cannot possess God, as the Song shows God is always just out of reach to inflame love more. Then the coquettish lover gives just enough hope that we are off in pursuit again. What Augustine's way of reading does is open up the Old Testament so Christians can learn more about Jesus Christ. Then it is not a Marcionite wasteland misleading us. It is a book of lovers transfiguring us and others. I do not know enough about Jewish readings of the Song to know this, but I bet they are not a lot different. There can be readings that are verbally and theologically linked but are dismissed: Job is wrong about the arrows, Solomon is right. It's a rule, a weird one to us, but not to the ancients. Which reading delights your hearers more?

Previously in Ps 143:6 Augustine comments on this line: "I stretch out my hands to you; my soul thirsts for you like a parched land" (NRSV). I think my dull exegetical senses might say something like this: the psalmist is "just" using poetic language to say she needs God. True enough. But Augustine the interpreter thirsts too. He longs too. We can feel his hands aching, feel the thirst in the desert. "I can thirst for you, but I cannot irrigate myself."[21] Augustine at his best sounds like an African American preacher riffing off Scripture, jazz riffs improvised but not random or unrehearsed. His mind goes to Ps 104 [103] about how we are dust, but the Spirit of God can renew dust, and often does. Then he concludes with a riff on 2 Cor 5:17–18 and John 12:24–25.[22] He is echoing a theme, here as elsewhere, in Paul that has often been read as supercessionist: the letter kills but the Spirit gives life. But stay with me. "In your Spirit all old things have passed; in your Spirit all are made new." Did you hear him say Paul's word "all?" Here Paul's universal vision pushes Augustine to say

20. Augustine, *Expositions II*, 149–50.
21. Augustine, *Expositions VI*, 354.
22. Augustine, *Expositions V*, 165.

all things are being made new. Wait, you mean some of the things? No. Most of the things? No. All the things. That includes the dust we are. God makes life out of dust and new resurrection life out of dust. That includes the Scripture we read. Hebrew Bible and New Testament, the fathers and the rabbis. If Christ is making all things new as Ps 104 promises and 2 Cor 5:17 insists, then not a speck of dust or ash will be forgotten. It will be resurrected and made whole. Augustine is showing us what desire is for. It is there to be inflamed for God, as the Song of Song shows, as his *Confessions* demonstrates, as every preacher knows but we usually can't deliver on. The advice I most often give to preachers is to pretend you're dying the day after you preach this. One day that will be true. Now go back and rewrite it. With desperation. Longing. And aching hope.

Now that is a little better than my "this-is-just-so-much-poetry" dismissal. This hunger and thirst are what being alive is for. And let us never again use the word "just" to dismiss anyone's exegesis. Ever.

A final rule for this essay: doctrine guides Augustine's reading of the psalms. That may not surprise you: doctrine guides everyone's reading of everything, especially perhaps those who insist they have no doctrine. They are just not fessing up. Augustine is clear about the doctrine that guides his readings so we can interrogate it. It is held pretty loosely, as doctrine done right always is. And it doesn't come up often, as rules for reading should not. But occasionally we can glimpse it. So Ps 50:4 for Augustine says, "For I admit my wrongdoing, and my offense confronts me all the time."[23] The NRSV of Ps 51:3 reads, "For I know my transgressions, and my sin is ever before me." Augustine interprets, "I have not thrust my deed behind my back; I do not look askance at others while forgetting myself."[24] David does not because Nathan will not let him. Psalm 51's superscription is about Nathan's confrontation after Bathsheba. Perhaps the greatest Old Testament parable is Nathan's before his king. It calls to Augustine's mind Jesus' parable about the woman caught in adultery. Is the New Testament a book of mercy, the Old a book of harsh law? By no means. *Me genoito*. Hell no.

> Remember that the Father had not given the law apart from the Son. If heaven and earth and all things in them were made through him, do you suppose that the law was written without the Word of God? No, God does not contradict his own law, any

---

23. Augustine, *Expositions II*, 415.
24. Augustine, *Expositions II*, 415.

more than an emperor acts in opposition to his laws when he pardons someone.[25]

It is basic Christian grammar that the Son is not lesser in power than the Father. That doctrine is a rule. Now go read as you will. Make it beautiful, convert us, do no harm.

Another doctrinal guideline is that God does not change. Cannot change. Basically agreed on by ancient Jews, Christians, and Muslims, though there are some stories whose letter you have to bend to get there. But it is also a biblical rule, our Ps 102:27 (NRSV): "But you are the same, and your years have no end." Divine immutability is a biblical doctrine. A minority report, maybe, that becomes dominant, but it's in there too. So it's a rule for reading. The psalmist is flying high:

> Long ago you laid the foundation of the earth,
> and the heavens are the work of your hands.
> They will perish, but you endure;
> they all wear out like a garment.
> You change them like clothing, and they pass away;
> but you are the same, and your years have no end.
> Ps 102:25–27 (NRSV)

We are the ones who change. Constantly. But that's not a bad thing, as in some more Platonist accounts of permanence versus fluidity. Creatures changing is the very possibility of creation's growth into union with God. Augustine preaches:

> You hear clothes mentioned, and a garment: can you interpret them otherwise than as the body? Let us hope that even our bodies will be transformed, but only by him who existed before we did, and abides after us, by him whose act has made us what we are, by him to whom we shall come when we have been changed. He changes us but is not changed himself; he creates us but is uncreated; he moves all things but abides in stillness; he it is who, as far as flesh and blood can understand him, is the I AM WHO I AM.[26]

God uses creatures' constant change to transfigure creation ever more closely to God's self, the *idipsum* in Latin, the selfsame, the one who is his own being. Augustine is often spoken of as baptizing Platonism, but this is a good example of him Hebraizing it. Not all change is bad.

---

25. Augustine, *Expositions II*, 416.
26. Augustine, *Expositions V*, 75–76.

Human change is hard, but necessary, for growth toward the unchanging one who loves us.

Because Augustine holds doctrine tightly, he can hold interpretations of this or that verse loosely. Some Christians have insisted Ps 51:11, "Do not take your holy spirit from me," has to be a reference to the Holy Spirit: "Some have understood this to be a reference to the Trinity in God, to God himself, apart from the incarnation." That would be a prooftext of the sort modern biblical scholars deplore and mock. Augustine has Jerome in mind as a source he often quibbles with, but respects: "This may be correct. Alternatively, the psalmist may have meant the upright spirit in a human being. . . . Neither option is heretical."[27] Textbook accounts of figural exegesis say they correct the letter to accord with orthodoxy. Some do that: Origen on the immoralities of the patriarchs perhaps, though he borrows from Jewish interpreters to offer up more morally salutary readings. But by Augustine's time the doctrines of the Spirit and the Trinity are settled. He doesn't need this verse. So he can shrug at it and move on.

I need to conclude. I hope you are seeing that I think Christians should read the Bible like Jews long have. I suspect we do not because they do—in the mutual recoil Irving Greenberg and others write about. But Augustine is into trades, so perhaps we can make an exchange here? There is no reading of Israel's Scripture without what this rabbi says about what this rabbi says about what this rabbi says about Moses. If Moses shows up to clarify we ask him, "Wait, have you read rabbi so and so, and rabbi so and so, and rabbi so and so?" Moses gets a voice, but only filtered through the tradition that bears him to us. If you want to master that tradition, you get a voice too. That's what preachers do. Augustine shows us he is reading David, with others living and dead, to pry delight out of hearers of his sermons on their way to work on weekday mornings in Roman North Africa. A final glimpse: our Ps 143:4, "My heart within me is appalled." Jesus Christ prays that, the whole Christ, head and members. "He took over into himself our lowly body and transformed it, configuring it to his own glorious body."[28] There is no depth to which Christ does not descend. Once there, he "slew death, broke bonds, and captured captivity." God in Christ makes a raid on hell to lift out Adam and Eve. The speaker is appalled with death, like we all are, but he can actually do something about it.

27. Augustine, *Expositions II*, 425.
28. Augustine, *Expositions VI*, 352.

BIBLIOGRAPHY

Augustine. *Expositions of the Psalms I: 1–32*. Edited by John E. Rotelle. Translated by Maria Boulding. Hyde Park, NY: New City, 2000.

———. *Expositions of the Psalms II: 33–50*. Edited by John E. Rotelle OSA. Translated by Maria Boulding. Hyde Park, NY: New City, 2000.

———. *Expositions of the Psalms V: 99–120*. Edited by Boniface Ramsey. Translated by Maria Boulding. Hyde Park, NY: New City, 2003.

———. *Expositions of the Psalms VI: 121–150*. Edited by Boniface Ramsey. Translated by Maria Boulding. Hyde Park, NY: New City, 2000.

Byassee, Jason. *Praise Seeking Understanding: Reading the Psalms with Augustine*. Grand Rapids: Eerdmans, 2007.

Cameron, Michael. *Christ Meets Me Everywhere: Augustine's Early Figurative Exegesis*. Oxford: Oxford University, 2012.

Dodd, C. H. *The Parables of the Kingdom*. London: Charles Scribner's Sons, 1961.

Frederiksen, Paula. *Augustine and the Jews*. New Haven, CT: Yale University Press, 2008.

Frei, Hans W. "The 'Literal Reading' of Biblical Narrative in the Christian Tradition: Does It Stretch or Will It Break?" In *Theology and Narrative: Selected Essays*, by Hans W. Frei, edited by George Hunsinger and William C. Plachier, 117–52. New York: Oxford University Press, 1993.

Taylor, Charles. *Sources of the Self: The Making of the Modern Identity*. Cambridge: Cambridge University Press, 1992.

4

From the Sixth Century to the Thirteenth Century

MARK J. WHITING

INTRODUCTION

THE PREVIOUS CHAPTER EXPLORED Augustine's sermons on the seven psalms that came to be known as the Penitential Psalms. In addition, key aspects of his theology seem inextricably bound to them. There is, however, no conclusive evidence that he knew these seven psalms as a fixed group. Our first task in this chapter is to explore the role of Cassiodorus (c. 487–c. 580) in the origin story of the Penitential Psalms. To put it another way: how did Pss 6, 32, 38, 51, 102, 130, and 143 [6, 31, 37, 50, 101, 129, and 142] become the definitive Penitential Psalms? The second, and much larger, goal of chapters 4 and 5 is to chart how this group of seven psalms, unrecognized as such by the biblical writers, came to occupy the foreground of liturgical practice in the Middle Ages. We shall see that for a millennium or so, these psalms were so important in both faith and praxis that they had the status of a canon-within-the-canon.

Our goals must be addressed somewhat selectively. Fittingly we will view the Seven Psalms through seven medieval windows—three in this chapter and four in the next. The life and work of Cassiodorus provides our first window. The second window is the practice and doctrine of penance. The third window is the liturgical use of these psalms in the high Middle Ages. The Fourth Lateran Council of 1215 provides a logical closing terminus for this chapter and an appropriate point of departure for chapter 5. The four windows of the next chapter will showcase the diverse ways in which the Seven pervaded Western culture, liturgy, and daily life in the thirteenth to sixteenth centuries.

CASSIODORUS AND THE ORIGIN STORY OF THE SEVEN PSALMS

Flavius Magnus Aurelius Cassiodorus Senator (c. 487–c. 580) lived a life of two halves. In the first half he lived a privileged life as one of ruling elite of the Ostrogothic Kingdom, also known as the Kingdom of Italy. Such status necessitated working hard to stay alive as he climbed to the top of the precarious political ladder. His famous compatriot, the philosopher Boethius (c. 480–524) failed to survive the vicious politics of this time. He was executed for what was judged to be treasonous correspondence with Justin I (c. 450–527), the Eastern Roman emperor. This was despite the possibility he might well have been making genuine attempts to bring peace and unity by facilitating dialogue between the increasingly alienated Roman and Constantinopolitan Sees.[1] Cassiodorus ran similar risks as he too sought good relations between East and West. Although his last name "Senator" is just that, a name, he did occupy very senior political positions on his journey up the ladder. He was variously *quaestor*, *consul ordinarius*, *magister officiorum* (in this specific role succeeding Boethius), and eventually *praetorian prefect*.[2] In these political roles Cassiodorus served in the administrations of five Ostrogothic rulers, first Theodoric (454–526) and finally Witigis (c. 500–542). The challenging politics of his day demanded artful rhetoric in the form of the official letters that got things done (or sometimes preserved the status quo). In the late 530s Cassiodorus published a selection of these, known as the *Variae*, as models of good practice.[3] His mastery of rhetoric, so clearly evident in this work, was later a key tool in his analysis of the Psalms and has a central role in his distinctive rhetorical approach to the Penitential Psalms.

The nature of the second half of Cassiodorus' life, at least in part, was a consequence of world events outside his control—though he might have seen the hand of providence at work, for at around this time

---

1. See Morton, "Death of Boethius," for an analysis of the date and circumstances of Boethius' death.
2. Copeland, "Cassiodorus' Hermeneutics," 160.
3. Cassiodorus, *Variae*.

it appears he underwent a conversion experience.[4] There is more than a hint of this half-time conversion in the introduction to his *Expositio Psalmorum* (Explanation of the Psalms):

> Some time ago at Ravenna I thrust aside the anxieties of official positions and the flavour of secular cares with their harmful taste. Once I had sampled that honey for souls, the divine psalter, I did what longing spirits often do, and plunged eagerly in to examine and to drink in sweet draughts of the words of salvation after the deep bitterness of my active life.[5]

The earlier, and more measured, fruits of Cassiodorus' active life, the *Variae*, bear only the merest hint that all was not well in the Ostrogothic Kingdom. We see, for example, an occasional nod to foreign armies.[6] These armies were those of Justin I who had decided to wrest Italy back into the Eastern See. It is reasonable to assume that when Ravenna, capital of the Ostrogothic Empire, fell in 540 and Witigis the Gothic king was taken captive to Constantinople, that Cassiodorus was part of his accompanying retinue.[7] Whilst it is possible that Cassiodorus might have commenced his *Expositio Psalmorum* in the 530s it appears to have been largely written during his time in Constantinople and completed around 550.[8]

Although written in what was essentially exile from his native Italy it appears that Cassiodorus was writing for the Italian monastic foundation—the Vivarium—founded in 544 on his family estate at Squillace. His *Expositio Psalmorum* was not only a full commentary on the biblical psalms but aimed to provide a broader education for its intended audience of monks.[9] The skills that he used in his political career to both administer effectively, and survive the times, were now turned to religious and educational ends. Unlike Augustine's *Enarrationes in Psalmos* (*Expositions on the Psalms*), Cassiodorus' work is a true commentary in the modern sense, i.e., written as purposeful sequential analysis of each psalm. In his commentary Cassiodorus speaks of the Penitential Psalms

---

4. See O'Donnell, *Cassiodorus*, 103–30, for a detailed rehearsal of the various possibilities.
5. Walsh, *Psalms* 1:23.
6. Olsen, *Honey of Souls*, 74.
7. O'Donnell, *Cassiodorus*, 132.
8. Heydemann, "Orator," 21.
9. This function of Cassiodorus' work is helpfully explored in Olsen, *Honey of Souls*, 114–46.

in a manner indicating he expects his readers to know of the Seven Psalms as a defined and closed group. It is helpful at this point to hear Cassiodorus on Ps 6 when he introduces them:

> Remember that this is the first of the penitents' psalms. It is followed by Psalms 31, 37, 50, 101, 129, and 142. We shall discuss each of these in its due place as opportunity allows. Do not believe there is no significance in this aggregate of seven, because our forbears said that our sins could be forgiven in seven ways: first by baptism, second by suffering martyrdom, third by almsgiving, fourth by forgiving the sins of our brethren, fifth by diverting a sinner from the error of his ways, sixth by abundance of charity, and seventh by repentance.[10]

As is common with early interpreters he is quick to ascribe significance to the number seven by connecting the Seven Psalms to the "seven means of forgiveness." In this way Cassiodorus is not offering exegesis, but explanation of a wider principle he considers to be part of reality. As was suggested in chapter 1 it is highly likely that this sort of celebration of the number seven might have provided part of the context in which seven, rather than six or eight, psalms were linked as a group of penitential psalms.

Although Cassiodorus is presenting the Penitential Psalms as a familiar group, the alignment of his interpretation of them with his expertise in rhetoric indicates he is putting his own stamp on their interpretation. He takes the well-known legal terminology of a *concessio*, in which a plaintiff concedes to a crime,[11] and turns it into an admission of guilt. The fourfold framework he employs, in following the *concessio*, fits some of the Penitential Psalms better than others. Despite the rather anachronistic use of a Roman legal framework as a reading lens placed in front of the text, it coheres surprisingly well with the structure of Ps 6. More specifically, it matches what is termed "prosopological exegesis" where a psalm is read by asking who is speaking its various strophes.

Examining Cassiodorus' application of the *concessio* to Ps 6 is instructive at this point. Despite opening in the form of an *exordium* to the judge, Cassiodorus makes it clear that the words of the psalmist must, of necessity, have a different content, for "only confession of faith can acquit a man whom no arguments defend. Such a course is permitted

---

10. Walsh, *Psalms* 1:90–91.
11. Copeland, "Cassiodorus," 168.

to those who truly repent, who in seeking pardon for themselves strive instead to condemn their own actions."[12] For Cassiodorus, the opening of the *exordium*—"O Lord, do not rebuke me in your anger, or discipline me in your wrath" (NRSV 6:1 [6:2])—is figurative, using metaphorical language: for "in fact the Lord is not maddened with anger or confounded with fury, but ever continues in one and the same tranquility of His glory."[13] As the psalmist continues, his plea for mercy, verse 2a [3a], and his appeal to a sickness of the bones, verse 2b [3b], is met with kindness from the God who is, after all, our physician. The *exordium* continues for three more verses and then the *narration*, which captures the attitude of repentance of the psalmist, follows. Whilst Cassiodorus' interpretation of the copious tears of the psalmist, verse 6 [7], is rather labored because of a misreading of the literary function of the parallelism between 6b [7b] and 6c [7c], he eventually concedes that the account might be hyperbolic and that these tears are evidence of repentance.[14]

Verses 8–9 [9–10], according to Cassiodorus, is the *correctio*. It is here that the psalmist embarks on self-correction, seeking to avoid the influence of the wicked. The psalm concludes with a *confirmatio* (verse 10) in which the journey from tears to joy is complete and the psalmist prays that his enemies might turn to God: "When he says let them be ashamed, he wants them to be enlightened by such contrition as to be ashamed of their previous acts, and to realize that the deeds which they long considered beneficial are wicked."[15]

Cassiodorus applies the same fourfold rhetorical legal framework to Ps 32 [31].[16] Although it makes broad sense of the psalm, the fit is weaker as the approach does not account for how the psalmist is looking back on their past experience of repentance, rather than working through a judicial rhetorical case. The same approach is employed for Ps 38 [37] which works in a similar fashion to its application to Ps 6. This is unsurprising as these two psalms, as we saw in chapter 2, share much in common in both form and content.[17] Once again, when Cassiodorus examines Ps 51 [50] he explains that it follows the *concessio* he introduced earlier: "We must remember that in this psalm the status of the argument is that called

12. Walsh, *Psalms* 1:92.
13. Walsh, *Psalms* 1:93.
14. Walsh, *Psalms* 1:96.
15. Walsh, *Psalms* 1:97.
16. Walsh, *Psalms* 1:304–13.
17. See Walsh, *Psalms* 1:376–87.

'concession' in this the defendant does not defend his action by argument, but simply asks for pardon. There is no doubt that this can be seen as a general rule in the penitential psalms."[18] Despite this statement of uniformity in approach, much of what then follows does not use the rhetorical method of *concessio*. Rather the approach recedes into the background as Cassiodorus, verse by verse, considers both doctrine and various literary devices he finds in this psalm.

In explaining Ps 102 [101] Cassiodorus essentially follows the now familiar fourfold steps of the *concessio* but with little reference to the technical language. At the conclusion of his exposition, he returns to the unitary nature of the Penitential Psalms as he exhorts his readers to appreciate the grace experienced by sinners turned penitent:

> What a blessed condition is that of penitents! It converts the guilty into the just, the sad into the unfailingly joyful, the mortal into the wholly immortal. In this world they associate with the wicked for the moment, but in the next they will gain partnership with the angels in eternal blessedness. So let us realise that this man is the fifth in the role of penitent, who defended himself by not defending himself, who washed himself clean by not washing himself, who cleansed himself by not cleansing himself. If we deserve to attain his poverty, we undoubtedly overcome all the kingdoms of the world.[19]

When Cassiodorus turns to the "sixth of the psalms of the penitents," from the outset he explains that its brevity leads to a curtailing of the fully developed fourfold approach applied to the previous five of these psalms. Here in Ps 130 [129] we instead find the opening *exordium* in which the penitent is heard "asking to be freed from the depths of sins"[20] and a hasty move to the joyful *confirmatio*. For the last of the Seven, Ps 142 [143], Cassiodorus employs his now well-worn fourfold *concessio* and makes several lengthy references back to the other six Penitential Psalms. In summarizing the conclusions that can be drawn from this psalm he provides a fitting close to this set of psalms:

> The affliction of the suppliants and the course of their blessed ears are brought to a close. But we must examine more carefully the meaning of the seventh prayer of penitents. Beginning with Psalm 6, he proceeded to Psalm 31, then to 37, to 50, to 101, to

18. Walsh, *Psalms* 1:494.
19. Walsh, *Psalms* 3:18.
20. Walsh, *Psalms* 3:312.

129, and finally here to 142. It is perhaps the case that just as we sin in the seven days which represent the extent of a week in the world, so we may be saved by the gift of healing repentance through this same number.... So let us aspire to the repentance which is the saving remedy of the human race, the consolation of those who weep, the seed of blessed joys, for it bestows the most sure hope on one and all, and imparts to suppliants *en masse* the gift of heavenly grace.[21]

Relatively few early Psalms commentaries have survived by being adopted wholeheartedly during the medieval period. Two accounts of the psalms dominated, with Augustine's rather different work of collected sermons vying with Cassiodorus' more unified commentary for first and second place for centuries. Given that the latter celebrated the Penitential Psalms as a coherent group, and the former a theological outlook so coherent with them, they were assured a prominent place in theology, liturgy, and personal devotion.

PENANCE AND THE PENITENTIAL PSALMS

In the midst of the fog of uncertainty lying over the origin of the Seven Psalms, Cassiodorus points to them as a beacon of mercy for the sixth-century faithful who desire to come before God for forgiveness. Although the rise of the Penitential Psalms owes much to Cassiodorus' work and those who promulgated it faithfully in monastic houses, they seem to already have a life of their own. It seems likely that part of the appeal of reading these seven psalms as a group is their collective coherence with the doctrine and practice of penance. We shall see that the seven Penitential Psalms provided a nexus of connections to a doctrinal and practical solution to a troubling theological conundrum.

From the earliest days of the church, anxious debate was had over how serious post-baptismal sin was to be handled. One of the earliest texts that gives insight into this debate is *The Shepherd of Hermas*, a second-century allegorical vision. A small section of what is termed "Mandate 4" from the Shepherd is illuminating in this regard:

> For, the person who has received remission of sins must no longer sin, but live in purity. However, since you are enquiring accurately into everything, I shall also clarify this matter for you,

---

21. Walsh, *Psalms* 3:412–13.

> without giving an excuse either to those who now believe or are destined to believe in the Lord. For, those who now believe or are destined to believe do not have repentance for sins, but they do have remission of their former sins. The Lord, then, has prescribed repentance for those who were called before these days. For, the Lord has knowledge of hearts and knows all things in advance, the weakness of human beings and cunning craft of the Devil, the evil he will do to the servants of God and his wickedness against them. Therefore, the Lord in His exceeding mercy took pity on His creatures and prescribed this occasion for repentance. Authority over this repentance has been given to me. "But this I say to you," he said. "After that solemn and holy call, if a man sins after severe temptation by the Devil, he has one chance of repentance. But, if he sins and repents offhandedly, it is unprofitable for such a man. Only with difficulty will he live." Mandate 4.3.2b–6[22]

The quotation above, and the wider text, indicate that some held that there was no possibility of a second remission of sin. The context of this document is one of persecution, under which some Christians might renounce their faith under extreme pressure. Hence, the question being addressed is one of dealing with a lapsed Christian rather than a Christian guilty of smaller misdemeanors. The view of *The Shepherd of Hermas* is that the lapsed Christian can repent and be forgiven afresh but argues against a further possibility of forgiveness.

Given the seriousness of the questions raised by post-baptismal sin, it is hardly surprising that a doctrine of penance developed as theologians sought to provide clarity and certainty over just how someone guilty of sinning after baptism was to achieve fresh reconciliation with God. Over time, acts of penance became a standard, and repeatable, part of the solution to post-baptismal sin. As penance evolved over the centuries, it was enshrined in church practice and instruction, as we will see in the next section of this chapter. Indeed, by the seventh century, the Council of Chalon-sur-Saône (647–53) decreed that penance should be made available whenever a sinner had fallen back into sin.[23]

Our interest in the Penitential Psalms requires some consideration of the practice of penance because of the close connection between what became a sacrament in the church—and remains one in some streams, most notably the Catholic Church—and the Penitential Psalms. The rise

---

22. Glimm et al., *Apostolic Fathers*, 266.
23. Meens, *Penance*, 80.

in prominence of these psalms is arguably due in some measure to the importance of penance to medieval life in Western Europe. Waltke et al. explain the history of penance with reference to a fourfold periodization:

> Public confession in the early church; secret or tariff penance in the sixth and seventh centuries (originating in Celtic society); tariff penance along with the revival of public penance in the late eighth and ninth centuries under the Carolingian reformers; and scholastic systematization of penance and the promotion of annual confession to a priest (by decree of the Lateran Council of 1215) in the twelfth and thirteenth centuries.[24]

This fourfold outline is a variation on a long-held consensus of a threefold development of penance. Although such a straightforward systemization is questionable[25] (and Waltke et al. are aware of this),[26] schemas such as these at least point to the immense variety of praxis around penance. For our purposes it can be noted that the Penitential Psalms, both individually and collectively, had an organic relationship with medieval penitential practice in all its various expressions. The rest of this section navigates some key aspects of the development of penance with a view to indicating the intimate connection between the theology and practice of penance and our seven psalms.

"Tariff penance" is a term traditionally given to a movement which began in Celtic Christianity where an emphasis was placed on matching an act to be performed with the perceived gravity of a sin. Hence the term "tariff" is used in the sense of a matched payment. Such an approach is often equated with a private, as opposed to public, form of penance. This is, however, an oversimplification. This can be seen in the following quotation from very early in ninth-century France. It also makes a good example of the level of prescription found in medieval handbooks of penance and shows how the Penitential Psalms might form part of the satisfactory act of penance:

> Presbyters ought to admonish the parishioners committed to them that everyone who knows himself to be stricken with the mortal wound of sin should, on the fourth day before Lent, return with all haste to the life-giving mother, the Church; where, confessing with all humanity and contrition of heart

24. Waltke et al., *Christian Worship*, 447.

25. So, for example Meens, *Penance*, 6–7, and Hamilton, *Practice of Penance*, 2–24. Both these studies question and challenge the long-held consensus.

26. Waltke et al., *Christian Worship*, 450.

> the evil that he has committed, he shall receive the remedies of penance according to the scale prescribed by the canonical authorities.... At the beginning of Lent all penitents who are undertaking or have undertaken public penance shall present themselves to the bishop of the city before the doors of the church, clad in sackcloth, with bare feet, with their faces downcast toward the earth.... Here the deans ought to be present, that is the archpriests of the parishes, with witnesses, that is the presbyters of the penitents, who ought carefully to examine their conversation. And he shall enjoin penance, according to the measure of guilt, through the appointed grades. Thereafter he shall lead them into the church and, prostrate upon the floor, he shall chant with tears, together with all the clergy, the seven penitential psalms, for their absolution.[27]

One of the challenges for the medieval church was the proliferation of such instructions. Medieval handbooks flourished, and this meant not only that the prescribed penance differed from country to country and region to region, but that the underpinning explanation of penance pointed to differences of emphasis in both practice and theology. Such disparities provided a key motivation for the Fourth Lateran Council, as we shall see below.

By the twelfth century, Peter Lombard (c. 1100–160) produced his famous *Sententiae in quatuor libris distinctae*—"sentences divided into four books"—designated simply as *Sentences* for short. The fourth volume concerns the sacraments and eschatology with almost a quarter of the text devoted to penance.[28] This work became essentially the theological textbook for the next three centuries or so.[29] Despite Lombard's book being compiled in the high Middle Ages much of the underpinning ideas about the theology of penance come from much earlier. Lombard cites the church fathers, especially Chrysostom and Augustine, when he delineates the three stages of penance: *compunctio cordis*, *confessio oris*, and *satisfactio operis*.[30] The first step, *compunctio cordis*, means "compunction of the heart." The Latin *compunctio* is a sudden awareness of one's moral fragility and need for repentance. This term, which refers to pricking, can be traced as a theological idea in Acts 2:37, its only direct biblical

---

27. McNeill and Gamer, *Medieval Handbooks*, 314–15.
28. Distinctions XIV to XXII, see Lombard, *Sentences* 4:69–135.
29. See Rosemann, *Sentences*, 21–183, for the remarkable impact of this book from the twelfth to fifteenth century.
30. Lombard, *Sentences* 4:88–135.

precedent. There we read, "Now when they heard this, they were cut to the heart and said to Peter and to the other apostles, 'Brothers, what should we do?'" (NRSV). The phrase "cut to the heart" was translated from the Greek into Latin as *compuncti sunt corde* in the Vulgate and other Latin versions. Psalm 32 [31] offers a clear connection with this idea in that the Vulgate's Ps 31:5 reads "*Conversus sum in aerumna mea dum configitur mihi spina.*" Kuczynski, in his exploration of the role of David in the medieval interpretation of the Psalms, translates this as "I am turned in my anguish, while the thorn is fastened in me."[31] Throughout the Seven Psalms the psalmist's ailments can also be read as evidence of true compunction of the heart, thus furthering the connection between the Penitential Psalms and the practice of penance. In this way these psalms have a direct connection with a key aspect of penance.

In the second step of *confessio oris*, or "confession of the mouth," we have even more connectivity between praxis and biblical text. Once penance was a universal practice in the Western Church, it was entirely natural that the Seven Psalms would become part of the language available to the confessor. Indeed, so natural and vital is this relationship between the shape of penance and the form and content of the Penitential Psalms that it seems likely that they informed the development of the doctrine in a complex "chicken-and-egg" scenario that cannot be unpacked here.

In the third, and final, step of penance, *satisfactio operis* or "satisfaction of deeds," reciting the Penitential Psalms was one of the options for appropriate actions to provide satisfaction.[32]

LITURGICAL USE OF THE SEVEN PSALMS IN THE HIGH MIDDLE AGES

Despite the relationship between the Penitential Psalms and penance their connectivity to both the liturgy and personal devotion is much broader and deeper. It is this wider role that is central to the place of the Fourth Lateran Council in the story of the Seven Psalms. It has been pointed out that although the Holy Land occupied the largest section of this Council's output, much of the rest of its diverse concerns are pastoral in nature.[33]

---

31. Kuczynski, *Prophetic Song*, 11.

32. See King'oo, *Miserere Mei*, 15–16, and see Sutherland, "Performing the Penitential Psalms," 16, and throughout, for performative usage of the Penitential Psalms, including their use to articulate penitence.

33. Boyle, "Fourth Lateran Council," 30.

As we shall see, this emphasis related to the ordering of church life, especially the monastic movement and to issues pertinent to the individual. The Penitential Psalms sit amidst a nexus of other texts, societal changes, cultural shifts, and developments in church life in the Council's constitutions. In this way we shall see that the reach of the Penitential Psalms goes well beyond their complex relationship with penance in its various forms. Before we examine the Council, some commentary is needed about the wider role of the Penitential Psalms in the life of the religious and wider populace at this time.

It would be difficult to overstate the importance of the Penitential Psalms in the Western monastic tradition. A good example of this is the *Regularis Concordia* from c. 973:

> Coming down to us from the great period of national prosperity, the reign of Edgar (959–75), when the political union of England had been in some sort achieved, it marks the final settlement, as it were, of the Benedictine revival in which a spiritual movement that had been gathering strength for well-nigh a hundred years found its highest expression.[34]

Examples of the prescribed use of the Penitential Psalms include their use in Lent throughout the monastic hours such that "at every hour one Penitential and one Gradual psalm shall be said, whereby being freed from the bonds of sin we may rise to heavenly things by the steps of the virtues."[35] Elsewhere these psalms feature prominently during nightly prayer throughout the year, on Good Friday, in the anointing of unwell brothers, in the burial office for a deceased brother, and on news of the death of a brother from another monastery.[36]

Just as the psalms were central to the regular worship in the monasteries of the early thirteenth century with the Penitential Psalms being especially prominent, around this time the Psalms generally, and the Seven in particular, began to be part of the experience of some outside the monasteries. In particular, women in the more socioeconomically privileged section of medieval society began to seek texts that might feed Christian piety. It has been suggested that Anselm (c. 1033–1109) was a pioneer in this movement with his prayers and meditations with Mathilda of Tuscany (c. 1046–1115) being key in the preservation and

---

34. Symons, *Regularis Concordia*, ix.
35. Symons, *Regularis Concordia*, 34.
36. Symons, *Regularis Concordia*, 12, 43, 64, 66, 67.

promotion of these texts.[37] Whilst the Penitential Psalms don't dominate Anselm's writings, they are cited and alluded to, and, in addition, they cohere with what might be termed the "affective piety" of Anselm's work.[38] Anselm opens his series of Prayers with a "Prayer to God." Its opening is a Penitent's call for mercy:

> Almighty God, merciful Father, and my good Lord,
> have mercy on me, a sinner.[39]

In a later prayer addressed to St. John the Baptist, there is a sustained allusion to motifs in Ps 51 as a direct acknowledgment of the need for ongoing forgiveness:

> In sin I was conceived and born,
> but you washed me and sanctified me;
> and I have defiled myself still more.
> Then I was born in the sin of necessity,
> but now I wallow in it of my own free will.
> In sin I was conceived in ignorance,
> but these sins I commit willingly, readily, and openly.[40]

Just one further example must suffice. In a prayer to St. Nicholas, Anselm desires to be a faithful penitent, both internally and externally:

> I fall away quickly, but do you be more swift to help.
> Certainly if my heart was contrite,
> if my heart was moved within me,
> if my soul was turned to water,
> if rivers of tears flowed from my eyes,
> Then I might hope that Nicholas would hear my prayers.[41]

Here in Anselm's Prayers and Meditations, a century before the Fourth Lateran Council, we see examples of an individualistic piety which takes the individual penitent seriously. The Council would in some ways continue this trajectory, perceiving individuals as needing a more bespoke cure rather than a prescribed tariff. Just how far the affective dynamic grew in medieval religious literature and practice will be one concern of the next chapter, given the even greater role of the psalms in

37. Ward, *Saint Anselm*, 9–10.
38. Ward, *Saint Anselm*, 9.
39. Ward, *Saint Anselm*, 91.
40. Ward, *Saint Anselm*, 128.
41. Ward, *Saint Anselm*, 188.

general and the Penitential Psalms as an inner canon in this role. Now we return to the Council's relevance to our exploration of the Seven.

The Fourth Lateran Council was the twelfth of what are termed the ecumenical councils of the Catholic Church. The Lateran Councils were the first of these councils to take place after the Great Schism of 1050 and so only had representatives of the Western Church in attendance. They took place in Rome and take their name from the Lateran Palace that had been in the hands of the Roman See since it was gifted in 311 by the Emperor Constantine. The Fourth Lateran Council was convoked by Pope Innocent III in April 1213 and opened at the Lateran Palace in Rome on November 11, 1215. Whilst the Council had a number of concerns, such as the defense of the Holy Land and dealing with heresy, its major emphasis can be understood as genuine pastoral concern.[42] Murray argues that "the parish priest gained a new significance in the wake of the Fourth Lateran Council's reforming program."[43] A number of the canons from this council fit with such an agenda.

Even if the Fourth Lateran Council was more consolidation and unification than innovation, canon 21 created waves in its systemization of penance. This canon, one of seventy-one, had implications for this doctrine, and ensured the continued importance of the Penitential Psalms within the church, personal piety, and wider culture. The full title of this canon is *De confessione facienda et non revelanda a sacerdote et saltem in pascha communicando* (On confession being made, and not revealed by the priest, and on communicating at least at Easter). This canon is informally named *Omnis utriusque sexus* (literally, "all of both sexes") because these are the opening words in Latin:

> Every Christian of either sex, after attaining years of discretion, shall faithfully confess all his sins to his own priest at least once a year, and shall endeavour according to his ability to fulfill the penance enjoined him, reverently receiving the sacrament of the Eucharist at least at Easter, unless perchance, on the advice of his own priest, for some reasonable cause, he determines to abstain for a time from receiving it. Otherwise he shall both be withheld from entrance to the church while he lives and be deprived of Christian burial when he dies. Wherefore this salutary enactment shall be frequently published in the churches lest anyone assume a veil of excuse in the blindness of ignorance.

---

42. Minnis, "Culture and History," 69–71.
43. Murray, "Gendered Souls," 81.

But if anyone for a right reason wishes to confess his sins to a priest who is not his own, he shall first ask and obtain permission from his own priest, since otherwise the other priest cannot loose or bind him. The priest, moreover, shall be discreet and cautious, so that in the manner of the skilful physician he may pour wine and oil upon the wounds of the injured, diligently searching out the circumstances both of the sinner and of the sin, that from these he may prudently understand what manner of advice he ought to offer him and what sort or remedy he ought to apply he ought to apply, employing various measures in order to heal the sick. Further, he is to give earnest heed that he does not in any wise betray the sinner by word or sign or in any other way; but if he needs more prudent advice he shall seek this cautiously without any divulging of the person, since we decree that he who shall presume to reveal a sin made known to him in the adjudication of penance, is not only to be deposed from the priestly office but also to be thrust into a strict monastery to do perpetual penance.[44]

CONCLUSION

If the connections and synergies between the evolution of the doctrine of penance—as well as purgatory and indulgences—can be unpacked from the rise of the Penitential Psalms, this is not the place for such a complex endeavor. More modestly we can note that the synergies between aspects of these central medieval doctrines and the Penitential Psalms ensured them a special place in the theology and practice of the medieval church.

BIBLIOGRAPHY

Augustine. *Expositions of the Psalms 33–50*. Edited by John E. Rotelle. Translated by Maria Boulding. Vol. 16 of *The Works of Saint Augustine*. Hyde Park, NY: New City, 2000.

Boyle, Leonard E. "The Fourth Lateran Council and Manuals of Popular Theology." In *The Popular Literature of Medieval England*, edited by Thomas J. Heffernan, 30–43. Knoxville: University of Tennessee Press, 1985.

Cassiodorus. *The Variae: The Complete Translation*. Translated by M. Shane Bjornlie. Oakland, CA: University of California Press, 2022,

---

44. McNeill and Gamer, *Medieval Handbooks*, 413–14.

Copeland, Rita. "Cassiodorus' Hermeneutics: The Psalms and the Arts of Language." In *Patristic Theories of Biblical Interpretation: The Latin Father*, edited by Tarmo Toom, 160–82. New York: Cambridge University Press, 2016.

Glimm, Francis X., et al., trans. *The Apostolic Fathers*. Vol. 1 of *Fathers of the Church Patristic Series*. Washington, DC: Catholic University of America Press, 2008.

Hamilton, Sarah. *The Practice of Penance, 900–1050*. London: The Royal Historical Society, 2001.

Heydemann, Gerda. "The Orator as Exegete: Cassiodorus as a Reader of the Psalms." In *Reading the Bible in the Middle Ages*, edited by Jinty Nelson and Damien Kempf, 19–42. London: Bloomsbury, 2015.

King'oo, Clare Costley. *Miserere Mei: The Penitential Psalms in Late Medieval and Early Modern English*. Notre Dame, IN: Notre Dame University Press, 2012.

Kuczynski, Michael P. *Prophetic Song: The Psalms as Discourse in Late Medieval England*. Philadelphia: University of Pennsylvania Press, 1995.

Lombard, Peter. *The Sentences, Book 4: On the Doctrine of Signs*. Translated by Giulio Silano. Toronto: Pontifical Institute of Medieval Studies, 2010.

McNeill, John T., and Helena M. Gamer. *Medieval Handbooks of Penance: A Translation of the Principal Libri Poenitentiales*. New York: Columbia University Press, 1938.

Meens, Rob. *Penance in Medieval Europe 600–1200*. Cambridge: Cambridge University Press, 2014.

Minnis, Alastair. "1215–1349: Culture and History." In *The Cambridge Companion to Medieval English Mysticism*, edited by Samuel Fanous and Vincent Gillespie, 69–90. Cambridge: Cambridge University Press, 2011.

Morton, Catherine. "Marius of Avenches, the 'Excerpta Valesiana,' and the Death of Boethius." *Traditio* 38 (1982) 107–36.

Murray, Jacqueline. "Gendered Souls in Sexed Bodies: The Male Construction of Female Sexuality in Some Medieval Confessors' Manuals." In *Handling Sin: Confession in the Middle Ages*, edited by Peter Biller and A. J. Minnis, 79–93. Vol. 2 of *York Studies in Medieval Theology*. Woodbridge, Suffolk: York Medieval Press, 1998.

O'Donnell, James J. *Cassiodorus*. PhD diss., University of California Press, 1979.

Olsen, Derek A. *The Honey of Souls: Cassiodorus and the Interpretation of the Psalms in the Early Medieval West*. Collegeville, MN: Liturgical, 2017.

Rosemann, Philipp W. *The Story of a Great Medieval Book: Peter Lombard's Sentences*. Peterborough, ON: Broadview, 2007.

Sutherland, Annie. "Performing the Penitential Psalms in the Middle Ages." In *Aspects of the Performative in Medieval Culture*, edited by Manuele Gragnolati and Almut Suerbaum, 15–38. Berlin: De Gruyter, 2010.

Symons, Dom Thomas, ed. *Regularis Concordia: The Monastic Agreement of the Monks and Nuns of the English Nation*. London: Thomas Nelson and Sons, 1953.

Walsh, P. G., ed. *Cassiodorus: Explanation of the Psalms, Volume 1*. Ancient Christian Writers. Mahwah, NJ: Paulist, 1990.

———. *Cassiodorus: Explanation of the Psalms, Volume 3*. Ancient Christian Writers. Mahwah, NJ: Paulist, 1991.

Waltke, Bruce K., et al. *The Psalms as Christian Worship: A Historical Commentary*. Grand Rapids: Eerdmans, 2010.

Ward, Benedicta, trans. *The Prayers and Meditations of Saint Anselm*. Harmondsworth: Penguin, 1973.

5

From the Fourteenth Century to the Sixteenth Century

MARK J. WHITING

INTRODUCTION

IN CHAPTER 4 WE saw Cassiodorus' celebration of the Penitential Psalms as a coherent group. Along with their association with the theological giant Augustine, this resulted in the Seven's prominence in early medieval Western theology. We also saw how these psalms meshed with the evolving doctrine and practice of penance, making them central to early medieval piety. The Fourth Lateran Council's normalization of annual Lenten penitential practice, with its emphasis on the use of the Penitential Psalms in that season, cemented their place in religious life and wider medieval culture. In this chapter, we celebrate these psalms at their height of popularity through four individuals who found profound consolation and spiritual sustenance in the Seven. More than twenty individuals—religious, clerical, and lay—could have been selected as our four late medieval windows on the Penitential Psalms. We shall see that our four chosen figures are diverse—a hermit, a religious, a woman born to nobility, and a bishop—and range across more than two hundred years. Despite their differences, they are united in their commitment to the ongoing spiritual veracity of the Psalter and more specifically the Penitential Psalms. Their contributions are wide-ranging in form too: a full English prose Psalter, a poetic paraphrase of the Penitential Psalms, a prose commentary on the Seven, and a series of ten sermons on the Penitentials. The four individuals have been chosen so that a short chronological recounting of their work sheds light on the immense value placed on these psalms across three centuries of the late medieval period.

RICHARD ROLLE AND THE ENGLISH PSALTER

Richard's year of birth is uncertain with some scholars speculating it was c. 1300 and others suggesting an earlier date of c. 1290. Other biographical details are clearer. He died in Hampole in Yorkshire some thirty miles or so from the place of his birth, Thornton, in the same county. He lived as a hermit from around the age of nineteen within his native Yorkshire, settling eventually in Hampole. He was known in popular discourse as "Richard of Hampole" and "Blessed Richard, confessor and hermit" until at least the seventeenth century.[1] His decision to follow a religious life as a mystic, preacher, and hermit followed an abrupt end to his studies at the University of Oxford.

In his capacity as a spiritual guide, he modeled the mystic tradition to his disciples and sought to enable others to experience the love that he felt for God and the saints. He wrote in both Latin and Middle English. Many of his diverse texts, such as *Incendium Amoris* and the *Emendatio Vitae*, are extant in multiple manuscripts.[2] Their survival attests to the immense influence Rolle had during his life and the number of people who valued his writings to warrant their wide transmission and preservation. During his life it appears that his spiritual guidance was mostly given to nuns and anchoresses. In some cases, the surviving literature informs us of the identity of the original recipients of the work. For example, *Ego dormio* is a letter to a nun of Yedingham, Yorkshire, and *The Form of Living* is written for Dame Marget (Margaret) Kyrkby.[3] Interesting though this type of correspondence is, our concern here is with a singular massive project, Rolle's *English Psalter*.

Rolle's endeavor stands as an important milestone in the appropriation of the Psalms by ever larger audiences. Because of the course of Western Christianity the book of Psalms was, at the start of the medieval period, available only in Latin translation. Over time Latin Psalters were copied with ever more glosses of explanation added. Eventually

---

1. Ward, "Rolle," 336.
2. Ward, "Rolle," 336.
3. Renevey, "Women," 214.

in a parallel development, excerpts from the Psalter were popularized through the innovation of books of hours. These lay literary artifacts selected some key biblical and liturgical texts to create a lay person's echo of the monastic hours.[4] At first they appear to have been for the privileged few, but eventually technology made them easier to produce and they shifted in nature to become Primers in both language and faith.[5] Rolle's work was another development in opening up the Psalms to those who only knew the vernacular. His presentation of the psalms in the English Psalter was straightforward. The Latin text is given, a line at a time, and beneath each Latin verse there is a Middle English translation. This is followed by a short explanation which unpacks and applies the verse. Rolle's endeavor to bring the Psalms to a wider audience took place at a time when it was illegal under canon law to translate the Bible from Latin into the vernacular. Rolle's project was not opposed because the vernacular sat alongside the Latin text (i.e., the Vulgate). The story of the Bible venularization is a complex one, which cannot detain us here.[6]

Though Rolle, unlike our other three witnesses in this chapter, did not author a work specifically on the seven Penitential Psalms, he achieved the more monumental task in celebrating all 150. His English Psalter is a translation into Middle English of the entire Psalter, as well as the Canticles.[7] He makes his motivation clear at the outset:

> Sothly this shynand boke is a chosen sange byfor God, als laumpe lyghtnand oure lyf, hele of a seke hert, huny til a bittire saule. Dignyte of gastly persons, tonge of priue vertus, the whilke heldes the proud til meknes, and kynges til pore men make vndire loute, fosterand barnes with hamlynes.[8]

Here we see echoes of the distinctive claims of Cassiodorus to the veracity of the Psalter. Cassiodorus refers to the Psalter as a shining book (Rolle's "shynand boke" above) and as the honey of souls ("huny til a

---

4. See Duffy, *Stripping*, 233–65

5. Sutherland, *English Psalms*, 17–34.

6. Lawton, "Englishing," 454–82, provides an engaging and sobering exploration of the Englishing of the Bible, positing that its legacy is with us today.

7. The canticles are various psalm-like biblical texts found elsewhere in both Testaments.

8. Bramley, *Psalter*, 3. The original Middle English is given here, as well as in other quotations in this chapter. Readers new to Middle English are encouraged to persevere, and I suggest reading the text aloud. Very quickly the key words and broad sense can be gained in this way.

bittire saule" above).⁹ Whilst he echoes Cassiodorus with regard to the nature of the Psalms, it is Augustine he is most indebted to in his underlying hermeneutic. Rolle's commentary is usually little more than a gloss on his Middle English translation, but in his reading of Ps 51 [50] he captures the essence of Augustine's sermon on this psalm. Rolle explains that David was set as an example to all, not to fall. If one does fall, however, then David is again an exemplar of repentance.¹⁰ For Rolle the right response to sin is to come meekly before God to ask forgiveness. Rolle goes on to point to Ps 51's [50's] special place as the most used psalm in the holy church.¹¹

A case might be made that in places Rolle's glosses enable a reading of the psalms that is more Augustinian than Augustine himself. Rolle's commentary on Ps 130 [129] is a case in point. For Rolle *De Profundis*, the penultimate Penitential Psalm, is an acutely single-minded and desperate call for forgiveness by means of penance.¹² For Rolle the whole Psalter is read through Augustine's penitential theology and a theology of penance that, in part, evolved from it. Kuczynski puts it well: "For many medieval audiences, however, they [the psalms] were the prayerbook of the Church, common property of the faithful and a guide to appropriately 'laborious' penitential behaviour."¹³ This is Rolle's motive for writing—he is writing for effect. Because he adopted a single-minded quest for the hard work of closeness to God, he wants his disciples to know the same benefit. Frequently, one of the effects he wishes to evoke are the outward sobs of the penitent, which are the mark of inward contrition.

Today we tend to see the psalms as able to evoke emotion by means of their poetic form. No doubt this was part of the implicit medieval understanding too. Yet, for Rolle and his contemporaries, there is a further dynamic at work centered on King David. Middle English texts frequently speak of David as a prophet and generally interpret the whole Psalter as the words of David.¹⁴ Rolle does this implicitly throughout his prose Psalter, and on occasions explicitly, as here in his commentary on the first verse of Ps 32 [31]: "Here the prophet [David] spekis in his person that

9. Walsh, *Cassiodorus*, 24 and 23 respectively.
10. Bramley, *Psalter*, 183.
11. Bramley, *Psalter*, 183.
12. Bramley, *Psalter*, 448.
13. Kuczynski, "Social Action," 212n13.
14. Kuczynski, *Prophetic Song*, 7.

does penaunce for his synn."[15] Rolle also understands the voice of the prophet as conveying a message that needs to be passed on. For Rolle this idea is synergistically wrapped up in his expectation of the effect of the Psalms. We see this in his explanation of Ps 51:13 [50:14]:

> I sall lere [teach] the wicked thi ways, and synful sall be turnyd til the. He that gret is [wept] before, now is he doctor, as whasay, conferme me, and confirmed i sall not be vnkynde, bot i sall lere with goed ensaumpile and worde wicked men thi ways, that is, mercy & sothfastnes. And swa synful men sall turnyd til the.[16]

Thus, here in the chief Penitential Psalm we find Rolle's ministry as a once-sick doctor who can now bring healing by enabling others to turn to the God who has healed him. In his translation and explanation of Ps 32:4 [31:4] we have a reminder that, in medieval thinking, penitence was understood to be a much more central and ongoing enterprise than is typical in most Christians streams today:

> For night and day your hand was heavy upon me.
> I am twisted in my anguish, while the thorn is fastened in me.[17]

The experience of David, and of Rolle, is more intense and extreme than today's appropriation of the image in the expression of "the pricking of one's conscience." The modern mindset, typified in our culture, suggests passive or even active suppression of this "pricking." For the devotionally oriented medieval Christian, such compunction was to be lived and breathed.

Our brief effort to see through Rolle's eyes indicates that, though Rolle did not write a specific work on the Seven Psalms, his wider project celebrates them, and their content coheres with his wider ministry. He models, around a millennium after the infamous resident of Hippo, a thoroughly Augustinian understanding of sin and penitence and shows how the Psalter resonates so readily with such a reading.

---

15. Bramley, *Psalter*, 111.

16. Bramley, *Psalter*, 187, with some translated words in square brackets after Kuczynski, *Prophetic Song*, 16–17.

17. My translation of Ps 32:4 [31:4] from Bramley, *Psalter*, 112.

RICHARD MAIDSTONE AND THE PENITENTIAL PSALMS

Alongside Rolle's prose English psalms, other works that enabled lay people to engage with the psalms in the vernacular flourished. This included a family of works known as paraphrases, a number of which survive to this day. They are poetic works based either on individual psalms or a small group of psalms. Of those on individual psalms it is Ps 51 [50] that was the most common subject, if the number of extant manuscripts is anything to go by. For example, in the Auchinleck and Thornton manuscripts paraphrases of Ps 51 [50] are found rubbing shoulders with a diverse assortment of texts.[18] For those works that include multiple psalm paraphrases it is the Penitential Psalms as an entire group of seven that eclipse the occasional, more eclectic groupings of a handful of psalms (such as Lydgate's Pss 43 [42], 54 [53], 103 [102], and 130 [129]). This is further evidence of the Penitential Psalms providing a lens through which the rest of the psalms might be understood, perhaps even a lens that offers insight into the backbone of English spirituality in the fourteenth to sixteenth centuries. Two paraphrases of the Penitential Psalms are attested in multiple manuscripts: those of Richard Maidstone (d. 1396) and Thomas Brampton (he wrote his paraphrase in 1414, but neither his year of birth nor year of death are known). We have chosen the slightly earlier work of Richard Maidstone here.

Maidstone was a Carmelite Friar, and the limited biographical information available for his early life suggests he was most likely born in the 1340s and educated at a Carmelite house in Aylesford, which is known to have had a good library around this time.[19] It is probable his birthplace was Maidstone, or somewhere close to it like Aylesford, hence his name. He was later educated in theology at Oxford where he obtained a doctorate in theology, and there are records of him engaging in debate on controversial issues of the day.

What motivated him to write an English paraphrase on the Seven Psalms is based on conjecture. Their language suggests that they are for a lay audience. There is a short opening introductory stanza of eight lines with an "abababab" rhyming scheme which is presumably to aid memorization. The rest of the work continues in eight-line stanzas with the same rhyming convention. After the opening stanza the Seven Psalms

---

18. Explored in Sutherland, *English Psalms*, 34–37.
19. Edden, *Maidstone's Penitential Psalms*, 10.

are introduced one at a time. Each English stanza is preceded by a single verse of the Latin Vulgate. In most manuscripts the Latin and English text are distinguished by the use of color.[20] Typically the first two to four lines of each stanza provide a close translation of the Latin, with the later lines elaborating and explaining the biblical text. Among the twenty-seven extant manuscripts there are some significant variations which are helpfully documented and explained in a critical edition by Valerie Edden.[21] Edden helpfully traces the unfolding story captured in the paraphrase with each psalm providing a different stage in a penitential journey:

Ps 6	Acknowledgment of sin
Ps 31 [32]	The penitent's need of a clear conscience and true shrift
Ps 37 [38]	Confession
Ps 50 [51]	Prayer for grace
Ps 101 [102]	Dramatic dialogue between Christ and the sinner, assuring him of Christ's atoning action at the crucifixion
Ps 129 [130]	Contemplation of judgment
Ps 142 [143]	Direct address to Christ. Prayer for grace to resist further temptation[22]

From the narrative arc of Edden's summary above it is immediately obvious that the poem goes beyond a paraphrase in its modern sense. Maidstone's work, in common with Rolle's prose and other efforts from this period to communicate the Penitential Psalms, is an imaginative, affective work which goes beyond explaining the text by modern conventions. Maidstone, like most of his contemporaries, reads through a rich cultural lens which is helpfully termed "penitential hermeneutics" by King'oo.[23]

The last two stanzas of Ps 51 [50] are reproduced below to help illustrate a number of instructive points about Maidstone's versification of the Penitential Psalms and wider aspects of interpretation of these psalms in the fourteenth century. The Latin text of vv. 20, 21 is included in italics so as to give at least some sense of the form of the work.

---

20. Sutherland, *English Psalms*, 234.
21. Edden, *Maidstone's Penitential Psalms*.
22. Edden, *Maidstone's Penitential Psalms*, 10.
23. See King'oo, *Miserere Mei*, 8–13, for a definition of penitential hermeneutics and throughout for its exploration.

Benigne fac, Domine, in bona uoluntate tua Syon, ut edificentur muri Ierusalem.
    Wiþ[24] meke wille do to Syon
    Þat Ierusalem walles were wel wrou3t![25]
    Ierusalem, as seiþ seynt Ion,
    Is holy chirche þat erreþ nou3t.
    Two testaments acorde in oon;
    Þese walles were togider brou3t
    Whenne Crist himself was cornerstoon,
    Þat mannes soule þus dere haþ bou3te.

Tunc acceptabis sacrificium iusticie oblaciones & holocausta; tunc imponent super altarem tuum uitulos.
    Þenne shaltou sacrifise accepte
    Of ri twisnesse and treuþe entere;
    And calueren aftir þi precepte
    Shulun be leyd on þin autere.
    On caluery a calf þer crepte,
    Cryst on cros boþe clene and clere;
    For teres þat his moder wepte
    He shilde vs alle from helle fyre.[26]

    In Maidstone's entire paraphrase the figure of David, so central to much Psalms interpretation of the Middle Ages, is absent. This is especially acute at the start of Ps 51 [50] where the Vulgate's superscript that speaks of David's double sin and Nathan's role in confronting David is omitted. Maidstone has chosen to foreground Christ in what might be termed a more figurative and less literal reading.[27] This casts an interpretive perspective across the whole poem, making the penitential journey, summarized above, the glue that binds the seven together, rather than David as the model sinner and ideal penitent. The extent of this figurative reading is evident in the identification of the calves of the Latin text in the one calf *par excellence*, Christ on the cross.[28] Maidstone is simply

---

    24. The þ is a lowercase thorn, one of two Middle English letters that did not survive the evolution to Modern English. A capital thorn is denoted Þ. Those new to Middle English can make instant headway by reading the thorn as "th." Thus "Wiþ" is "With."

    25. The 3 is a lowercase yogh, one of two Middle English letters that fell by the way as English developed. Here, in Maidstone's poems, it frequently appears in words where it should be read as "gh," so "wrou3t" becomes "wrought," in both pronunciation and meaning.

    26. From Edden, *Maidstone's Penitential Psalms*, 81.

    27. In agreement with Staley, "Maidstone's Psalms," 258.

    28. Edden, *Maidstone's Penitential Psalms*, 114.

using an interpretive paradigm that had been used for a millennium. He even explicitly references the church father who is generally recognized as defining it. The "seynt Ion" in line 3 above is John Cassian (360–435) who famously defined the four senses of Scripture, or *quadriga*. Cassian's explanation of the literal, allegorical, moral, and anagogical senses of Scripture, with Jerusalem as an example, was a ubiquitous textbook lesson. For our purposes we note that Jerusalem can be the literal city with that name, but can also be understood as the body of Christ, the church. It is this twin meaning of "Syon" (in the Vulgate) as "Ierusalem" and "Cryst" that is explored in the first eight-line stanza above.

In a parallel move, whilst Rolle majors on David as the archetypal penitent sinner, Maidstone's focus is on Christ who has made the penitent's forgiveness possible. We should not see these as mutually exclusive; indeed both can be readily traced back to Augustine and are complementary interpretive paradigms rather than inchoate alternatives. For medieval readings of the Penitential Psalms, they are the two poles of penitential hermeneutics. The affective and literal reading which has David at its heart is an exhortation based on a sinner who has gone before us. The more theological figural reading is more explanatory, and for Maidstone focuses on the cost of dealing with all such sinners. This approach can also be emotive as is evident, by way of example, from the reminder of the "teres þat his moder wepte."

ELEANOR HULL AND THE SEVEN PENITENTIAL PSALMS

Dame Eleanor Hull (c. 1394–1460) was, until recently, a marginal voice in modern appraisals of Middle English literature. Her two recognized works—including her commentary on the seven Penitential Psalms—are each known from single extant manuscripts. This perhaps led to the conclusion that her work was less widely celebrated in its day, and consequentially of less value. It also seems likely that until recently modern scholarship marginalized her significance simply because she was a woman. A third aspect that might explain the relative neglect of her voice is that the single manuscript of Hull's work states that it is a translation of a thirteenth-century French original. Since Alexandra Barratt's critical edition of her commentary, however, Eleanor Hull has been treated more frequently and much more positively.[29] Lawton, for example, in his assessment of her work points out:

> We do not scruple so delicately when writing on Chaucer: if we were to find a single French source for the Miller's Tale, it would probably not lead us to question the quality of Chaucer's writing. If we were to find that we have been describing Hull's source more than her own invention, we are nonetheless reading the text that exists. We should continue looking for sources, without qualifying a judgement that Hull writes extremely fine prose.[30]

Whatever the nature of any French antecedent, Hull's work is singular in nature given its length and complexity, and remarkable for a commentary in this period on the Seven Psalms.

Biographically we know that Eleanor was firmly rooted in the Lancastrian Dynasty. Her father was Sir John Malet of Enmore (Somerset), a retainer of John of Gaunt. Eleanor was well connected not only by birth but in marriage too, as her husband, John Hull, was also a retainer of John of Gaunt. It is likely that he is the John Hull who later became ambassador to Castile during the reigns of both Henry IV and Henry V.[31] John Hull died when Eleanor was around twenty-six years of age. After his death she frequently resided at the Benedictine priory of Sopwell in St. Albans. It was at this time that she translated the commentary on the Penitential Psalms.[32] After her son died in 1453, she retired to another Benedictine priory, over 120 miles away as the crow flies, in Cannington, Somerset. She died there in 1460 and was buried there in accordance with her wishes.[33]

We suggested above that King David and Christ provide two poles of penitential hermeneutics, the lens through which the Penitential Psalms are generally read in the medieval period. At the very heart of her commentary, in covering the middle Penitential Psalm, Hull celebrates Ps 51 [50] as Davidic by way of its title:

> This tytyl seythe, "in þe end, of þe psalmis of Dauid." Here byfore ye haue herd what a tytyl ys. The tytyl ys þe entre of þe techyng for-to vndyrstond þe psalme. Psalme, he seythe, ys þe preysyng of God with song that is browht forthe by suetnes of

29. Barratt, *Hull*.
30. Lawton, "Hull's Voices," 300.
31. Barratt, *Hull*, xxiv.
32. Koster, "Dame Eleanor Hull," forthcoming.
33. Koster, "Dame Eleanor Hull," forthcoming.

> þe euerlastyng ioye, and for that Dauid had for-ʒete the prey-syng of God al-myghty for þe veyne pleasance of his flessche, he made þis psalme wher-of þe tytyl sownyth, 'in þe end, of þe psalmis of Dauid'. And hit sownyth as moche as þer-of he seyd, 'Y haue be wykkid and wrecchyd al my lyfe vn-to now, but now schal y drawe towards hym that is þe ende of al euelys, and in þis proffytable ende that is þe begynnyng of al goodness that euer were and euer schal be y schal begynne my presyng besechyng þe al-myghty that he make me worþy to preylse hym aftyr his gret mercy and that he forʒeue me my mysdedys. And þer-for with gret repentance y seye and with feruent dezyre of myn hert: *Miserere mei deus secundum magnam misericordiam tuam.*[34]

The title is a celebration of how David's story arc goes from sinful failure to forgiven penitent through God's mercy. As Hull put it, David has arrived at a "profitable end" through penance and forgiveness; he has made a new "beginning of goodness" founded in God's mercy.

Elsewhere in the commentary on Ps 143 [142], for example, Hull presents David as speaking prophetically in Christ's voice: "Aftir his crye he prophecyeht agen and spekyth in the person of Cryst, that the cryes of verrey repentantis he rehercyth and presentith to God his fadre."[35] Lawton argues, however, that there is more going on in Hull's work than David and Christ functioning as two voices. He argues that Hull has a highly sophisticated approach to the literary relationship between voices in her text, and in its relationship to other key texts such as Augustine's *Enarrationes* (*Expositions of the Psalms*).[36] He goes further in exploring Hull's approach as one that makes use of "public interiorities":

> Augustine's precedent is formative, and much of his writing, not just the *Enarrationes*, engages with the voice of the Psalms in his interweaving of the many and the one, being at once the voice of another, available to others to voice, and an address to God that may be limitlessly personal. Augustine kept a copy of Psalm 31 on the wall of his chamber, as if it were a personal memento or manifesto. In the *Confessions* he speaks of his delight in the Psalms: "My God, how I cried to you when I read the Psalms of

---

34. Barratt, *Hull*, 100.
35. Barratt, *Hull*, 199.
36. Lawton, "Psalms as Public Interiorities," 302. See chapter 3 for more on Augustine and his *Enarrationes*.

David!" He felt the impulse "to recite them, were it possible, to the entire world."[37]

Hull does not just echo Augustine, Cassiodorus, and other commentators, but rather increases the reach and resonance of their voices. Other voices are what might be termed "intertextual relationships" with other literary works, but *a priori* for Hull the personal religious dynamic of the Penitential Psalms requires something like Lawton's richer concept of public interiorities. The nature of the voices also goes beyond an experiential encounter with ancient authors to include voices that span the original Seven Psalms and multiple texts. As Lawton explains:

> If it remains difficult to talk about Eleanor Hull's own voice, that is because she is so deft at outrunning it. Her voice is a line of flight into multiplicity: voices for David, Christ, Augustine, Isaiah, Cassian, body, soul, young, old, Jew, sultan, "fools," righteous, damned, living, dead, true penitent and, not least, the "I" of exposition.[38]

With Rolle and Maidstone, we noted the consensus as to their respective audiences. Maidstone's simple, plain verse was surely written to be propagated far and wide to fulfill a hunger for the Penitential Psalms among those who did not know Latin. Despite Rolle's stated audience as religious individuals, his prose Psalter soon had a much broader lay readership.[39] A similarly broad audience has been suggested as the destination for Hull's translation. Lawton rightly questions this. The sophistication of her work suggests a community closer to her experience: the Benedictine nunnery where she most likely lived after being widowed. Space does not permit fuller discussion, but Lawton's case opens up the possibility that rather than simply being the translator of an earlier work, Hull is at the very least a cocreator of a rich premodern commentary to stand alongside the likes of Augustine and Cassiodorus.

Before we move on to our fourth and final window on the Penitential Psalms in this chapter—our seventh for the Middle Ages as a whole—we should note that the Penitential Psalms are especially well placed to realize the full richness of Lawton's concept of public interiority. The idea provides, at least in part, an answer as to Augustine's role in the origin of the seven Penitential Psalms as a single entity. The Seven arose out of a rich dialogue,

---

37. Lawton, "Psalms as Public Interiorities," 302.
38. Lawton, "Psalms as Public Interiorities," 316.
39. Lawton, "Englishing the Bible," 470.

a dialogue in which Augustine's voice is especially clear and fruitful. In this way two apparently opposing claims are both true. As Byassee claimed in chapter 3, "Augustine does not know the medieval Christian liturgical tradition of the seven psalms of penitence,"[40] and as Gillingham suggests, he is also the source[41] of the Penitential Psalms as an entity.

JOHN FISHER: BISHOP AND MARTYR

John Fisher (1469–1535) was variously a Catholic cardinal, chancellor of the University of Cambridge, and bishop of Rochester. It is sobering to remember that he was also a martyr. He became a victim of the wrath of Henry VIII and was beheaded on Tower Hill on the morning of June 22, 1535. His head was displayed on London Bridge for some two weeks after his death. Such an ignominious end to his life would have been unthinkable in 1508 when his sermons on the Penitential Psalms were published. These ten sermons were published at the request of Lady Margaret Beaufort (the mother of Henry VII) following Fisher preaching them to her household in 1504.[42] Fisher's life was a rich and complex one, not least because of the religious turmoil that saw him move from religious exemplar to martyr. Duffy poignantly picks up on the singular nature of this fate for a cardinal of the Catholic Church:

> Catholic piety conventionally explains the scarlet robes that Cardinals wear as a sign of their readiness to shed their blood for the sake of the Christian gospel. This is an edifying thought: but as a matter of fact, in the whole millennium-long history of the cardinalate, only one member of the Sacred College has actually ever suffered martyrdom. That man was John Fisher.[43]

Of course, Fisher might have been the only cardinal to suffer this fate, but he was sadly hardly alone within the wider body of the church. Like many of those who died in this time of religious trouble he is said to have quoted from a psalm immediately prior to his execution, in his case Ps 31:1 [30:2]: "*In te, Domine, speravi, non confundar in aeternum,*"

---

40. See chapter 3.
41. See the foreword.
42. Hatt, *English Works of John Fisher*, 7.
43. Duffy, *Saints, Sacrilege and Sedition*, 150.

which in the NRSV reads: "In you, Lord, I have taken refuge; let me never be put to shame."[44]

Fisher's work on the Penitential Psalms is very different to the English prose Psalter, Penitential Psalms paraphrase, and commentary on the Seven already considered in this chapter. We get a taste of this in the following short excerpt:

> If a tablet has been foul and filthy for a long time, first we scrape it, and after it has been scraped we wash it and make it clean. Our soul can be compared to a tablet on which nothing was painted. Nevertheless, with many misdeeds and spots of sin we have defiled and made it deformed in the sight of God. Therefore, it is necessary that it should be scraped, washed, and wiped. It shall be scraped by the inward sorrow and compunction of the heart when we are sorry for our sin; it shall be washed with tears from our eyes when we acknowledge and confess our sin; and lastly, it will be wiped and made clean when we try to make amends and do satisfaction by good deeds for our sins.[45]

This quotation is instructive in a number of ways. There is direct use of the language of the Seven: "wash," "washed," and "tears." Here also is the more developed penitential language of the "soul," "compunction," and "satisfaction by good deeds." The latter prefigures the vigorous disagreements he would have with Luther more than a decade later, and his adherence to the highly developed late medieval doctrine of penance. Fisher's first oral public opposition to Luther's theology was a sermon on May 12, 1521—some three and a half years after Luther nailed his *Ninety-five Theses* to the door of the Schlosskirche in Wittenberg.[46] This was only the start of Fisher's public disputation. His *Assertionis Lutheranae confutatio* of 1523 would see nineteen editions—and four reprints of a German translation[47]—and was "regarded as the definitive work against the German reformer."[48]

Fisher's opposition to Luther was concerned with a rich tapestry of theology, including: "Scripture, the papacy, justification, free will,

---

44. Reynolds, *St. John Fisher*, 285.
45. Fisher, *Penitential Psalms*, 102.
46. Hatt, *English Works of John Fisher*, 48. Fisher had already been promulgating anti-Luther writings such as Leo X's *Exsurge Domine* a year earlier; see Rex, *Theology of John Fisher*, 78–79
47. Hatt, *English Works of John Fisher*, 10.
48. Hatt, *English Works of John Fisher*, 9.

penance, the eucharist, purgatory and indulgences."[49] The Penitential Psalms, as well as the penitential hermeneutics they engendered, are threaded intimately into this weave of doctrinal concerns. We've already seen in chapter 4 how penance evolved over the centuries. By the early sixteenth century the centrality of penance to belief and religious practice meant that many earnest Christians feared that they could not achieve justification and so escape purgatory. Such anxieties—and we'll explore Luther's acute angst in the next chapter—led to acute questions around the extent and nature of the third stage of penance, *satisfactio operis*.[50] For Luther, as we will see, the answer was that the cross of Christ eclipses the necessity of purchasing forgiveness, whether directly with indulgences or indirectly by works of satisfaction. For Fisher "the sacrament of penance is not the expression of an essentially fearful and works-bound theology, but the form the divine graciousness takes in liberating us from the need to endure the consequences of our own sins."[51] We can see Fisher's adherence to the late medieval consensus on penance:

> But since penance has three different parts, that is to say, contrition, confession, and satisfaction, the more diligently anyone exercises himself in each of them, the nearer he is to eternal bliss, for by those three, as by so many instruments, we erase and cleanse our soul perfectly from sins. When we are about to erase and remove any sort of writing, we first scrape the paper and, by that erasing or scraping, remove something of the letters, like a defacing of true, perfect knowledge, so that these letters can only be perceived and discerned dimly. If we erase the paper again, the letters shall be utterly removed and be put out of knowledge. And if we do so the third time, then shall nothing of the least letter be seen, but the paper shall be as clean as ever it was. In this way the three parts of penance achieve in our souls the removal of sins. By the virtue of contrition, our sins are forgiven; by confession, they are forgotten; but by satisfaction, they are so fully removed that no sign or token remains of them of any sort, but we are as clean as ever we were.[52]

This is not the only place where Fisher explains penance; indeed Fisher's sermons on the Penitential Psalms have been described as "an

---

49. Rex, *Theology of John Fisher*, 80.
50. See chapter 4.
51. Duffy, "Spirituality of John Fisher," 209.
52. Fisher, *Penitential Psalms*, 26.

extended meditation on the sacrament of penance in its three parts—contrition, confession and satisfaction."[53] We can see why Luther might read Fisher's metaphorical description above as exemplifying salvation by works.

We will, however, conclude our brief exploration of Fisher and the Penitential Psalms with a quote from one of many passages that demonstrates how he sees God's grace at the heart of the forgiveness made possible through the sacrament:

> Lord, our faith is so clear and assured by the merit of the Passion of your Son, our Lord Jesus Christ, who by the effusion of his holy blood has given so great efficacy and strength to the holy sacraments of his Church that when we receive any of them we shall be sprinkled and made clean by the virtue of his precious blood, as with hyssop.... None can express how joyful the sinner is when he knows and understands himself to be delivered from the great burden and heaviness of sin, when he sees and perceives that he is delivered utterly and brought out of the danger of so many and such great perils he was in while he continued in sin, and when he also perceives the clearness of his soul, and remembers the tranquillity and peace of his conscience.[54]

CONCLUSIONS

The four figures examined in this chapter are part of a wider phenomenon in which the Penitential Psalms seem to have uniquely cohered with the "mood" of the late Middle Ages, as well as more specifically the doctrines of penance, purgatory, and indulgences. It is unclear whether the Seven Psalms simply bolstered these doctrines or to what extent they functioned coherently as an impetus for the evolution of Augustinian penitential hermeneutics. Within this framework they potentially (i) helped define penance, (ii) provided a remedy for postmortem time in purgatory, and (iii) inadvertently founded the soteriological "solution" of indulgences. What is clear is that there was a collective appetite for the Seven themselves and diverse ways in which they could be imbibed and digested.

---

53. Duffy, "Spirituality of John Fisher," 208.
54. Fisher, *Penitential Psalms*, 114–15.

BIBLIOGRAPHY

Barratt, Alexandra, ed. *The Seven Psalms: A Commentary on the Penitential Psalms Translated from the French by Dame Eleanor Hull.* Oxford: Oxford University Press, 1995.

Bramley, Henry Ramsden, ed. *The Psalter or Psalms of David and Certain Canticles with a Translation and Exposition in English by Richard Rolle of Hampole.* Oxford: Clarendon, 1884.

Duffy, Eamon. *Saints, Sacrilege and Sedition: Religion and Conflict in the Tudor Reformations.* London: Bloomsbury, 2012.

———. "The Spirituality of John Fisher." In *Humanism, Reform and the Reformation: The Career of John Fisher,* edited by Brendan Bradshaw and Eamon Duffy, 205-31. Cambridge: Cambridge University Press, 1989.

———. *The Stripping of the Altars: Traditional Religion in England 1400-1580.* New Haven, CT: Yale University Press, 1992.

Edden, Valerie J. "Richard Maidstone's Penitential Psalms." *Leeds Studies in English* 17 (1986) 77-94.

Edden, Valerie J., ed. *Richard Maidstone's Penitential Psalms.* Vol. 22 of *Middle English Texts.* Heidelberg: Carl Winter, 1990.

Fisher, Saint John. *Exposition of the Seven Penitential Psalms.* San Francisco: Ignatius, 1998.

Hatt, Cecilia A. *English Works of John Fisher, Bishop of Rochester: Sermons and Other Writings, 1520 to 1535.* Oxford: Oxford University Press, 2002.

King'oo, Clare Costley. *Miserere Mei: The Penitential Psalms in Late Medieval and Early Modern England.* Notre Dame, IN: University of Notre Dame Press, 2012.

Koster, Josphine A. "Dame Eleanor Hull." In *The Palgrave Encyclopedia of Women's Writing in the Global Middle Ages,* edited by Michelle M. Sauer, et al. Cham, CH: Springer, 2026.

Kuczynski, Michael P. *Prophetic Song: The Psalms as Discourse in Late Medieval England.* Philadelphia: University of Pennsylvania Press, 1995.

———. "The Psalms and Social Action in Later Medieval England." In *The Place of the Psalms in the Intellectual Culture of the Middle Ages,* edited by Nancy Van Deusen, 191-214. Albany: State of New York University Press, 1999.

Lawton, David. "Englishing the Bible." In *The Cambridge History of Medieval English Literature,* edited by David Wallace, 454-82. Cambridge: Cambridge University Press, 1999.

———. "Psalms as Public Interiorities: Eleanor Hull's Voices." In *The Psalms and Medieval Literature: From the Conversion to the Reformation,* edited by Tamara Atkin and Francis Leneghan, 298-317. Cambridge: D. S. Brewer, 2017.

Renevy, Denis. "Women and Devotional Compilations." In *Women and Medieval Literary Culture: From the Early Middle Ages to the Fifteenth Century,* edited by Corinne Saunders and Diane Watt, 206-26. Cambridge: Cambridge University Press, 2023.

Rex, Richard. *The Theology of John Fisher.* Cambridge: Cambridge University Press, 1991.

Reynolds, E. E. *St. John Fisher.* London: Burns & Oates, 1955.

Staley, Lynn. "Maidstone's Psalms and the King's Speech." In *The Psalms and Medieval Literature: From the Conversion to the Reformation*, edited by Tamara Atkin and Francis Leneghan, 255–70. Cambridge: D. S. Brewer, 2017.

Sutherland, Annie. *English Psalms in the Middle Ages 1300–1450*. Oxford: Oxford University Press, 2015.

Walsh, P. G., ed. *Cassiodorus: Explanation of the Psalms, Volume 1*. Mahwah, NJ: Paulist, 1990.

Ward, Benedicta. "Rolle, Richard." In *The SCM Dictionary of Christian Spirituality*, edited by Gordon S. Wakefield, 336. London: SCM, 1983.

6

Fear and Hope in the Life of the Justified

Luther's Reading of the Penitential Psalms

CHANNING L. CRISLER

INTRODUCTION

ALTHOUGH IT MAY COME as a surprise to many, *The Ninety-five Theses* (1517) do not constitute the first major publication of the often celebrated and maligned Reformer, Martin Luther.[1] That distinction goes to a work he penned six months prior entitled *The Seven Penitential Psalms* (*Die sieben Bußpsalmen*).[2] While the Saxon Hus had severed ties with the medieval Roman Catholic penitential system, he held on to these psalms

---

1. For a helpful discussion on Luther's first major publication, see Wengert, "Martin Luther's First Major Publication," 166–80. Additionally, for a wonderful work on Luther and the psalms of lament, see Ngien, *Fruit for the Soul*. Luther left behind a massive literary corpus. In this essay "*LW*" together with a number refers to specific volume of *Luther's Works* in Concordia's project to translate his most important work into English; see the bibliography at the end of this chapter for the volumes cited here.

2. Wengert renders the full German title as "The Seven Penitential Psalms with a German Interpretation According to the Literal Sense, Fundamentally Oriented towards Christ's and God's Grace Alongside Its Own True Meaning" (Wengert, "Martin Luther's First Major Publication," 168). Luther later revised this 1517 work in 1525, a revision he said was characterized by relying on the "right text," that is the Hebrew text (*LW* 14:140). Jonathan Seiling argues that the 1525 revision reflects Luther's attempt to tamp down the revolutionary fervor associated with the 1525 Peasants' Revolt. See Seiling, "'Radical' Revisions," 28–47.

as "an expression of Christian repentance."³ This is not penance as an ecclesiastical prescription or an absolving act. Rather, repentance became a way of life for Luther, and he found in these seven psalms, which the church had long grouped together, a way of understanding and experiencing that life before God in Christ.⁴ He conceived of this life, which he found embedded in the Penitential Psalms according to the central "subject" that dominated the totality of his exegesis and theological formation, namely the interplay between "the sinful and lost human being and the justifying or saving God."⁵ Luther, of course, locates that justification in divinely given faith, which is far from a static experience given that faith has the dynamic person and presence of the crucified and risen Christ as its object. This theological "subject" is not a concept to be mastered but lived out as a perpetual oscillation between "sentences of divine address and human response."⁶ Justification by faith, to put it another way, is lived out in prayer, where there exists "an exchange of words" between God and the sinner.⁷ In the Penitential Psalms that "exchange" is jarring, painful, desperate, and yet paradigmatically hopeful for the believer, as Luther well understood.⁸

Given this interplay between Luther's theological "subject" and his reading of the Penitential Psalms, the guiding assertion of the present essay is simply this: Luther finds in the Seven Psalms a rich depiction of how the justified must live out their faith before God in a paradoxical and yet complementary way, namely in the simultaneous experience of fear and hope. That Luther centered his reading of the Penitential Psalms on the relationship between fear and hope is self-evident in his reflection on Ps 130:5a, wherein the psalmist asserts "I wait for the Lord." Luther remarks:

---

3. *LW* 1:ix. For a discussion on how Luther's shift in his understanding of penance is reflected in his work *The Seven Penitential Psalms*, see Kingóo, *Miserere Mei*, 82–94.

4. See chapters 3 and 4 of this volume for their origins with Augustine and Cassiodorus, and chapters 4 and 5 which give an account of their rise to prominence in the medieval period.

5. This is Oswald Bayer's translation of Luther's Latin text which reads "*subjectum Theologiae homo reus et perditus et deus justifcans vel salvator.*" See Bayer, *Theology the Lutheran Way*, 18, and 216n12.

6. On the nature of this divine address and human response in Luther's thought and its relation to the Penitential Psalms, particularly Ps 51, see Bayer, *Theology the Lutheran Way*, 18.

7. Bayer, *Theology the Lutheran Way*, 18.

8. It is clear from some of the final remarks in Luther's work on these psalms that this "subject" helps guide his interpretation of the Penitential Psalms, as I will discuss later in this essay. See *LW* 14:204.

> Up to this point the psalmist has described the *fear*, the cross of the old man, and also how this is to be borne. Now he describes the *hope*, the life of the new man, and how one should walk in it. *These two things* are taught in all the psalms, in all Holy Writ. For God deals strangely with His children, He blesses them with contradictory and disharmonious things, for hope and despair are opposite. Yet His children must hope in despair; for *fear* is nothing else than the beginning of despair, and *hope* is the beginning of recovery [emphasis added].[9]

Luther weds the interplay between fear and hope to his "subject" of theology throughout his reading of the Penitential Psalms. What he then finds necessary for the life of the justified is an ever-present fear of divine judgment that constantly sustains and renews hope in the promise of Christ.

Four brief comments on the approach implemented in this essay are in order. First, I am solely interested in Luther's reading of Penitential Psalms. Space limitations prohibit historical-grammatical exegesis of these psalms alongside of what Luther offers.[10] Second, I will work through each of Luther's readings of the Penitential Psalms with a primary focus on how he describes the nature of fear and hope in the lives of the justified. Third, given the fact that Luther regarded Christ as the *sensus literalis* of all biblical texts, special attention will be given to his christological reflection with an eye towards how that reflection informs the "fearful" and "hopeful" lives of the justified.[11] Fourth, in the conclusion of this essay, I will consider the implications of this essay for contemporary readers of the Penitential Psalms.

With respect to this fourth and final step, although the academy and church today seem to welcome the prescription of hope, I would surmise that many within these institutions might not embrace the prescription

---

9. *LW* 14:191. Readers should note that I am following the translation of the Penitential Psalms as they appear in *LW* 14.

10. This includes dealing with translational issues related to the Hebrew, Greek, Latin, German, and English versions of the Penitential Psalms.

11. For a helpful study on Christ as the *sensus literalis* in Luther's reading of Scripture, see Marsh, *Martin Luther*. However, although Luther routinely found Christ in the Psalms, Robert Kolb explains, "By no means did Luther see Christ in every passage of the Old Testament. He sometimes expressed doubt whether a psalm should be interpreted as the voice of Christ or should be seen as only the voice of David (although in many cases it could be both). On occasion he tried to distinguish when the psalmist was speaking in his own voice and when his voice turned into a prophecy of Christ's words" (Kolb, *Martin Luther*, 127). See, for example, *LW* 14:324.

of fear with the same enthusiasm. It likely strikes many as surprising, perhaps even offensive, that Luther privileges hope and fear in his reading of the Penitential Psalms.[12] Space does not permit an apology of the scriptural validity of fearing God or its logical necessity. What I can offer is a brief explanation of how Luther understood the interplay between fear and hope in the life of the justified based on his reading of the Seven Psalms. Moreover, besides the historical benefit of examining how Luther read a cherished collection of psalms, the ultimate purpose of this study is to offer contemporary readers a way to approach the Penitential Psalms in a theologically informed way. We never approach a biblical text as if our minds are a *tabula rasa*. Rather, our cognitive tablets are teeming with historical curiosities, theological commitments, and personal concerns (even hurts). What Luther offers us is a model for how to read the Penitential Psalms in relation to what he finds as the defining "subject" of theology and vice versa. The "payoff" is that neither Scripture nor theology are reduced to concepts which one masters but the place where one experiences a fearful and hopeful encounter with the crucified and risen Christ. It is in this spirit that I will conclude this essay with a set of hermeneutical theses for reading the Penitential Psalms which I have inferred from Luther's very first publication.[13]

PSALM 6—HOPE HIDDEN IN DIVINE CHASTISEMENT

Luther frames his understanding of this entire psalm around its opening request: "O Lord, rebuke me not in Thy anger, nor chasten me in Thy wrath" (Ps 6:1). From here he prefaces his subsequent reflection around two points which exemplify the way he privileges fear and hope throughout his reading of the Penitential Psalms: (1) the justified must accept that all trials ultimately come from God; and (2) the justified must know that God either chastens graciously and presently as a father or wrathfully and eternally as a judge.[14] Failure to accept point (1) engenders an impatient

---

12. This is despite clarion calls in the early church for fear such as Paul's admonition to the Philippians, "Work out your salvation with fear and trembling [μετὰ φόβου καὶ τρόμου]" (Phil 2:12b).

13. Moreover, in the spirit of full disclosure, Martin Luther is an academic "hobby" for me. My primary field of research is New Testament studies and early Christianity. Experts on Luther will likely detect the deficiencies of my analysis. My apologies in advance for plowing in their field with dulled instruments. But even a dull plough can till enough soil in which something can grow.

14. *LW* 14:140.

despising of God. Alternatively, the justified must accept and fear that all their trials ultimately come from God, because it prompts the justified to cry out for chastening from a father rather than a judge. As Luther characterizes the psalmist's opening request, "Thus he implores here, not that he wants to go unpunished altogether, for this would not be a good sign, but that he be punished as a child by his father."[15] In this way, the hope of God's grace is hidden and sought within the fear of his chastisement. The rest of Luther's engagement with Ps 6 reveals various aspects of this hidden hope as he sees it in this psalm.[16]

What is particularly pronounced is his point that God only gives an understanding of this hidden hope within sorrow over sin and in the face of potentially fatal disaster which can take many forms. Luther responds to Ps 6:2, noting, "And here it must be noted that this psalm and others like it will never be thoroughly understood unless disaster stares man in the face as it does in death and at the final departure."[17] One only tastes the fullness of paternal hope within, not apart from, tears, laments of "how long," grief that destroys the body, the machinations of evildoers, and the concern with divine wrath which hovers above all kinds of afflictions. God then shrouds hope within his chastisement, and it is only in experiencing that affliction that the justified truly understand their paternal hope. As Luther puts it, "Thus all God's chastisements are graciously designed to be a blessed comfort, although through weak and despairing hearts the foolish hinder and distort the design aimed at them, because they do not know that God *hides* His goodness and mercy under wrath and chastisement" [emphasis added].[18]

How then does Luther regard Christ in this experience of hidden hope? Two points stand out. First, Luther reads Ps 6:7a, "My body wastes away because of my grief," in concert with Jesus' parable of Lazarus and the rich man in Luke 16:19–30. He observes, "The world cares for the body with silk, gold, and sumptuous eating, like the rich man in the Gospel; but through the wrath of God I have become the poor and deformed Lazarus."[19] Christ then teaches the justified that the wrath of God must reduce one to the poverty like that of Lazarus to experience the hope

---

15. *LW* 14:141

16. As is well known, Luther's fascination with divine hiddenness is ubiquitous throughout his works. See, e.g., McGrath, *Luther's Theology of the Cross*, 164–68.

17. *LW* 14:141.

18. *LW* 14:142.

19. *LW* 14:144–45.

hidden in it. Second, Luther detects in the psalmist's request "Depart from me, all you workers of evil" (Ps 6:8a) Christ's rebuke of those who do not experience God's wrath and thereby have no hope. While noting that Matt 7:22 contains a citation of Ps 6:8, Luther interprets the two texts in relation to one another, concluding:

> These wise and holy ones are called workers of evil by Christ because they do not perform the good in the right way. And now he attacks the proud holy ones who have never felt the wrath of God or come to a knowledge of their sins. Therefore they do not believe, trust, call upon, now, or teach the goodness of God; but they mislead themselves and others through works and the bold presumption of merit before God. He wishes that these, too, would have to experience the wrath of God, so that they would finally recover from their bold presumption and regain their senses.[20]

In this way, Luther presents Christ as one who taught his disciples that hope is hidden in divine chastisement. He did so, like the psalmist in this instance, namely by using "workers of evil" who appeared to be righteous as a foil for those who experience hope in the divine chastisement of a father rather than a judge.

PSALM 32—SELF-IMPUTATION OF SIN ON THE ROCK OF JUSTIFICATION

Perhaps the most influential verses in Luther's reading of this second Penitential Psalm are its opening lines, "Blessed he is whose transgression is forgiven. Whose sin is covered. Blessed is the man to whom the Lord imputes no iniquity. In whose spirit there is no deceit" (Ps 32:1–2). While Luther certainly believes that God does not impute iniquity, he transfers what God does not do to what the justified must do, though this interpretive move is not ultimately an imposition on the text.[21] As he often does, Luther explains this necessity by employing the self-righteous as an instructive foil for the justified, noting, "That is not blessed but unblessed is he who does not impute sins to himself, is well pleased with himself, thinks himself pious, has no qualms of conscience, considers

---

20. *LW* 14:145.

21. Luther interprets Ps 32:1–2 with an eye towards 32:3–7 wherein the psalmist highlights confession of sin, which Luther characterizes as a kind of self-imputation of sin.

himself innocent, and takes this for comfort and hope."[22] He then identifies the truly blessed as "those who constantly impute manifold sins and transgressions to themselves."[23] In short, Luther prescribes the self-imputation of sin which is the antithesis of "the basic spirit of all men" wherein outwardly one "seems to be righteous," but inwardly that righteousness is self-serving and in no way carried out because of God.[24]

According to Luther, such self-imputation is synonymous with confession of sin and indispensable for justification. This is clear from several of his comments on the psalm including his reflection on the speaker's confession "I did not hide my iniquity" (Ps 32:5). Luther responds, "As soon as he realizes that he is a sinner and brings his complaint to Thee, he is justified and acceptable to Thee."[25] Self-imputation of sin is then a clearly forensic experience with God wherein "I will accuse myself; then God will acquit me."[26]

The self-imputation of sin also shapes Luther's christological reflection in at least two ways. First, he finds in this psalm the specific kind of self-imputation to which Christ himself speaks a word of acquittal. Luther establishes an intertextual link between the psalmist, particularly the confession in verse 5, and the notoriously sinful woman in Luke 7:36–50 who washes Jesus' feet with her tears.[27] The woman's gesture complements and further illustrates the nature of the psalmist's confession, or self-imputation of sin. From here Luther hears Christ's acquittal, "I will speak against myself; then God will speak for me. I will speak of my guilt; then 'he will speak' about my merit, as he did to Mary Magdalene in the house of Simon the leper" [emphasis added].[28] Second, from the complaint about a "rush of great waters" in Ps 32:6, Luther crafts a christological metaphor that weds the self-imputation of sin to the hope of justification. Luther suggests:

---

22. *LW* 14:148.

23. *LW* 14:148.

24. Regarding this self-serving righteousness, Luther continues "Thus a man is pious out of fear of hell or hope of heaven, not because of God" (*LW* 14:149).

25. *LW* 14:150.

26. *LW* 14:151.

27. Though Luther identifies the woman in Luke 7:36–50 as Mary Magdalene, Luke simply refers to her as "a woman [γυνή] in the city who was a sinner [ἁμαρτωλός]" (Luke 7:37).

28. *LW* 14:151.

> That is, that person is holy who stands, not on his own holiness but on the Rock of Thy righteousness which is Christ. Everyone who is his own accuser, punisher, and judge is founded on Him when many blows and cruel tribulations come over him like a great flood of water, or when he is persecuted on account of his humble life.[29]

While self-imputation is "like a great flood of waters," only those who do so can stand before God. Specifically, to follow the metaphor, only the person flooded by their own confession of sin can stand firmly upon the rock of righteousness who is Christ himself.

PSALM 38—THE PIERCING OF THE PENITENT HEART

Luther prefaces his remarks on Ps 38, noting, "This psalm portrays most clearly the manner, words, acts, thoughts, and gestures of a truly penitent heart."[30] He proceeds to describe the nature of this heart according to his interpretive frame for the Penitential Psalms, which as we have noted, revolves around the interplay between fear and hope. I will highlight three of his observations that represent the overall way he understands the nature of a "penitent heart" in this psalm which is nothing less than a "pierced" heart.

First, the penitent heart is one that fears God's anger, or "arrows," in a way that promotes the hope of justification. The psalmist cries out, "O Lord, rebuke me not in Thy anger. Nor chasten me in Thy wrath! For Thy arrows have sunk into me. And Thy hand has come down on me" (Ps 38:1–2). The reference to divine arrows in Ps 38:2 makes quite an impression on Luther as he carries the anthropomorphism forward in his reading of Ps 38:3–6 and 38:10. He identifies the arrows as God's rebukes and threats within Scripture which when felt elicit the cry "O Lord, rebuke me not in Thy anger."

Second, the penitent heart lives in the paradox of both being with and without sin.[31] Luther detects this paradox at multiple points. For example, in Ps 38:4, the psalmist laments, "For my iniquities have gone over my head. They weigh like a burden too heavy for me." Luther argues that

---

29. *LW* 14:151.

30. *LW* 14:156.

31. Here we hear echoes of Luther's well-known dictum *simul est iustus et peccator* ("at the same time justified and a sinner"). See, e.g., *LW* 26:232–34.

the psalmist can only utter this cry because he lives "in righteousness and grace."[32] He explains, "One devil does not drive out the other; sin does not accuse its kind; and one wolf does not cry out against the other. And yet it is impossible for him who cries out against sin to be without it, for he dare not speak to God in fiction. It must be true that 'he has sin,' as he says, and yet also true that 'he is without sin'" [emphasis added].[33]

Third, the penitent heart is attacked outwardly by enemies and thereby inwardly by God. This dynamic is clearest in Luther's comments on Ps 38:12a, which reads, "Those who seek my life lay their snares." Luther finds here the interrelated "sources" of affliction for the penitent heart, explaining, "He is attacked 'outwardly' by tyrants and evil people for the sake of God's Word and His justice. This makes him tremble 'inwardly' and fear the wrath of God. Then all the old sins appear which he otherwise never felt or remembered, and which have become foul. Misfortune never comes alone" [emphasis added].[34]

Christologically, the person, work, and presence of Christ appear in Luther's comments on Ps 38 in at least four ways. I only have space to enumerate them: (1) The experience of being with and without sin is a kind of crucifixion with Christ;[35] (2) the speaker in Ps 38:6 and the tax-collector Luke 18:9–14 reflect the "true signs" of repentance;[36] (3) the justified can hope in the fact that Christ was likewise struck by God's "arrows" of anger; and (4) Jesus teaches in Ps 38:18 and John 12:25 hatred of sin.[37]

PSALM 51—FEAR IN ADAM AND HOPE IN CHRIST

One of the dominant features of Luther's reading of Ps 51 is his juxtaposition of Adam and Christ, a contrast which appears to varying degrees throughout his engagement with many of the Penitential Psalms. In short, Luther suggests that the justified must fear the Adam who still resides in them if they are truly to find hope in Christ. The Adam-Christ motif emerges early in Luther's exegesis which in turn shapes much of his subsequent analysis. In Ps 51:2, the psalmist cries out, "Wash me

---

32. *LW* 14:158.
33. *LW* 14:158.
34. *LW* 14:160.
35. *LW* 14:158
36. *LW* 14:159
37. *LW* 14:162.

thoroughly from my iniquity, and cleanse me from my sin!" Luther sees this washing as both punctiliar and ongoing. There is a "first grace" which is a "beginning of washing and cleaning."[38] At the same time, "there is no end of washing and cleansing in this life."[39] The middle term here is the Adam-Christ dynamic. As Luther explains, "Now with us the situation is that Adam must get out and Christ must come in, Adam must become as nothing, and Christ alone remain and rule."[40] He sees the "old Adam" within the believer as one who "makes sinful and nullifies also the good works." The solution, or hope, in this internal anguish is that God looks upon "the grace and cleansing which has begun."[41]

Luther goes on to locate an eschatological hope in which Adam is finally nothing and Christ is everything. He works along protological and eschatological lines by using the oft-debated Ps 51:5: "Behold, I was brought forth in iniquity, and in sin did my mother conceive me." Here Luther reflects on original sin, as he understood it, explaining, "How could I be without sin if I was made in sin and sin is my nature and manner? I am an evil tree and by nature a child of wrath and sin."[42] Even for those justified in Christ, Adam's sin perpetually deprives the justified of "complete purity."[43] This perpetual experience then shapes the eschatological hope of the justified which is paradoxically found in death. Luther explains, "Adam must die and decay before Christ can arise completely, and this begins with a penitent life and is completed through death. Hence death is a wholesome thing to all who believe in Christ; for it does nothing else than destroy and reduce to powder everything born of Adam, so that Christ alone may be in us."[44] Penitence in Christ then begins the death of Adam in the justified and death completes it.

PSALM 102—A STORY OF MISERY IN THE KINGDOM

Luther begins his reflection on this psalm with one pregnant sentence: "The 'prayer' is his desire for grace; the 'cry' is his *story of misery*"

38. *LW* 14:167.
39. *LW* 14:167.
40. *LW* 14:167.
41. *LW* 14:167.
42. *LW* 14:169.
43. *LW* 14:171.
44. *LW* 14:169.

[emphasis added].⁴⁵ He narrates this "story of misery" as one marked by fear and hope in the kingdom.

Fear in this story stems from multiple interrelated sources scattered throughout Ps 102: (1) justified divine wrath (Ps 102:2); (2) futility of life caused by Adam's sin (102:3–5, 11); (3) enemies who revile repentant people (102:5); (4) the loneliness and mocking of a life of faith (102:6–8); (5) an indeterminate span of waiting for God's help (102:13); and (6) God's permissive and/or direct assault on his saints (Ps 102:23–24).⁴⁶ These sufferings and the cries they elicit become a "mark" of the people in God's kingdom "who suffer much on His account."⁴⁷ Along these lines, the reference to "the groans of the prisoners" in Ps 102:20 prompts Luther to conclude:

> It is, as stated above, the characteristic of His kingdom that God permits His own to suffer much and to be children of death and sheep for the slaughter, as St. Paul says (Rom 8:36). But they are not forsaken on this account; they are certain that He hears their groans and their misery.⁴⁸

That Luther appeals to Rom 8:36 is interesting given the fact that Paul both cites a lament psalm (Ps 44:22) and does so to summarize the experience of the righteous which he lays out in Rom 8:31–39.⁴⁹

Hope in the psalmist's "story of misery" stems from God's answer in Christ. To be clear, Luther does not detect in the psalm a linear progression whereby the first step is fear, then the second is a cry, and the third is an answer. Rather, the suffering, fear, accompanying cries, and hope are bound up with another and in fact defined by one another.⁵⁰ Luther refers

---

45. *LW* 14:178.

46. Luther's discussion on these causes of misery includes some vivid imagery. For example, in discussing the psalmist's complaint "I lie awake, I am like a lonely bird on the housetop," Luther explains, "The world is a house in which all men are enclosed and sleeping. I alone am outside the house, on the roof, not yet in heaven and still not in the world. The world is below me, and heaven is above me. I hover between the life of the world and eternal life, lonely in the faith" (*LW* 14:181).

47. *LW* 14:184.

48. *LW* 14:185.

49. On this point, see Crisler, *Intertextual Commentary on Romans* 2:241–43.

50. In this way, at least from my perspective, Luther rightly understands the true nature of the much-debated "shift" in mood within the Penitential Psalms or the larger form of lament psalms. It is a mistake to believe that the psalmist moves on from his pain when he shifts from a cry to a statement of trust or praise. Rather, statements of trust and praise emerge from within, and in fact despite, affliction.

to this reality in Ps 102 as the "whole repentant life" whereby one realizes how profoundly "original sin has corrupted us."[51] The whole lifelong cry for help is essentially "a call to Christ and to His grace."[52] Outwardly the justified are crushed by God; however, inwardly they are made strong by Christ. In short, Luther describes the "story of misery" in the kingdom as follows:

> This is the way it goes in Christ's kingdom according to the outer man. He breaks, punishes, and humbles His beloved saints and permits them to be tortured here in time that they may be strong and powerful, not outwardly but inwardly."[53]

PSALM 130—HOPE MUST BE UNDERSTOOD BY WAITING IN THE DEPTHS OF DESPAIR

Luther's reading of this psalm reflects his larger epistemological commitment to "experiential wisdom" (*sapientia expermentalis*). As Bayer explains, "In response to the question posed to him about what type of knowledge is involved in theology, Luther opted for an understanding of theology according to which it is more wisdom (*sapientia*) than science (*scientia*)—already the early Luther spoke of theology as a *sapientia experimentalis* (an experiential wisdom), as a wisdom that comes by experience, and he stays with that understanding; *scientia* is not utterly distinct from *sapientia* but is included within it."[54] For Luther, this kind of wisdom emerges in the experience of affliction described in Ps 130. In his interpretation of Ps 130, the justified can only come to know hope in the depths of their despair. Such exclusivity is evident in his engagement with the opening cry "Out of the depths I cry to Thee, O Lord!" (Ps 130:1). Luther expounds:

---

51. *LW* 14:180. Similarly, in his comments on Ps 102:24, Luther writes, "Although He breaks me asunder and oppresses me, I will not on this account run away from Him; but '*I will hope in Him, cry to Him*,' and plead with Him all the more, as all His saints do" (*LW* 14, 186 [emphasis added]).

52. *LW* 14:182.

53. *LW* 14:186.

54. Bayer, *Martin Luther's Theology*, 30.

These are noble, passionate, and very profound words of a truly penitent heart that is most deeply moved in its distress. In fact, this cannot be understood except by those who have felt and experienced it. We are all in deep and great misery, but we do not all feel our condition.[55]

Fear of God's judgment, such as what Luther detects in Ps 130:3, leads to a cry for help which leads to an experience of grace. However, the latter experience does not materialize apart from despair.

Luther acknowledges that this experience is strange while also generating the requisite "constant waiting" that must characterize the life fearful and hopeful life of the justified. It is strange in the sense that God involves the justified in two "disharmonious things" given that "hope and despair are opposite."[56] Luther explains, "And these two things, direct opposites by nature, *must be* in us, because in us two natures are opposed to each other, the old man and the new man. The old man *must* fear, despair, and perish; the new man *must* hope, be raised up and stand. Both of these are in one person and even in one handiwork at the same time [emphasis added]."[57] This strange divine work then results in "constant waiting," a theme that dominates Luther's reading of verses 5–8. For example, Luther glosses the psalmist's assertion "I wait for the lord" in verse 5 with "My soul has become a 'waiter.'"[58] Waiting then is *the* occupation of the "new man."[59]

This waiting, of course, is christologically defined in Luther's reading of Ps 130. The justified wait in fear of judgment and in the hope of grace; however, they experience both with Christ. Prior to hope being fulfilled, Luther describes the life of fear and hope as a crucifixion:

> And just as the judgment of God produces fear, so fear results in crying out, and the cry brings mercy. As long as the old man lives, the fear, that is, the crucifixion and execution of this old man, must not cease; nor dare the judgment of God be forgotten.

---

55. *LW* 14:189.

56. *LW* 14:191.

57. *LW* 14:191. Luther continues, "Just as a wood carver, by chiseling and taking away the wood that does not belong to the carving, enhances the form of his work, so hope, which forms the new man, grows in the mist of fear that cuts down old Adam" (*LW* 14:191).

58. *LW* 14:192. He continues, "So here: I have waited so firmly for the Lord that my soul has become a 'waiter'; and its whole life has become a tarrying, a hoping, and waiting" (*LW* 14:192).

59. *LW* 14:193.

And whoever would live without this crucifying and this fear and the judgment of God, does not live aright."[60]

Nevertheless, despite Luther's insistence that the justified must live in fear, he wants it to be rightly understood. As he notes towards the close of his comments, "To know God aright is to recognize that with Him there is nothing but kindness and mercy. But those who feel that God is angry and unmerciful do not know Him aright. Therefore they rather flee from Him and do not wait for Him."[61] There is then a misguided fear that does not lead to a hope for Christ and one that does. Those who are justified by faith do not flee from God even as they fear his judgment. Rather, in keeping with the theology of the psalms, they run to him for mercy which is ultimately found in the crucified and risen Christ.

PSALM 143—ONLY TAKING FROM GOD THE RIGHTEOUSNESS WHICH IS ONLY PRESENT IN THE CRUCIFIED CHRIST

Luther frames the seventh and final penitential psalm in relation to Christ, noting in his preface to Ps 143, "Every psalm, all Scripture, calls to grace, extols grace, searches for Christ, and praises only God's work, while rejecting all the works of man. Therefore this psalm can be readily understood in the light of the foregoing, for it speaks the same *language*" [emphasis added].[62] The "language" in question is the interplay between the Penitential Psalms and Luther's Christocentric reading of them. The specific dialect in Luther's reading of Ps 143 can be identified as "taking" from God the righteousness *who* is Christ. Two brief points on this.

One of the main themes that emerges from Luther's interpretation of Ps 143 is that those who live in fear and hope can only take, or receive, from God. For example, the psalmist complains, "Therefore my spirit faints within me; my heart within me is appalled" (Ps 143:4). Luther responds, "This is the right kind of sacrifice, one that pleases God, as already stated in the fourth of these psalms (51:7), namely, a soul that has no comfort among creatures and is even forsaken and persecuted by itself, so that it looks for nothing but the pure grace of God."[63] While the

---

60. *LW* 14:190.
61. *LW* 14:193–94.
62. *LW* 14:196.
63. *LW* 14:198.

self-righteous are presently comforted by their own righteousness, those living in fear and hope only find comfort in God himself—"All comfort, help, and blessedness are due to Thy work alone."[64] The comfort stems from this realization: "Only when Thou doest our works, and our works are not ours but Thine, then they are pleasing, right, true, and good before Thee."[65] Similarly, when the psalmist confesses "I stretch out my hands to Thee" (Ps 143:6), Luther responds, "That is, since everything depends on Thy work and grace, I justly seek only grace and never feel secure in my own efforts, as my enemies do."[66]

What those living in fear and hope take from God is not the mere "imputation" of righteousness but the person and work of Christ himself. Within his comments on Ps 143, Luther rejects the "naked act of imputation" of righteousness, as Arnold Guebert puts it, which separates justification from Christ himself.[67] As Luther sees it, "Christ, I say, not as some express it in blind words, 'causally,' that He grants righteousness and remains absent Himself, for that would be dead. Yes, it is not given at all unless Christ Himself is present, just as the radiance of the sun and the heat of fire are not present if there is no sun and fire."[68] In this way, the justified who live in fear and hope do so in the presence of Christ whose own sufferings as the crucified are reflected in the suffering of the justified.[69]

CONCLUSION

In closing this brief overview, I want to consider how Luther's work might shape contemporary engagement with both the Penitential Psalms and, really, the entire Psalter. After all, Luther's work on these seven psalms essentially reflects how he reads all of them.[70] One reads them, simply, in

64. *LW* 14:199.
65. *LW* 14:199.
66. *LW* 14:200.
67. See *LW* 14:204n29.
68. *LW* 14:204.
69. For a reading of Paul's doctrine of justification along these lines, see Seifrid, *Christ Our Righteousness*, 183–86.
70. Luther's fondness for the psalms is well known and reflected in statements such as, "The Psalter ought to be a precious and beloved book, if for no other reason than this: it promises Christ's death and resurrection so clearly—and pictures his kingdom and the condition and nature of all Christendom—that it might well be called a little Bible" (*LW* 35:254). Additionally, as Paul Althaus puts it in summarizing Luther's view of the Psalms, "The experience of God's wrath and of his grace speaks in this book. For

fear *and* hope. It is in this spirit that I offer the following hermeneutical theses for reading and responding to the Penitential Psalms and thereby every psalm:

1. When God chastises, see the hope of Christ in the chastisement (Ps 6).

2. Confess sin to stand more firmly upon the rock of your righteousness who is Christ (Ps 32).

3. When your penitent heart is pierced by divine "arrows," hope in the Christ who was as well.

4. Be fearful of indwelling sin that has beset you since Adam but hope in your death with Christ (Ps 51).

5. Trust that the kingdom's "story of misery" crushes you only to strengthen you in Christ (Ps 102).

6. Taste the hope that emerges when you wait for Christ in the depths of your despair (Ps 130).

7. Take from God the righteousness *who* is the crucified and risen Christ (Ps 143).

BIBLIOGRAPHY

Althaus, Paul. *The Theology of Martin Luther*. Translated by Robert C. Schultz. Philadelphia: Fortress, 1966.
Bayer, Oswald. *Theology the Lutheran Way*. Minneapolis: Fortress, 2017.
Crisler, Channing L. *An Intertextual Commentary on Romans, Volume 2: Romans 5:1—8:39*. Eugene, OR: Pickwick, 2021.
King'oo, Clare Costley. *Miserere Mei: The Penitential Psalms in Late Medieval and Early Modern England*. Notre Dame, IN: Notre Dame University Press, 2012.
Kolb, Robert. *Martin Luther and the Enduring Word of God: The Wittenberg School and Its Scripture-Centered Proclamation*. Grand Rapids: Baker, 2016.
Luther, Martin. *Lectures on Galatians Chapters 1–4*. Edited by Jaroslav Pelikan et al. Vol. 26 of *Luther's Works*. St. Louis, MO: Concordia, 1968.
———. *Lectures on Genesis Chapters 1–5*. Edited by Jaroslav Pelikan et al. Vol. 1 of *Luther's Works*. St. Louis, MO: Concordia, 1958.
———. *Selected Psalms III*. Edited by Jaroslav Pelikan et al. Vol. 14 of *Luther's Works*. St. Louis, MO: Concordia, 1958.
———. *Word and Sacrament I*. Edited by Helmut T. Lehman. Vol. 35 of *Luther's Works*. St. Louis, MO: Concordia, 1960.

---

this reason, it is a contemporary book for Christians and presents them a picture of themselves" (Althaus, *Theology of Martin Luther*, 101).

Marsh, William M. *Martin Luther on Reading the Bible as Christian Scripture*. Eugene, OR: Pickwick, 2017.

McGrath, Alister E. *Luther's Theology of the Cross: Martin Luther's Theological Breakthrough*. Oxford: Blackwell, 1985.

Ngien, Dennis. *Fruit for the Soul: Luther on the Lament Psalms*. Minneapolis: Fortress, 2015.

Seifrid, Mark A. *Christ, Our Righteousness: Paul's Theology of Justification*. Downers Grove, IL: InterVarsity, 2000.

Seiling, Jonathan R. "The 'Radical' Revisions of the Commentary on the Seven Penitential Psalms: Luther and His 'Enemies' (1517–1525)." *Reformation & Renaissance Review* (2006) 28–47.

Wengert, Timothy J. "Martin Luther's First Major Publication." *Lutheran Quarterly* 36 (2022) 166–80.

7
"A Limited and Restrained Form"
John Donne Reads the Penitential Psalms

Emma Rhatigan

INTRODUCTION

IN 1621, INSPIRED MOST likely by the death of Mary Sidney, countess of Pembroke,[1] Donne paid tribute to the Sidney psalm translations in verse.[2] His poem "Upon the Translation of the Psalms by Philip Sidney and the Countess of Pembroke His Sister" is a celebration of the Sidneys' work, but in amongst the praise, Donne also bemoans the lack of English metrical translations of the psalms. In a dig at the most widely used metrical version, "Sternhold and Hopkins" (a translation by Thomas Sternhold, John Hopkins, and others, first printed in 1562) Donne complains that the Psalms are "well-attired abroad" but "ill at home" (line 38), insisting he can "scarce call that [the English Church] Reformed" until the psalms too "be reformed" (lines 40–41).[3] Donne himself, however, did

---

1. Mary Sidney (1561–1621) was a poet and literary patron who, along with her brother, Philip Sidney (1554–86), wrote the Sidney Psalter. The first forty-three psalms of this remarkable poetic translation of the biblical psalms were written by Philip, and Mary wrote the remaining 107 to complete the work following his death.

2. Robin Robbins dates the poem to October/November 1621. See Robbins, *Complete Poems of John Donne*, 580. All quotations from Donne's poems in this chapter are from this edition, cited in the text by line number.

3. The "Sternhold and Hopkins" translation was printed with the *Book of Common Prayer* and often appended to English Bibles. It was frequently derided for its clumsy attempts to capture the psalms in English verse. Hannibal Hamlin identifies Marot's

not answer this call for a new verse translation. He concludes his poem by instructing his readers to tune their voices to the Sidneys' "sweet, learned labours" (line 54) and did not write any further celebrations or translations of the psalms in poetry.[4] Rather, Donne was to attend to the psalms not in poetry, but in prose, through a sustained engagement with them in his pulpit oratory.

Even when Donne engaged with the psalms in the pulpit, he remained highly attentive to their status as poetry, often evoking what his contemporaries might call a rhetorical (what we might term a "literary") interpretative framework alongside his theological analysis.[5] As he insists in a sermon on Ps 6:8–10:

> It is easie to observe, that in all Metricall compositions, of which kinde the booke of Psalmes is, the force of the whole piece, is for the most part left to the shutting up; the whole frame of the Poem is a beating out of a piece of gold.[6]

The psalm requires interpretation as a "Metricall composition." Moreover, as this evocative echo of his poetic allusion to "gold to aery thinness beat" (line 24) in "A Valediction Forbidding Mourning" suggests, Donne was not just attuned to the psalms as poetry, but self-consciously aware that his reading of them would be shaped by his own experience of writing verse. Thus, in this chapter I want to explore how Donne's interest in the psalms as poetry might have influenced his exegesis. In what follows I will focus on two rhetorical figures: metaphor and prosopopoeia. These two figures have long been associated with Donne's poetry, but here I want to consider how they shaped his reading of the Penitential Psalms.

---

and Beza's French psalms as "possible candidates" for the "well-attired" psalms which Donne claims could be enjoyed on the continent; see Hamlin, "Piety and Poetry," 211.

4. For important studies of early modern verse translations of the psalms, see Hamlin, *Psalm Culture*; Quitslund, *Reformation in Rhyme*; and Zim, *English Metrical Psalms*. For specific attention to verse translations of the Penitential Psalms, see Hamlin, "Sorrowful Souls," and King'oo, *Miserere Mei*.

5. As Hamlin explains, "In early modern England, the Hebrew psalms were seen as poems," despite the fact that their form is "based on syntactic and semantic parallelism . . . rather than meter or rhyme"; see Hamlin, "Piety and Poetry," 203n1. Barbara Lewalski discusses the ways early modern readers categorized books of the Bible as different forms of poetry in Lewalski, *Protestant Poetics*, 31–71.

6. From Potter and Simpson, *Sermons of John Donne* 6:41.

"A FORM AS IS BOTH CURIOUS AND REQUIRES DILIGENCE IN THE MAKING"

Of Donne's 160 extant sermons, thirty-four are on texts from the Psalms, and of these the majority, twenty-one, are on one of the Penitential Psalms.[7] These sermons are, however, dispersed in terms of chronology and preaching venue. Donne preached three series of sermons on the Penitential Psalms: a series of six sermons on Ps 6, a series of eight sermons on Ps 32, and a series of six sermons on Ps 38. He also preached one sermon on Ps 51.[8] There is no evidence to indicate whether this sermon was also part of a longer series. We also have no information about where or when the series on Ps 6 or the individual sermon on Ps 51 were preached. However, we do have more contextual information about the other two series. George Potter and Evelyn Simpson assigned the sermons on Ps 32 to St. Paul's, where Donne was dean from 1622 until his death in 1632. This series has recently been dated by Mary Ann Lund to 1626.[9] Meanwhile, in *Fifty Sermons* (1649), the series on Ps 38 is described as being preached at Lincoln's Inn, where Donne was reader in divinity from 1616 to 1622. This series was most likely preached in the spring or summer of 1619.[10] This would mean, rather counterintuitively, that Donne preached the Ps 38 series before the Ps 32 series. However, we know Donne re-preached sermons in different venues, and it is possible that the Ps 32 series was originally preached at Lincoln's Inn but then reworked for delivery at St. Paul's. Indeed, it could be that all three series on the Penitential Psalms were initially preached at Lincoln's Inn during

---

7. The remaining sermons on the psalms include a series on Donne's prebendary psalms and eight sermons which are not part of a longer series.

8. The Ps 6 and Ps 32 series are extant in Donne, *LXXX sermons*, as numbers fifty to fifty-five and fifty-six to sixty-three respectively. In Potter and Simpson, *Sermons of John Donne*, the Ps 6 series was printed in volume 5 as numbers fifteen to nineteen (counting sermons fifty-two and fifty-three in *LXXX sermons* as a single sermon) and the Ps 32 series was printed in volume 9 as numbers eleven to eighteen. Four of the Ps 32 sermons have now been printed in Lund, *Oxford Edition Volume XII*. The Ps 38 series is extant in Donne, *Fifty sermons*, as numbers nineteen to twenty-three. One sermon from this series (on Ps 38:9) was not printed in the seventeenth century and is extant only in manuscript. The Ps 38 series was printed in volume 2 of Potter and Simpson, *Sermons of John Donne*, as numbers 1 to 6. The sermon on Ps 51 was printed as number sixty-four in *LXXX sermons* and as number fifteen in volume 5 of Potter and Simpson, *Sermons of John Donne*.

9. See Lund, *Oxford Edition Volume XII*, xxix.

10. See Potter and Simpson, *Sermons of John Donne* 2:13–14.

the first years of Donne's ministry and then revised and re-preached on later occasions.[11]

The sermon series are more discontinuous than we might expect. Only the series on Ps 32 includes sermons on every verse of the psalm. In the case of the other series Donne may not have written out all the sermons after delivery, but it is also possible that he never preached on every verse in the first place.[12] While some verses lack a sermon, however, other verses are treated across multiple sermons and sometimes multiple verses are considered in a single sermon. In one of his sermons on Ps 38 Donne even admits to taking the verses out of order.[13] It is also evident that Donne did not always pursue a single course of sermons over successive weeks. These are sermons which could be appreciated individually, as well as part of a series.[14]

There are, then, certain challenges in considering Donne's sermons on the Penitential Psalms as a group. These sermons were preached, and quite possibly re-preached, at different times and in different pulpits, and Donne seems to have resisted the sort of linear verse-by-verse analysis that we might find in a commentary on the Psalms.[15] Nonetheless, Donne himself referred to his sermons on the Psalms collectively. In a sermon on Ps 38:2 he tells his congregation:

> My spirituall appetite carries me still, upon the *Psalms of David*, for a first course, for the Scriptures of the Old Testament, and upon the *Epistle of Saint Paul*, for a second course, for the New ... because they are Scriptures, written in such forms, as I have been most accustomed to; Saint *Pauls* being Letters, and *Davids* being Poems.[16]

Donne's words are testimony to his recurring personal interest in the psalms, but also suggest that his sermons on the psalms, albeit preached

11. This possibility is explored by Stanwood, "Donne's Earliest Sermons," 366–79.

12. Donne, like many of his contemporaries, preached from notes. Often, his sermons were only written out in full after delivery in the pulpit. See Rhatigan, "Margins of Error," 423–44.

13. In the sermon on Ps 38:9 Donne tells his congregation that he has already preached on verse 10, but has "reserved" preaching on verse 9. See Potter and Simpson, *Sermons of John Donne* 2:144.

14. Lund, *Oxford Edition Volume XII*, xxxix–xli.

15. See, for example, Martin Luther's *A Commentarie vpon the XV. Psalmes*, translated by Henry Bull (London, 1637). This commentary was derived from Luther's lectures on the Gradual Psalms and moves sequentially through each verse of each psalm.

16. Potter and Simpson, *Sermons of John Donne* 2:49.

in different times and places, warrant collective study on the basis of their shared response to the book of Psalms as poetry. Indeed, Donne continues this reflection on the psalms by elaborating on the specific virtues of verse. He claims:

> God . . . gives us our instruction in cheerfull forms, not in a sowre, and sullen, and angry, and unacceptable way, but cheerfully, in *Psalms*, which is also a limited, and a restrained form; Not in an *Oration*, not in *Prose*, but in *Psalms*; which is such a form as is both curious, and requires diligence in the making.[17]

Donne is thinking here of set forms of poetry: poetry which is "limited" and "restrained" by formal considerations such as meter, rhyme, and stanzas. Such poetry requires "diligence in the making," words which work as an invitation to recall Donne's own poetry, not least the verse which he had written at Lincoln's Inn and shared with some of the members of his congregation twenty years earlier.[18] What, though, did it mean for Donne to read the psalms as Scripture written in a "limited" form? By attending to Donne's interest in the psalms as poetry I want to suggest that his commitment to reading with an eye to form also had consequences for the meanings he extracted from these texts in the pulpit. Specifically, I want to suggest that his attention to the rhetorical figures of metaphor and prosopopoeia generated modes of exegesis which both "limit" and "restrain," but also extend and enable meaning.

"REMOTE AND PRECIOUS METAPHORS"

Donne's delight in metaphor has been both celebrated and derided by readers of his poetry from the seventeenth century through to the present day. However, one of his most hyperbolic celebrations of figurative language is expressed in relation to Scripture. In his *Devotions Upon Emergent Occasions*, he exclaims:

> Thou art a *figurative*, a *metaphoricall God* . . . A *God* in whose words there is such a height of *figures*, such *voyages*, such

---

17. Potter and Simpson, *Sermons of John Donne* 2:49–50.

18. On Donne's relationship with Lincoln's Inn as both student and preacher, see Ettenhuber, *Sermons of John Donne* 5:xiii–lii, and Rhatigan, "Donne's Readership at Lincoln's Inn," 576–88. Ironically, Donne himself did not write in set forms very often; Ben Jonson complained that "for not keeping of accent [formal rhythm or meter]" Donne "deserved hanging"; see Smith, *John Donne*, 67–70. Donne's *Holy Sonnets* are an important exception.

peregrinations to fetch remote and precious *metaphors* [emphasis original].[19]

To read Scripture, he suggests, is to embark on a voyage into metaphorical language. The Penitential Psalms are no exception. Preaching on Ps 32:6, Donne observes that the Holy Ghost "is a direct worker upon the soule and conscience of man, but a Metaphoricall, and Figurative expresser of himselfe."[20] In the pulpit, however, Donne's celebrations of this "Metaphoricall God" are tempered with anxiety; surely as a preacher his role must extend beyond extolling the poetry of Scripture? Thus in a sermon on Ps 32:1–2 he offers a careful corrective:

> As we say justly, and confidently, That of all Rhetoricall and Poeticall figures, that fall into any Art, we are able to produce higher straines, and livelier examples, out of the Scriptures, then out of all the Orators, and Poets in the world, yet we reade not, we preach not the Scriptures for that use, to magnifie their Eloquence.[21]

Donne then continues to explain that this caveat about the value of the Scriptures' eloquence is especially relevant when approaching the poetry of the psalms. David, he insists, was indeed "the sweet Psalmist" with "an harmonious, a melodious, a charming, a powerfull way of entring into the soule," but, crucially, "he employed his faculties for the conveying of the God of Israel, into the Israel of God." Attending to his text, Donne explains that when David claimed "*The spirit of the Lord spake by me,*" he was referring not to "the spirit of Rhetorique, nor the spirit of Poetry . . . but, *The spirit of the Lord.*" David's way, Donne stresses, was "to establish the Church of God upon fundamentall Doctrines."[22] The poetry of the psalms and, indeed, the oratory of the preacher, must convey, not detract from, their central task of teaching doctrine.

We see Donne working to bring metaphor and exegesis together in his treatment of the recurring references to "bones" in Ps 6. Preaching on Ps 6:2–3, Donne structures his sermon according to David's "Petitions" and then the "Reasons" which underpin them, one of which is David's

---

19. Donne, *Devotions Upon Emergent Occasions*, 99. This approach to Scripture is strongly influenced by the medieval *quadriga*, the fourfold sense of Scripture, whereby a biblical text would be read according to the literal, the allegorical, the tropological (or moral), and the anagogical senses. On early modern readings of metaphor in Scripture, see Lewalksi, *Protestant Poetics*, 72–86, and, more recently, Knight, *Dark Bible*, 228–70.

20. Potter and Simpson, *Sermons of John Donne* 9:328.

21. Potter and Simpson, *Sermons of John Donne* 9:252.

22. Potter and Simpson, *Sermons of John Donne* 9:252–53.

claim that "my bones are vexed." Donne's starting point is "the naturall and ordinary acceptation" of bones, which is, he argues, that "they are these Beames, and Timbers, and Rafters of these Tabernacles, these Temples of the Holy Ghost, these bodies of ours."[23] For an "ordinary" sense, Donne's definition is highly metaphorical, extending St. Paul's description of man's body as a temple in 1 Cor 6:19 to imagine bones as "Beames" and "Timbers." At the same time, Donne is also echoing his own poetical bone metaphor in "A Valediction: Of My Name in the Window" where he describes the scratched name in the window as "ragged, bony" and comparable with a skeleton, a "ruinous anatomy" (lines 23–24). He extends this metaphor so that the scratched name becomes a "house" in which, as in the sermon, his bones are "rafters," tiled by "muscle, sinew and vein" (lines 28–30). In the sermon, however, Donne develops the metaphor still further. Taking his cue from Basil, who questions (to use Donne's paraphrase) "Shall we dwell upon the native and naturall signification of these *Bones*," Donne moves from the body to the soul, insisting, again following Basil, "The soule hath her Bones too."[24] Thus David is referring not just to the bones of his body, but "the strongest powers and faculties of his soule, and the best actions and operations of those faculties."[25] However, even when the "bones" of his text have been transformed from physical bones to "good actions," Donne continues to press his metaphor. He continues:

> The Bones themselves have no sense, they feele no paine. We need not say, That those good works themselves, which we doe, have in their nature, the nature of sinne . . . But *membrane dolent*; Those little membrans, those filmes, those thin skins, that cover, and that line some bones, are very sensible of paine, and of any vexation [emphasis original].[26]

Donne brings the eye of the anatomist to his metaphor, extending it into a visceral dissection of human tissue. In so doing, however, he is committed not just to a display of rhetorical skill, but to extracting the relevant

---

23. Potter and Simpson, *Sermons of John Donne* 5:352.

24. Potter and Simpson, *Sermons of John Donne* 5:352–53. See Basil, *Homilia in Psalmum XXXIII* (PG 29.383): "Iam vero juxta eamdem rationem fuerint etiam quædam hominis interni ossa, quibus colligatio harmoniaque facultatum animæ continetur" ("Now truly in the same vein of thinking there would even be within man's frame some bones in which the binding and harmony of the soul's faculties are contained").

25. Potter and Simpson, *Sermons of John Donne* 5:353.

26. Potter and Simpson, *Sermons of John Donne* 5:353.

doctrines or teachings from his text. It is, after all, not just membrane which Donne is probing here, but the corrupting work of original sin, a disease which "festers beyond the bone, even into the marrow it selfe."[27]

At this point, Donne moves on to the next part of his *divisio*, a discussion of David's second "Reason"; "my soule is also sore troubled." However, he does not turn away from the metaphorical potential of "bones," returning to them in his analysis of the "trouble" which assails both David's bones and his soul. He explains, "This then is the force of *Davids* reason in the Petition, *Ossa implentur vitiis*, as one of *Iobs* friends speaks, *My bones are full of the sins of my youth*" [emphasis original],[28] before initiating an extended survey of biblical bones:

> *Adhaeret os meum carni*, as *David* also speaks, *My bones cleave to my flesh*, my best actions taste of my worst; And *My skin cleaves to my bones*, as *Ieremy* laments, That is, My best actions call for a skin, for something to cover them. . . . Thou that art my Messias, be my *Moses*, and carry these bones of thy *Ioseph* out of Egypt; Deliver me, in this consideration of mine actions, from the terror of a self-accusing, and a jealous, and suspicious conscience: *Bury my bones beside the bones of the man of God*; Beside the bones of the Son of God: Look upon my bones as they are coffin'd, and shrowded in that sheet, the righteousnesse of Christ Jesus. *Accedant ossa ad ossa*, as in *Ezekiels* vision, Let our bones come together, bone to bone. . . . My bones being laid by his, though but gristles in themselves, my actions being considered in his, though imperfect in themselves, shall bear me up in the sight of God [emphasis original].[29]

This is virtuosic exegesis and demonstrates how Donne's attention to metaphor was informed by an early modern religious culture in which reading and study of the Bible were highly influenced by the practice of commonplacing.[30] This sort of biblical survey could have been constructed out of a concordance such as Robertus Stephanus' *Concordantiae Bibliorum vtriusque Testamenti, Veteris & Noui* (Geneva 1555), which specifically facilitated topic-based readings of Scripture.[31] Thus

27. Potter and Simpson, *Sermons of John Donne* 5:355.
28. Potter and Simpson, *Sermons of John Donne* 5:358.
29. Potter and Simpson, *Sermons of John Donne* 5:358–59.
30. Commonplacing was the practice of collecting and organizing interesting passages from selected texts. It was a way of reflecting on texts, making intertextual connections, and curating ideas for future literary projects.
31. See Green, *Print and Protestantism*, 124–29, 138–42, and Morrissey, "Nuts,

Donne makes the metaphor of bones as good works extend and resonate in different scriptural contexts. In Lam 4:8 they are covered with the skin of corrupt actions; in Exod 13:9 they are rescued from the Egypt of a "suspicious conscience"; in 1 Kgs 13:31 they are shrouded in the sheet of Christ's righteousness; before, finally, in Ezek 37:7, the "gristles" of man's good works are redeemed in the bones of Christ's perfection. This is certainly a metaphorical "peregrination"; Donne has taken his congregation from the "natural" bones which constitute their physical body to a vision of the spiritual bones which will gird their "recompacted" (to borrow a term from "A Valediction: Of My Name in the Window") resurrected body.[32] However, it is a metaphorical journey which is rooted in a tradition of biblical exegesis devoted to discovering the particular doctrines or teachings of a text. As Mary Morrissey has explained, a commonplace reading of Scripture enabled Reformers to read "discontinuously" across different biblical texts or "places" in order to explicate doctrine. In other words, a biblical verse not only belonged in its immediate place in a specific book of the Bible, but was also linked theologically with other verses throughout Scripture.[33] Reading metaphorically by tracking a particular figure through the Bible was one way of pursuing this sort of doctrinally led "discontinuous reading." Hence Donne connects the bones of Ps 32 with those of Ezek 37:7 in order explicate the doctrine of the resurrection. But doctrinally led reading is perhaps less radically expansive than Donne's celebration of a peregrination might suggest. Indeed, arguably, just as Donne was aware of poetry as "limited" in terms of form and meter, so too did his "metaphorical" reading of the psalms restrain meaning by limiting it to established doctrine.

"WE MAY FALL IN WITH THEM, AND SING OUR PART"

In his celebration of the Sidney translations Donne attends repeatedly to the sound of the psalms; the Sidneys are "the organ" and God the "harmony," and their translations "teach us how to sing" (lines 15, 22). This

---

Kernels, Wading Lambs," 84–103. Stephanus includes an entry for "ossis" on fol. 348r of his *Concordantiae*.

32. In the poem, the speaker anticipates a "return" which will "repair / And recompact my scattered body" (lines 31–32).

33. Morrissey, "Nuts, Kernels, Wading Lambs," 89. Morrissey takes the term "discontinuous" reading from Stallybrass, "Books and Scrolls," 42–79. On metaphorical readings which are led by doctrine, see also Knight, *Dark Bible*, 235–44.

attention to sound is not surprising given the long tradition of speaking or singing the psalms aloud. In the early modern period a psalm was a profoundly oral text.[34] However, Donne's interest in sound goes beyond a general appreciation of the aural world of the psalms to pay specific attention to the importance of voice. He describes how

> The songs are these, which Heav'n's high, holy muse
> Whispered to David, David to the Jews;
> And David's successors, in holy zeal,
> In forms of joy and art do re-reveal (lines 31–34).

Donne's coinage "re-reveal" captures not only the repeated process of encountering the psalms through translation, but also the way the psalms can simultaneously speak to and be spoken by numerous voices.[35] The poetical mode of translation or paraphrase means the psalms are always spoken by the Holy Spirit, David, and "David's successors," translators through the ages.[36] But this radical indeterminacy of voice also extends to readers of the psalms. Whether through silent reading, reading aloud, or song as we "fall in with them [the Sidneys], and sing our part" (line 56), we too voice the psalms.[37] In contrast to the limiting of a metaphorical reading rooted in commonplacing, prosopopoeia extends meaning by multiplying voices and speakers, offering opportunities to apply and reapply the biblical text to new circumstances. To articulate the concept in the terminology of early modern rhetoric, all translators and readers of the psalms are bound up in a complex process of prosopopoeia, in which, to take Abraham Fraunce's definition, "we represent the person of anie, and make it speake as though he were there present."[38] In other words, a

---

34. On the early modern practice of singing the psalms, see Quitslund, "Singing the Psalms for Fun," 237–58 and Temperley, *Music of the English Parish Church*, 22–99.

35. The *Oxford English Dictionary* cites Donne's use of the verb in this poem as their earliest example. *Oxford English Dictionary*, s.v. "re-reveal (v.)." On the complexity of voice in early modern translations of the psalms, see Hamlin, "My Tongue Shall Speak," 509–30.

36. On the tradition of associating the Penitential Psalms with David, see King'oo, *Miserere Mei*, 32–41.

37. King'oo, following Roland Greene, argues for a distinction between "ritualistic" translations or paraphrases of the psalms, in which the voice of the psalmist is universalized, and "fictional" versions which seek to construct the voice as that of David. Here Donne might be said to be describing a move from a fictional to a ritualistic reading of the psalms. In what follows I am indebted to Greene and King'oo's analytical framework, but draw in particular on the term "prosopopoeia" to think about how Donne might have read the psalms rhetorically as poetry.

38. Fraunce, *Arcadian Rhetorike*, G2r.

writer or speaker ventriloquizes the voice of another. Gavin Alexander has described how in classical rhetorical theory prosopopoeia became bound up with ethos, the way in which an orator might seek to produce emotion by moving himself, as well as an audience. As a consequence of this deliberate attempt to feel the emotion which is being "performed," Alexander argues that "the figure of prosopopoeia and the related doctrine of *ethos* have an innate tendency . . . to elide performance with identity."[39] In the context of a psalm, in particular a Penitential Psalm, this speaks directly to the way in which an individual not only seeks to inhabit the penitential sorrow of the psalmist, but also to use the psalm to speak to their particular experience of sin and repentance. To voice the psalms is to speak both as David and as an individual.

For Donne this plurality of voice in the psalms is something to be celebrated. Thus, preaching on Ps 51:7, he says of David:

> His example is so comprehensive, so generall, that as a well made and well placed Picture in a Gallery looks upon all that stand in severall places of the Gallery, in severall lines, in severall angles, so doth *Davids* history concerne and embrace all [emphasis original].[40]

Donne creates his own distinctive version of the conventional metaphor of a "mirror" to describe the universality of the psalms.[41] Like a mirror, Donne's "Picture" enables a sinner to identify their own experience even as they gaze on that of David. And this reflective process takes place "in severall places"; Donne's metaphorical "Gallery" reaches out universally in time and space. Any individual can see their sin in David's and, as a consequence, articulate their repentance by taking on his words. Indeed, in the pulpit, Donne explicitly adopts an exegetical approach which privileges plurality of voice over singularity. For example, in a sermon on Ps 32:7, he explains how "S. *Hierom* takes these words (and the whole Psalme) to be spoken collectively, others distributively; He in the person of the Church, They of every, or at least of some particular soules." Donne, however, refuses to limit himself to either interpretation, claiming (perhaps to the relief of his congregation) that "to examine their reasons is unnecessary, and would bee tedious; It will aske lesse time, and

---

39. Alexander, "Prosopopoeia," 102.

40. Potter and Simpson, *Sermons of John Donne* 5:299.

41. On the prevalence of the mirror metaphor in discussions of psalms' universality, see King'oo, *Miserere Mei*, 130.

afford more profit to consider the words both ways."[42] The psalms can speak in multiple voices.[43]

One of Donne's most striking responses to the prosopopoeia of the psalms comes in his sermon on Ps 51:7, when he transforms the psalm into a dramatic exchange between God and David. Taking as his precedent a sermon by John of Damascus which, he claims, is "a Dialogue, in which *Eve* acts the first part, and the blessed Virgin another,"[44] Donne constructs his own dramatic dialogue in which David pleads with God to "purge" and "wash" him. First, he tells us, "We heare *David* in an anhelation and panting after the mercy of God, cry out, *Domine Tu*, Lord doe thou that that is to be done." Then he provides us with God's reply: "We may have heard God . . . say *Purget natura, purget lex*. I have infused into thee a light and a law of nature . . . let the light of nature, or of the law purge thee, and rectifie thy self by that."[45] The exchange then continues: "We may hear *David* reply, *Domine Tu* . . . do Thou, Thou, that is to be done upon me," then "We heare God say, *Purget Ecclesia*, I have established a Church . . . for the purging and washing of souls there."[46] This "Dialogue" extends throughout this section of the sermon, with Donne voicing David and God in turn. Presumably in the pulpit Donne himself "performed" the different voices, shifting his intonation and perhaps using gesture to distinguish one voice from the next. Readers of Donne's poetry would already be familiar with his experiments in creating drama within a nondramatic text. In "The Flea," for example, Donne speaks through a first-person lyric voice, but this speaker vividly charts the response of his female addressee: both her physical response when "Cruel and sudden!" she kills the flea and her verbal reply when he complains, "Thou triumph'st, and says't that thou / Find'st not thyself nor me the weaker now" (lines 19, 23–24). Donne's approach to Ps 51 shows a similar interest in voice and playfulness with form. Speaking both the "parts" of David and God in the present tense, Donne turns the psalm into drama, making full use of the performative potential of the pulpit.

David's voice in this "Dialogue" is dramatically rendered and, as Donne elaborates on the words of the psalm, he emphasizes David's assertions of his suffering. The voice we hear is that of a self under pressure.

---

42. Potter and Simpson, *Sermons of John Donne* 9:334.
43. See chapter 5 and the exploration there of Dame Eleanor Hull.
44. Potter and Simpson, *Sermons of John Donne* 5:305.
45. Potter and Simpson, *Sermons of John Donne* 5:305.
46. Potter and Simpson, *Sermons of John Donne* 5:305.

At the same time, the structure of the "Dialogue" foregrounds the fact that Donne is ventriloquizing this voice. The voice we hear is unambiguously David in dialogue with God. However, when Donne moves into the next section of the sermon, the form of the "Dialogue" becomes less clear and the interplay between voices more complex. When David replies for the last time, his response is far longer and more self-reflexive:

> We may heare *David* reply, *Domine Me*; Nay but Lord, I doe not heare Peter preach, I live not in a time, or in a place, where Crownes of Martyrdome are distributed. . . . Lord, looke more particularly upon me, and appropriate thy selfe to me, to me, not onely as thy Creature, as a man, as a Christian, but as I am I, as I am this sinner that confesses now, and as I am this penitent that begs thy mercy now.[47]

Donne tells us we are hearing the voice of David, he says "we may heare *David* reply," but the voice we hear no longer sounds like the voice of David which we heard earlier in the "Dialogue." The references to St. Peter and martyrdom are blatantly anachronistic and the "now" which the speaker repeatedly insists upon resonates much more strongly with the moment of the performance than that of David. Surely a member of the congregation would have heard the complaint "I live not in a time, or in a place, where 'Crownes of Martyrdome' are distributed" as a reference to contemporary London (although, ironically, Catholics, including members of Donne's own family, still faced persecution). As the voice identifies itself as "a Christian" and circles around the first-person pronouns "me" and "I," it must have become increasingly difficult to distinguish it from Donne's own voice. The very nature of the sermon performance, which foregrounds the speaker's voice, would have worked to align this self which so insistently asserts his own identity ("as I am I") with Donne. Donne, then, not only explains the potential of the psalms to speak universally but demonstrates it by, paradoxically, allowing it to resonate with his own individual voice.

We encounter a comparable example in Donne's sermon on Ps 32:3–4. Donne is elaborating on the fact that David puts himself forward as an example. He explains, "He goes not far for his Example; He labors not to shew his reading, but his feeling; not his learning, but his compunction; his Conscience is his Library; and his Example is himselfe."[48] Donne is

---

47. Potter and Simpson, *Sermons of John Donne* 5:306–7.
48. Potter and Simpson, *Sermons of John Donne* 9:278.

speaking in the third person; the "he" and "his" clearly refer to David. But the analogy between David offering instruction through the psalm and Donne offering instruction through the sermon is hard to avoid. Is Donne as preacher seeking to engage his congregation through a display of "reading," or is he drawing on the rhetorical tradition of ethos and seeking to move his audience by recourse to his own "feeling?" Donne proceeds by offering further instances of those who offer instruction through self-example, starting with the example of Christ and moving through to St. Paul:

> Christ who could doe nothing but well, proposes himselfe for an example of humility, *I have given you an example*; Whom? what? *That you should doe as I have done.* . . . S. Paul, who had proposed Christ to himselfe to follow, might propose himselfe to others, and wish as he does, *I would all men were even as my selfe* [emphasis original].[49]

Donne speaks the words of Christ and St. Paul in the first person, but he clearly distinguishes between their voices and his. In print this distinction between the words of Christ and Donne's interjections is apparent visually through the use of italics; in performance Donne no doubt used intonation to distinguish between Christ's authoritative words and his own abrupt questions, "Whom? what," spoken in the part of the non-understanding listener. However, as Donne continues, these distinctions between his voice and those of his biblical examples become less clear.

> For, though that Apostle, by denying it in his own practise, seeme to condemne it in all others, To preach our selves, (*We preach not our selves, but Christ Iesus the Lord*) yet to preach out of our owne history, so farre, as to declare to the Congregation, to what manifold sins we had formerly abandoned our selves, how powerfully the Lord was pleased to reclaime us, how vigilantly he hath vouchsafed to preserve us from relapsing, to preach our selves thus, to call up the Congregation, to heare what God hath done for my soule, is a blessed preaching of my selfe.[50]

The passage is dominated by the first person: "To preach our selves . . . our owne history . . . how powerfully the Lord was pleased to reclaim us . . . preserve us . . . a preaching of my selfe." There is a case for reading this as a prosopopoeia in which Donne takes on the voice of

49. Potter and Simpson, *Sermons of John Donne* 9:278–79.
50. Potter and Simpson, *Sermons of John Donne* 9:279.

David. After all, Donne is reflecting on David's use of himself as an example, and the words speak directly to David's expression of repentance in the psalm. However, at the same time, the words also sound distinctly like Donne himself. Donne's ordination had come late in life after a youth which was, in popular opinion at least, often remembered as somewhat debauched. Donne ruefully observed of Lady Bedford's less-than-enthusiastic response to his newfound calling that "she had more suspicion of my calling, a better memory of my past life, then I had thought her nobility could have admitted."[51] Would, then, a congregation have heard Donne's words not as a ventriloquizing of David, but as a personal conversion narrative? This seems possible, but it might be more fruitful to think about how the sermon, like the psalms themselves, rejects a clear distinction of voices, providing instead a moment when Donne's voice is, to use his own term, "tuned" with that of the psalmist, inhabiting David's voice even as he directs it to his congregation. The sermon is, then, an example of how engaging creatively with the figure of prosopopoeia allows Donne to develop a mode of exegesis which extends meaning from the "limited" form of a poem.

CONCLUSION

In the introduction to their edition of Donne's sermons, George Potter and Evelyn Simpson argue that Donne was "essentially a poet" who wrote prose when "debarred from the ordinary forms of verse."[52] Later reassessments of the sermons have taken issue with this emphasis on their "literary" value, developing readings which emphasize Donne's place in the varied, and often conflicted, religious, political, and social worlds of the early seventeenth century.[53] In this chapter I have sought to use Donne's sermons on the Penitential Psalms to reframe these debates by starting with the questions of whether and how Donne read Scripture as a poet. As Mary Morrissey describes, early modern preaching manuals articulated a preacher's task as threefold. Firstly, they should "explicate" a text, in other words, "unfold it" to reveal the layers of meaning it contained; then they should apply it to their hearers; and finally they should

---

51. John Donne, *Letters to Severall Persons of Honour*, 2F1v.
52. Potter and Simpson, *Sermons of John Donne* 1:99.
53. See, for example, Shami, *John Donne and Conformity in Crisis*, 8–12.

"exhort" the congregation to follow these lessons.[54] Reading, then, in the form of "unfolding" or uncovering a biblical text, was the starting point for any of Donne's sermons, and, in the case of the psalms, this reading was informed by his interest in the psalms as fixed forms of poetry. Thus Donne's "explications" probe the psalms' rhetorical workings, including, as I have shown, the Holy Ghost's use of metaphor, which restrains meaning by guiding the reader to an exegesis shaped by doctrine, and voice, which extends meaning by allowing the reader to apply the texts to new circumstances. In turning to his "exhortation," Donne would then draw on his own rhetorical skill in order to persuade his listeners to attend to the lessons in the sermon. And in this context we can return to Potter and Simpson's assertion that Donne wrote as "a poet"; not, though, to insist upon a distinction between pulpit oratory and poetry, but to appreciate how both forms were indebted to the traditions and conventions of rhetoric. Indeed, for Donne, some of the most satisfying pulpit oratory was when the process of explicating Scripture rhetorically could develop organically into his own rhetorical exhortation. Hence his love of the psalms, "written in such forms, as I have been most accustomed to."[55]

BIBLIOGRAPHY

Alexander, Gavin. "Prosopopoeia: The Speaking Figure." In *Renaissance Figures of Speech*, edited by Sylvia Adamson et al., 97–112. Cambridge: Cambridge University Press, 2020.

Donne, John. *Devotions Upon Emergent Occasions*. Edited by Anthony Raspa. Oxford: Oxford University Press, 1975.

———. *Fifty sermons. The second volume preached by that learned and reverend divine, John Donne*. London: Printed by Ja. Flesher for M. F., J. Marriot, and R. Royston, 1649.

———. *Letters to Severall Persons of Honour*. 1651.

———. *LXXX sermons preached by that learned and reverend divine, Iohn Donne, Dr in Divinity, late Deane of the cathedrall church of S. Pauls London*. London: Printed [by Miles Flesher] for Richard Royston, in Ivie-lane, and Richard Marriot in S. Dunstans Church-yard in Fleetstreet, 1640.

Ettenhuber, Katrin, ed. *The Oxford Edition of the Sermons of John Donne. Volume 5, Sermons Preached at Lincoln's Inn, 1620–1623*. Oxford: Oxford University Press, 2015.

Fraunce, Abraham. *The Arcadian Rhetorike*. London, 1588.

Green, Ian. *Print and Protestantism in Early Modern England*. Oxford: Oxford University Press, 2000.

---

54. Morrissey, "Sermon-Notes," 295.

55. Potter and Simpson, *Sermons of John Donne* 2:49.

Hamlin, Hannibal. "My Tongue Shall Speak: The Voices of the Psalms." *Renaissance Studies* 29.4 (2015) 509–30.

———. "Piety and Poetry: English Psalms from Miles Coverdale to Mary Sidney." In *The Oxford Handbook of Tudor Literature, 1485–1603*, edited by Mike Pincombe and Cathy Shrank, 203–21. Oxford: Oxford University Press, 2009.

———. *Psalm Culture and Early Modern English Literature*. Cambridge: Cambridge University Press, 2004.

———. "Sorrowful Souls: Versions of the Penitential Psalms for Domestic Devotion." In *Private and Domestic Devotion in Early Modern England*, edited by Alec Ryrie and Jessica Martin, 211–35. London: Routledge, 2017.

King'oo, Clare Costley. *Miserere Mei: The Penitential Psalms in Late Medieval and Early Modern England*. Notre Dame, IN: University of Notre Dame Press, 2012.

Knight, Alison. *The Dark Bible: Cultures of Interpretation in Early Modern England*. Oxford: Oxford University Press, 2022.

Lewalski, Barbara. *Protestant Poetics and the Seventeenth-Century Religious Lyric*. Princeton: Princeton University Press, 1979.

Lund, Mary Ann, ed. *The Oxford Edition of the Sermons of John Donne: Volume XII, Sermons Preached at St Paul's Cathedral, 1626*. Oxford: Oxford University Press, 2017.

Morrissey, Mary. "Nuts, Kernels, Wading Lambs and Swimming Elephants' Preachers and Their Handling of Biblical Texts." In *The English Bible in the Early Modern World*, edited by Robert Armstrong and Tadhg Ó Hannracháin, 84–103. Leiden: Brill, 2018.

———. "Sermon-Notes and Seventeenth Century Manuscript Communities." *Huntington Library Quarterly* 80.2 (2017) 293–307.

Potter, George, and Evelyn Simpson, eds. *The Sermons of John Donne*. 10 vols. Berkely: University of California Press, 1953–62.

Quitslund, Beth. *The Reformation in Rhyme: Sternhold, Hopkins and the English Metrical Psalter, 1547–1603*. Aldershot: Ashgate, 2008.

———. "Singing the Psalms for Fun and Profit." In *Private and Domestic Devotion in Early Modern England*, edited by Alec Ryrie and Jessica Martin, 237–58. London: Routledge, 2017.

Rhatigan, Emma. "Donne's Readership at Lincoln's Inn and the Doncaster Embassy." In *The Oxford Handbook of the Sermons of John Donne*, edited by Jeanne Shami et al., 576–88, Oxford: Oxford University Press, 2011.

———. "Margins of Error: Performance, Text, and the Editing of Early Modern Sermons." *The Library* 21.4 (2020) 423–44.

Robbins, Robin Hugh A., ed. *The Complete Poems of John Donne*. Harlow: Pearson, 2008.

Shami, Jeanne. *John Donne and Conformity in Crisis in the Late Jacobean Pulpit*. Woodbridge: D. S. Brewer, 2003.

Smith, A. J., ed. *John Donne: The Critical Heritage*. London: Routledge, 1995.

Stallybrass, Peter. "Books and Scrolls: Navigating the Bible." In *Books and Readers in Early Modern England: Material Studies*, edited by Jennifer Andersen et al., 42–79, Philadelphia: University of Pennsylvania Press, 2002.

Stanwood, P. G. "Donne's Earliest Sermons and the Penitential Tradition." In *John Donne's Religious Imagination: Essays in Honor of John T. Shawcross*, edited by Raymond-Jean Frontain and Frances M. Malpezzi, 366–79. Conway, AR: UCA, 1995.

Temperley, Nicholas. *The Music of the English Parish Church: Volume 1*. Cambridge: Cambridge University Press, 1979.

Zim, Rivkah. *English Metrical Psalms: Poetry as Praise and Prayer, 1535–1601*. Cambridge: Cambridge University Press, 1987.

8

C. H. Spurgeon
Treasuring David's Penitential Psalms

Peter J. Morden

INTRODUCTION

Charles Haddon Spurgeon (1834–92) was, by common consent, the foremost popular preacher of Victorian Britain. In 1853 he became pastor of New Park Street Chapel in London, and within a remarkably short space of time turned around what had been a struggling, declining church. In 1861 his burgeoning congregation moved to the purpose-built Metropolitan Tabernacle, which could comfortably seat 5,500 people. To the amazement of skeptical observers, he filled the vast auditorium to overflowing Sunday by Sunday until just before his death. His reputation and influence traveled far beyond his British base. As early as 1858, when he was only twenty-four, the *North American Review* was reporting that Americans returning from a trip to England were invariably asked two questions, namely: "Did you see the Queen?" and "Did you hear Spurgeon?" The paper went on to declare that there was "scarcely any name more familiar" than his in the anglophone world.[1] By 1875 his sermons had been translated into languages as varied as French, Dutch, Telugu, Māori, and Welsh.[2] Soon to follow were some Russian editions of a few select messages. These were passed by the Tsarist censor and

---

1. "Sermons," 275.
2. Spurgeon, "Twenty Years of Published Sermons," 7.

approved by the Orthodox Church for official distribution. A staggering one million copies were printed.[3] Many additional examples could be adduced to demonstrate his global reach.[4] Spurgeon was a preacher of great international standing in the nineteenth century and his influence continues today through the enduring popularity of his freely available published works.[5]

Spurgeon the expositor was best known through the sermons that were printed weekly from 1855 in the *New Park Street/Metropolitan Tabernacle Pulpit*. But his multivolume commentary on the Psalms, the *Treasury of David*, was also influential.[6] The production of the seven volumes which made up the *Treasury* spanned over sixteen years and in many ways it was his *magnum opus*, a labor of love that was warmly received and widely appreciated. The commentary exhibited the same features which characterized his preaching: a resolute focus on Jesus and the gospel, an unwavering commitment to "sound" evangelical doctrine, a deep spirituality, a transparent love for people, and an extraordinary ability to communicate in language that was both vivid and accessible. It was a potent mix.

THE DIVINE AND THE HUMAN IN THE PENITENTIAL PSALMS

Underpinning Spurgeon's powerful exposition of the Psalter was an unshakable commitment to the full authority of both the Old and New Testaments of Scripture.[7] His ministry coincided with the growth of "higher criticism," a movement which represented a significant shift in biblical

---

3. Murray, *Full Harvest*, 353–54.

4. Spurgeon, "Twenty Years of Published Sermons," 7.

5. For a detailed study, see Morden, *Communion with Christ and His People*. Worth noting is that his story is one of triumph but not of triumphalism, for his life was marked by significant suffering. On this, see Morden, *Communion with Christ and His People*, 258–84.

6. Spurgeon, *Treasury Of David*, in 7 volumes. Hereafter cited as simply *Treasury* with a volume number. All citations in this chapter are from the original London editions. The text is freely available online at https://archive.spurgeon.org/treasury/treasury.php. For some excellent contemporary reflections drawing from the *Treasury*, see McKinley, *Psalms for Everyday Living*.

7. For more detail on Spurgeon's approach to Scripture in the context of his time, see Breimaier, *Tethered to the Cross*, 85–93; Morden, *Communion with Christ and His People*, 107–10.

scholarship. Critics such as Julius Wellhausen (1844–1918) and Benjamin Jowett (1817–93) treated Scripture, as Jowett put it, "like any other book."[8] They deployed a range of linguistic, archeological, and historical methods in order to—as they understood it—better understand the text. Whilst Spurgeon could draw on insights gleaned from higher criticism, he steadfastly resisted anything which in his view downgraded Scripture's divine inspiration and unique authority, which in practice many higher critics did. His own approach was straightforward and clearly communicated throughout his ministry. The Bible, he declared in 1855 at the beginning of his London pastorate, was "dictated by the Holy Spirit"; indeed, "each letter was penned with an Almighty finger" and "untainted by any error."[9] In a message preached in or after 1861 he repeated his belief that the "Spirit of God . . . dictated" the Scriptures.[10] And towards the end of his life, in August 1888, he spoke of the "infallible wisdom" of God "dictating every syllable."[11] In the face of the encroaching tide of higher criticism he thus took a firm stand in favor of verbal plenary inspiration. The Bible was certainly not "like any other book"—far from it. This foundational commitment is everywhere in evidence in his expositions of the Penitential Psalms, which were for him part of the divinely inspired infallible word of God.[12]

Spurgeon's understanding of biblical inspiration might seem unsophisticated and even mechanical. Yet the *Treasury* also reveals his deep appreciation of the humanity of the Psalms, and their ability to give voice to frail—indeed faltering and fallible—human experience. The Psalter provided fuel for a life of prayer that all could draw from, helping Christians give voice to feelings which otherwise would have "found no utterance."[13] So, the Psalter enabled believers to vocalize their praise, thankfulness, and petition.[14] It also helped them in the vital business of expressing penitence for sin, and in this task the Penitential Psalms occupied the central place, for they were full of material to inspire and direct prayers of confession and repentance. They showed the seriousness of sin, pointed the penitent to its only remedy, and encouraged him or her

---

8. Jowett, "On the Interpretation of Scripture," 338.
9. Spurgeon, "Bible," 110–12.
10. Spurgeon, "Renewing Strength," 700.
11. Spurgeon, "Message of Our Lord's Love," 711.
12. See, e.g., *Treasury II*, 71.
13. *Treasury VI*, vii.
14. See, e.g., Spurgeon, "Singing Pilgrim," 181–92.

to come to God in their brokenness. By expressing the cries of the sinner, these Penitential Psalms were especially "human"; indeed, the best known of these, Ps 51, was "very human," for "its cries and sobs are of one born of a woman."[15] Spurgeon was sure, contrary to many higher critics, that this Psalm's human author was King David.[16] In his exposition he identified strongly with the distress expressed by the penitent King as he came to God for mercy, and believed that others could and should do so as well. Here was authentic Christian spirituality, at one and the same time both deeply human and directed by God himself.

Spurgeon followed tradition in recognizing the seven Penitential Psalms under consideration in this present volume (Pss 6, 32, 38, 51, 102, 130, 143) as a distinct group.[17] Rather than dealing with each of the Psalms one by one, the following analysis takes a thematic approach, examining the central themes of the different expositions. Taken in sequence, these themes together make up what Spurgeon regarded as the pathway of true penitence which would lead to forgiveness and restoration.[18] For him, this pathway began with an awareness of the reality and terrible consequences of human sin.

SIN AND REBELLION

Spurgeon spent considerable time in his expositions setting out what he believed these Psalms taught about sin. Commenting on Ps 51:4, "Against thee, thee only, have I sinned,"[19] he stated the classic Reformed understanding of sin, that it was fundamentally rebellion against God. He asserted: "To injure our fellow men is sin, mainly because in doing so we violate the law of God. The Psalmist's heart was so filled with a sense of the wrong done to the Lord himself, that all other confession was

---

15. *Treasury II*, v.
16. *Treasury II*, 449.
17. E.g., *Treasury I*, 62, although note his comments on Ps 143, that he regarded as somewhat different from the others, a "mingled strain" containing some penitential elements but also other "ingredients." See *Treasury VII*, 323.
18. I have focused on the main expositions, not on the lists of quotations and "hints to village preachers" which accompany Spurgeon's comments. These were often compiled by others.
19. Spurgeon quoted from the Authorized (King James) version of the Bible. He was aware of errors in the AV and was willing to critique it and, on occasion, to emend the text. Even so, it remained his Bible of choice throughout his ministry. See Breimaier, *Tethered to the Cross*, 88–89.

swallowed up in a broken-hearted acknowledgment of offense against him."[20] So, whilst sin certainly involved doing "injury" to others, at its heart it should be understood as opposition to God. He further stated his belief in the Augustinian understanding of original sin held by the Magisterial Reformers. Reflecting on verse 5, "Behold I was shaped in iniquity," he declared how his text showed we are in "very nature" sinners and that our sin is "inbred." Deploying an agricultural metaphor, he insisted that our sin has "deep tap-roots." In a polemical passage he railed against commentators—again his main targets were the higher critics and those influenced by them—who downplayed the true meaning of Scripture on this point. "It is a wicked wresting of Scripture to deny that original sin and natural depravity are here taught. Surely men who cavil at this doctrine have need to be taught of the Holy Spirit what be the first principles of the faith."[21] This was a strong rebuke, but Spurgeon was sure that an Augustinian and Reformed doctrine of sin was foundational to a right understanding of the human condition.

Such pervasive sinfulness separated the sinner from a holy God, leaving them under his righteous wrath and in grave danger of eternal separation from him.[22] Spurgeon expressed this in unambiguous and expressive language in comments on Ps 32:2, stating: "Transgression, sin, and iniquity are the three-headed dog at the gates of hell."[23] He was clear that once someone began to realize the seriousness of sin and its awful consequences they would be deeply affected. Again, his language was vivid, pulling no punches. "What a killing thing is sin!" he exclaimed. "It is a pestilent disease! A fire in the bones!"[24] He continued: "Unconfessed transgression, like a fierce poison, dried up the fountain of the man's strength, and made him like a tree blasted by lightning, or a plant withered by the scorching heat of the tropical sun."[25] This was a harrowing yet accurate description of someone coming under conviction of sin for the first time. But Spurgeon was of course aware that the Psalm was written

---

20. *Treasury II*, 451. Spurgeon consistently used male language, and I have retained this when quoting him.

21. *Treasury II*, 451.

22. See e.g., *Treasury VII*, 70–71.

23. *Treasury II*, 90; a reference to Cerberus, the three-headed dog of Greek mythology who stood at the entrance to Hades. For further powerful language about sin and hell, see *Treasury I*, 63.

24. *Treasury II*, 90.

25. *Treasury II*, 91; cf. *Treasury II*, 221.

by a mature believer and they were describing their own experience. No Christian was ever completely free of sin; indeed, all Christians would continue to wrestle with personal sin and need to confess regularly.[26] The Penitential Psalms were thus essential both for the newly awakened sinner and the experienced saint. Psalm 6 set out a right attitude to sin, namely "sorrow" (vv. 3, 6-7), "humiliation"—by which Spurgeon meant anguish and abasement—(vv. 2, 4), and "hatred" (v. 8).[27] These points were vital to him, for only if the human condition was accurately diagnosed could the remedy God provided be sought and applied.

ATONEMENT AND THE CROSS

So, how could someone who was becoming ever more aware of their sin and precarious state before God respond? Granted, they would feel horrified and express their deep sorrow, but was any further response possible? Spurgeon's whole life was predicated on his belief that there was. Yet before a sinner could do anything, it was crucial to know that God had acted decisively on their behalf. In his mercy Jesus the incarnate Son of God had come to be their Savior. He had lived a perfect life and—crucially—died a perfect death for sinners. His terrible suffering on the cross was deeply purposeful, for Christ had given his life in our place as our sacrificial "substitute,"[28] bearing our "load" of sin so completely he had carried it "right away."[29] The language was redolent of John Bunyan's *The Pilgrim's Progress* and Christian's experience of being freed from his burden of sin as he approached the cross.[30] This book was much beloved by Spurgeon, and his dominant theology of the cross, that of penal substitution, was one shared by Bunyan. It was also the understanding typically held by evangelicals.[31] Christ died in the place of sinners, enduring the righteous wrath of God against sin on their behalf. As Spurgeon said when expounding the opening verse of Ps 32, the cross of Christ was the

---

26. Morden, *Communion with Christ and His People*, 250–51.
27. *Treasury II*, 91.
28. *Treasury II*, 92.
29. *Treasury II*, 89.
30. Spurgeon's spirituality was heavily indebted to Bunyan, especially to *The Pilgrim's Progress*. See Morden, *Communion with Christ and His People*, 26–30.
31. On evangelicalism and penal substitutionary atonement, see, e.g., Morden, "Evangelical Spirituality," 64. For Spurgeon's own resolute commitment to this doctrine, Spurgeon, *Autobiography* I:99; 113.

"propitiation" for our sin, completely "covering" it over and the making an end of it.[32] Our sinfulness is indeed great, but in the atonement God's provision is greater still. The cross covers it all.

How was Spurgeon able to write extensively about the cross and what it accomplished when commenting on these psalms, which were written many years before the coming of Christ? His comment on Ps 32:1 just cited shows us his method. He interpreted the sacrificial system set out in the Hebrew Scriptures as having been perfectly fulfilled in Christ. They were the "type" and Christ was the perfect "antitype"; they were the shadow that pointed to the reality. So, in expounding the phrase "sin is covered" in Ps 32:1, he firstly interpreted the word "covered" in the light of other Old Testament texts, for example, the ark of the covenant which was "covered by the mercy seat" which would be sprinkled with the blood of sacrifice.[33] With the basic point—"covering" comes through sacrifice—established, the commentator then traced a line from the old covenant sacrifice directly to the new covenant once-for-all-time sacrifice of Christ.[34] This christocentric and crucicentric approach to the interpretation and application of the Penitential Psalms was vital to Spurgeon.

WEEPING AND MERCY

The atonement still had to be responded to. The opening lines of Ps 130, "Out of the depths I cried unto thee, O Lord" (KJV), signposted the way for the penitent sinner.[35] The aforementioned threefold attitude to sin set out in Ps 6—sorrow, humiliation, and hatred—need not lead to despair because there was encouragement to confess all to God and ask for "mercy."[36] Spurgeon was an emotional man who did not deal in half measures. Such was the sinner's plight that weeping before God was not only appropriate but extremely likely if the penitent had truly comprehended their parlous situation. Commenting on Ps 6:8 and the phrase, "For the Lord hath heard the voice of my weeping," he asked the question:

---

32. *Treasury II*, 90.

33. Lev 16:15.

34. *Treasury II*, 89–90; cf. *Treasury II*, 455: "The Psalmist was so illuminated as to see far beyond the symbolic ritual; his eye of faith gazed with delight upon the actual atonement."

35. *Treasury VII*, 69.

36. *Treasury II*, 89, 91.

Is there a voice in weeping! Does weeping speak! In what language does it utter its meaning? Why, in that universal tongue which is known and understood in all the earth, and even in heaven above... weeping is the eloquence of sorrow. It is an unstammering orator, needing no interpreter, but understood by all. Is it not sweet to believe that our tears are understood even when words fail? Let us think of our tears as liquid prayers, and of weeping as a constant dropping of importunate intercession which will wear its way right surely into the very heart of mercy.[37]

Thus, the Penitential Psalms not only offered language the sinner could use, helping them give voice to their deepest feelings. They also legitimized nonverbal prayer, in this case weeping. This was a universal "language," one which in fact could be especially effective given that it was authentic and heartfelt. These were qualities he was sure God in his grace loved to respond to.[38] As he put it elsewhere: "Prayer with the heart is the heart of prayer."[39]

REPENTANCE AND FAITH

In crying to God for mercy, the penitent sinner would express repentance—a turning from sin—and faith—a turning to God to receive his grace. The importance of repentance would have been understood by most of his readers, but Spurgeon believed that many people's understanding and experience of it was shallow. In the course of his exposition of Ps 6 he cried out to God, "O Holy Spirit, beget in us the true repentance which needeth not to be repented of."[40] What he advocated was a deepening awareness of the corrosive nature of sin and the wrath of God against it. When this was in place a corresponding depth of "hatred" of sin would follow, as would a new appreciation of repentance.[41]

Such thoroughgoing penitence would likely be accompanied with fear and trembling, but there was a corresponding truth, that the worst sinner could still come to God with a humble, trusting confidence. This

---

37. *Treasury I*, 65.

38. In Spurgeon's comments on Ps 38 he made a similar point in respect of groans. See *Treasury II*, 222. God understands the deep meaning of these groans and responds to them, as he does our tears. See also *Treasury IV*, 418.

39. Spurgeon, "Thought-Reading Extraordinary," 536.

40. *Treasury I*, 62.

41. See *Treasury II*, 225.

was because—and only because—of the merciful and gracious character of God and the atonement he had made.[42] Spurgeon's exposition of the two clauses which make up the opening verse of Ps 38 are illustrative of the balanced approach he wanted to commend and is quoted here in full:

> "O Lord, rebuke me not in thy wrath." Rebuked I must be, for I am an erring child and thou a careful Father, but throw not too much anger into the tones of thy voice; deal gently although I have sinned grievously. The anger of others I can bear, but not thine. As my love is most sweet to thy heart, so thy displeasure is most cutting to my conscience. "Neither chasten me in thy hot displeasure." Chasten me if thou wilt, it is a Father's prerogative, and to endure it obediently is a child's duty; but, O turn not the rod into a sword, smite not so as to kill. True, my sins might well inflame thee, but let thy mercy and longsuffering quench the glowing coals of thy wrath. O let me not be treated as an enemy or dealt with as a rebel. Bring to remembrance thy covenant, thy fatherhood, and my feebleness, and spare thy servant.[43]

Firstly a comment about form. It is instructive that the whole quotation, like the previous one regarding repentance from Ps 6, took the form of a prayer with Spurgeon addressing God in direct speech. Here is evidence of the deep spirituality which many readers and hearers found compelling, and which marked the *Treasury* out from other commentaries which were more cerebral. As to content, the key notes struck in the course of the quotation will by now be familiar, especially the seriousness of sin which left the sinner under the wrath of God and crying to him for mercy. What is striking is the bold way God is addressed. In many ways the psalmist had no right to speak in the way he did, for he had "sinned grievously" and such sin "inflames" the "glowing coals of [God's] wrath." This he knew all too well. Yet the humble confidence he nevertheless displayed was still appropriate, predicated as it was on the merciful, "longsuffering" character of God and his sure promises, and this confidence is reflected in Spurgeon's prayer. God had established his covenant with his people, entering into relationship with them. This saving relationship was open to all who turned to him in repentance and faith. So, whether someone was coming to Christ for the first time, or whether they were a mature believer coming again for forgiveness, the way was gloriously open. Everyone could pray with a humble confidence:

---

42. See *Treasury VII*, 71–72.
43. *Treasury II*, 220.

"Bring to remembrance thy covenant, thy fatherhood, and my feebleness, and spare thy servant." The pathway of true penitence was one that was full of hope.

A number of points here echo the Puritan spirituality which was important to Spurgeon. The emphasis on human depravity, on what Jeremiah Burroughs (1600–46) called "the exceeding sinfulness of sin,"[44] and on the practice of pleading the character and the promises of God, were all typically Puritan, as was the stress on covenant.[45] Spurgeon read the Penitential Psalms—at least in part—through a Puritan lens.

ASSURANCE AND JOY

The one who comes to God in real repentance, whether that repentance is expressed verbally or merely by tears and groans, and then cries for mercy and puts their faith in Christ will receive forgiveness and pardon. To believe this is not arrogance or presumption because God has promised it in his word. Commenting on Ps 51:14, Spurgeon offered a mix of remarks directly on the text and some New Testament reflections. David had confessed his horrific sin openly and freely. Rightly he had believed he was worthy of death. Yet, he had come to God trustingly and received pardon. This was because Jesus is "our righteousness," and in his merits the repentant sinner stands "righteously accepted."[46] Even David the foul adulterer and vile murderer could have full assurance of forgiveness and salvation, and so could others who likewise trusted God. Spurgeon, in comments on Ps 32:1, insisted that all his readers could know this assurance for themselves. Where the atonement is "seen and trusted in, the soul knows itself to be now accepted in the Beloved," he declared. "It is clear from the text that a man may *know* he is pardoned: where would be the blessedness of an unknown forgiveness? Clearly it is a matter of knowledge, for it is the ground of comfort" [emphasis original].[47] This confident view of assurance was less typically Puritan and more commonly held by eighteenth-century evangelicals, so here is a point at which Spurgeon departed from the standard Puritan view. For him, full assurance was vitally important,

---

44. Burroughs, *Evil of Evils*. For Spurgeon's appreciation of Burroughs (sometimes spelt "Burroughes"), see Morden, *Communion with Christ and His People*, 32.

45. See Kapic and Gleason, *Devoted Life*, for an excellent introduction to Puritanism as a movement of spirituality.

46. *Treasury II*, 220.

47. *Treasury II*, 90; see also *Treasury VII*, 71.

for it was the ground not only of "comfort" but of confident discipleship.[48] He was certain that the Penitential Psalms supported his case.

Assurance of salvation led not only to confident discipleship, it also generated great joy which welled up in the heart of the believer to such an extent it could not fail to be expressed. Such joy was a repeated and perhaps surprising theme of Spurgeon's comments on these psalms, and balances the corresponding stress on sorrow over sin. He rejoiced that: "A full, instantaneous, irreversible pardon of transgression turns the poor sinner's hell into heaven, and makes the heir of wrath a partaker in blessing." Those who had received this blessing would be filled with joy; indeed, it was a "sure way to happiness." Reflection on the blessing of the gospel of forgiveness would "demand quiet contemplation," for "joy so great" could not adequately be expressed through language alone.[49] Once again, words were deemed insufficient to express the deep feelings engendered by the gospel, but this time, rather than weeping over sin, it was quiet contemplation which was appropriate to express gratitude and thankfulness for Christ.

However, quiet contemplation on its own would not be enough for the forgiven sinner. Reflecting on Ps 32:7, "Thou shalt compass me about with songs of deliverance," Spurgeon exclaimed: "What a golden sentence! The man is encircled in song, surrounded by dancing mercies, all of them proclaiming the triumphs of grace."[50] Such was his emphasis on exuberant joy he was prepared to push the boundaries of Victorian decorum:

> It is to be feared that the church of the present day, through a craving for excessive propriety, is growing too artificial, so that enquirers' cries and believers' shouts would be silenced if they were heard in our assemblies. This may be better than boisterous fanaticism, but there is as much danger in the one direction as the other. For our part, we are touched to the heart by a little sacred excess, and when godly men in their joy o'erleap the narrow bounds of decorum, we do not, like Michal, Saul's daughter, eye them with a sneering heart.[51]

The Penitential Psalms not only plumbed the depths, they also scaled the heights as they mapped out the joyful response of the forgiven penitent.

---

48. See Morden, *Communion with Christ and His People*, 70–76.
49. *Treasury II*, 92.
50. *Treasury II*, 92.
51. *Treasury II*, 94. 2 Sam 6:14–22.

SURRENDER AND SERVICE

Whilst joy was a logical and important outflowing of the penitent's experience of forgiveness and restoration, their responses to what God had done in Christ did not end there. Full devotion and commitment would surely follow. "When the heart can sincerely call Jehovah 'my God,' the understanding is ready to learn of him, the will is prepared to obey him, the whole man is eager to please him."[52] The one who had truly been brought into right relationship with God would want to grow in knowledge and understanding of his ways and press forward in obedient discipleship. Indeed, the whole person—body and soul—would be at his service. Here was full surrender.[53] A wide range of commitments flowed from this primary one of deep devotion and "hearty loyalty" to God.[54] Two will be considered here.

Firstly, there was a commitment to a life of prayer. This obviously included confession, thanksgiving, and adoration, all crucial types of prayer for the penitent sinner who knew the transforming grace of God. Intercession for others was also vitally important and a dimension of prayer Spurgeon often emphasized. As he expounded the closing verses of Ps 51 he urged intercession for the church, specifically for its revival. "God can make his cause to prosper, and in answer to prayer he will do so. Without his building we labour in vain; therefore are we the more instant and constant in prayer."[55] Such a revival for the church would have implications for the nation and indeed the whole world. Psalm 102 was interpreted as the cry of a mature believer lamenting over their land, standing with their people in their "miseries" and "afflictions," and praying passionately for revival.[56] "Zion" in this Psalm was treated as analogous to the church, and it was through the prosperity of Zion that revival for the land would come. Commenting on the phrase, "Thou shalt arise, and have mercy upon Zion," he declared that "God will not always leave his church in a low condition." Rather there will come a time when, in response to the prayers of his people, God will "arise" and act. Through a revived church the nation would

---

52. *Treasury VII*, 327.

53. See *Treasury II*, 455: "We can never do too much for the Lord to whom we owe more than all."

54. *Treasury VII*, 327.

55. *Treasury II*, 456. Ps 127:1.

56. *Treasury IV*, 417.

be renewed and "the Kingdom of Christ would extend its bounds."[57] Thus the prayers of Pss 51 and 102 were two sides of the same coin. National renewal would come through a renewed church. To pray for the latter was essentially to pray for the former as well.

Spurgeon's passion for the church is sometimes underappreciated but it was one he often expressed. In fact he had a well-thought-out and robust ecclesiology. As far as he was concerned, the church was glorious, at the very heart of God's purposes, and would ultimately be triumphant.[58] He had a particular love for the local congregation he was privileged to pastor.[59] His passion for intercession is better known, and he rarely missed an opportunity to stress the importance of the Monday night meeting for corporate prayer at the Tabernacle.[60] Speaking personally, he believed prayer was for him "as much a necessity" for his own spiritual life as breath was for his natural life. "We cannot live," he insisted, "without asking favours of the Lord."[61] His comments on the Penitential Psalms are consistent with the rest of his life and ministry and add to our appreciation of his thought and practice.

A second outworking of the desire for surrender and service was the believer's responsibility to share the gospel of forgiveness with others in evangelism. Indeed, this was not just a duty, but a Christian's delight. "Reader, what a delightful Psalm!" Spurgeon exclaimed in the course of his comments on Ps 32. "Have you, in perusing it, been able to claim a lot in the goodly land? If so, publish to others the way of salvation."[62] Those who had a share in the "goodly" inheritance of the people of God would surely need little invitation to joyfully proclaim the gospel to others. Spurgeon himself put his own exhortation into practice even as he wrote the pages of the *Treasury*. Expounding on the words "Purge me with hyssop" from Ps 51:7, he appealed to any reader who did not yet know Christ personally. "O that some reader may take heart, even now while smarting under sin, to do the Lord the honour to rely thus confidently on the

---

57. *Treasury IV*, 422; noting 425.

58. Spurgeon, "Glory, Unity, and Triumph," 253–64.

59. Spurgeon, "Crowning Blessings Ascribed To God," 289–300. This was a message Spurgeon preached to celebrate his twenty-five years of ministry in London.

60. See, for example, Spurgeon, *Sword and Trowel*, 609; see also Morden, *Communion with Christ and His People*, 141.

61. Spurgeon, "Secret of Power in Prayer," 15.

62. *Treasury II*, 94.

finished sacrifice of Calvary and the infinite mercy there revealed."[63] Such was his own evangelistic impulse the commentator became the preacher. The pilgrimage taken by the repentant sinner—from awakening through penitence and on to forgiveness and restoration—was so vital and so glorious it simply had to be shared with others. The pathway of penitence was open to all.

CONCLUSION

Reflecting on his experience of commenting on Ps 51 for the *Treasury*, Spurgeon confessed:

> I postponed expounding it week after week, feeling more and more my inability for the work. Often I sat down to it, and rose again without having penned a line. It is a bush burning with fire yet not consumed, and out of it a voice seemed to cry to me, "Draw not nigh hither, put off thy shoes from off thy feet."[64]

For Spurgeon, this Psalm was precious. This was in significant degree because it was "freighted with an inspiration all divine." It was as if, he said, "the Great Father were putting words into his child's mouth."[65] Yet, as we have seen, this Psalm was also precious because it was full of human frailty. It gave unsparing insight into the journey taken by a lost sinner who reached out to God and received mercy in place of judgment. The Psalm was nothing less than a meeting place between a righteous God and frail humanity. Here was holy ground indeed.

Although Spurgeon had a special affection for Ps 51, his love for each of the Penitential Psalms is hopefully clear for all who have read this present chapter. Interpreted through the lens of Christ and his cross, they plumbed the deepest valleys and scaled the highest heights of authentic Christian experience and offered a pattern of piety for all generations to come. Spurgeon's own comments help to illuminate this journey of penitence and restoration. As such they are a treasury indeed for Christians today.

---

63. *Treasury II*, 452.
64. *Treasury II*, v; see Exod 3:5.
65. *Treasury II*, v.

BIBLIOGRAPHY

Breimaier, Thomas. *Tethered to the Cross: The Life and Preaching of C. H. Spurgeon.* Downers Grove, IL: InterVarsity, 2020.

Burroughs, Jeremiah. *The Evil of Evils: Or The Exceeding Sinfulness of Sin.* London: Thomas Goodwyn, 1654.

Jowett, Benjamin. "On the Interpretation of Scripture." In *Essays and Reviews*, edited by John William Parker, 330–433. London: John Wm. Parker and Son, 1860.

Kapic, Kelly M., and Randall C. Gleason, eds. *The Devoted Life: An Invitation to the Puritan Classics.* Downers Grove, IL: InterVarsity, 2004.

McKinley, David J. *The Psalms for Everyday Living: A Year of Devotions with Charles Spurgeon's Treasury of David.* Eugene, OR: Resource, 2021.

Morden, Peter J. *Communion with Christ and His People: The Spirituality of C. H. Spurgeon.* Eugene, OR: Wipf & Stock, 2014.

———. "Evangelical Spirituality." In *The Routledge Research Companion to the History of Evangelicalism*, edited by Andrew Atherstone and David Ceri Jones, 57–72. Abingdon: Routledge, 2019.

Murray, Iain H., ed. *C. H. Spurgeon Autobiography, Volume 2: The Full Harvest, 1860–1892.* London: Banner of Truth, 1973.

"Sermons of the Rev. C. H. Spurgeon of London." In *North American Review*, edited by William D. O'Connor and F. H. Underwood, 275–80. Boston: Crosby and Nicholls, 1858.

Spurgeon, C. H. *Autobiography of Charles H. Spurgeon: Compiled from his Diary, Letters, and Records by his Wife and his Private Secretary.* 4 vols. London: Passmore and Alabaster, 1897–99.

———. "The Bible." *New Park Street Pulpit* 1 (1855) 110–12.

———. "Crowning Blessings Ascribed to God." *Metropolitan Tabernacle Pulpit* 25 (1879) 289–300.

———. "The Glory, Unity, and Triumph of the Church." *Metropolitan Tabernacle Pulpit* 25 (1879) 253–64.

———. "The Message of Our Lord's Love." *Metropolitan Tabernacle Pulpit* 34 (1888) 705–12.

———. "Renewing Strength." *Metropolitan Tabernacle Pulpit* 29 (1883) 697–708.

———. "The Secret of Power in Prayer." *Metropolitan Tabernacle Pulpit* 34 (1888) 13–24.

———. "The Singing Pilgrim." *Metropolitan Tabernacle Pulpit* 28 (1882) 181–92.

———. *Sword and Trowel* (1883) 609.

———. "Thought-Reading Extraordinary." *Metropolitan Tabernacle Pulpit* 30 (1884) 524–40.

———. *The Treasury Of David.* 7 vols. London: Passmore and Alabaster, 1869–85.

———. "Twenty Years of Published Sermons." *The Sword and The Trowel: A Record of Combat With Sin and Labour For The Lord* (1875) 3–8.

9

Bonhoeffer and the Penitential Psalms

Tim Judson

BONHOEFFER IN CONTEXT

BRIAN BROCK INFORMS US that Bonhoeffer's personal experience of English monastic life developed his deep appreciation for the Psalter.[1] His short (twenty-three page!) but profound work on the Psalms, *Prayerbook of the Bible* (*Das Gebetbuch der Bibel*), was his last book published during his lifetime. Without diminishing the critical importance of later writings that were made available posthumously, *Prayerbook* is arguably a good starting point for understanding Bonhoeffer's theology and ethics, as well as his liturgical imagination. It makes Bonhoeffer not only accessible, but appropriate within the context of this book on the Penitential Psalms.[2] As we will see, the psalms of penitence abided as an existential friend until his death by hanging in the Flossenbürg concentration camp on April 9, 1945.

Like many upper-middle-class people of his time, Bonhoeffer would often operate with a calm and reasoned approach to matters at hand, but would react more viscerally and irrationally if something either struck a chord with him (like the "Negro spirituals" did) or touched a nerve

---

1. Brock, *Singing*, 74.
2. He also writes on the psalms within *Life Together*, which was written at a similar time, though his thoughts there are brief. See Bonhoeffer, *DBWE* 5:53–58, where "*DBWE*" refers to *Dietrich Bonhoeffer Works in English*, the referenced volumes of which are cited in full in the bibliography at the end of this chapter.

in his ego.³ In prison, Bonhoeffer acknowledges his failures to his best friend and confessor, Eberhard Bethge, particularly the "patience and forbearance" that "bore my tyrannical and self-serving manner, which often made you [Bethge] suffer."⁴ What is wonderful about Bonhoeffer is that, despite his gifting and authoritative position, he was aware that he was hard work. He took the opportunity, where possible, to recognize the harm he caused others around him, thereby not taking people for granted, but in gratitude and penitence, acknowledging his own sin and the call to discipleship alongside his brothers and sisters. This required him to face the less virtuous aspects of his character.

An awareness of Bonhoeffer's theological influences also facilitate understanding his approach to the psalms of penitence. Martin Luther's writing was a tremendous influence on Bonhoeffer.⁵ The pseudo-Lutheranism that had emerged in his era, however, became problematic due to its extreme separation between church and state in a manner that surreptitiously absolved the church of any responsibility in relation to state action, which (in Bonhoeffer's mind) made the church guilty of apostasy.⁶ Karl Barth was another hugely significant influence on Bonhoeffer's thought.⁷ Bonhoeffer held a less polemical view towards liberal theology than Barth did, having grown up in the same neighborhood as Adolf von Harnack's family, and though Bonhoeffer embraced Barth's neoorthodoxy, he did not want (nor did he think it possible) to simply return to a premodern, pre-Enlightenment form of Christian thinking. For him, this would be a "sacrifice made at the cost of intellectual integrity."⁸ We must be careful not to accuse Barth of making this mistake, but the fact remains that in his last years, Bonhoeffer "recognized afresh his

---

3. Goebel, "Piano," 125. Johannes Goebel reflects on a notable occasion in Finkenwalde where he asked Bonhoeffer if he was composing or ever had composed something whilst playing the piano, which Bonhoeffer did regularly. Goebel observes that something "primeval" came over Bonhoeffer, where he "betrayed his concentration of will" and played "too loud" in what seems to be an unreserved and aggressive manner. Bonhoeffer then suddenly "stopped as abruptly as he had begun." Goebel wonders whether this reaction was a subtle way of this seminary principal criticizing Goebel's curiosity.

4. Bonhoeffer, *DBWE* 8:181.

5. See DeJonge, *Reception of Luther*; Barker, *Cross of Reality*; Hopkins, *Christ, Church, and World*. For a fuller list, see Oliveri, "Word for the Church."

6. See Bonhoeffer, *DBWE* 4:123; Bonhoeffer, *DBWE* 16:543.

7. Key examples are Pangritz, *Karl Barth*; Krötke, *Karl Barth and Dietrich Bonhoeffer*; Greggs, *Theology Against Religion*; Schlingensiepen, *Dietrich Bonhoeffer*, 101–3.

8. Bonhoeffer, *DBWE* 8:478.

indebtedness to the liberal Protestant legacy in which he had been nurtured at the University of Berlin, especially by Harnack."[9]

Another significant influence on Bonhoeffer was his experience in the Black church during his time in America from 1930–31. James H. Cone highlights Bonhoeffer as a standout exemplar of Christian solidarity and courage, observing Bonhoeffer's immersion in Black life, particularly in the Abyssinian Baptist Church in Harlem, whilst other Whites such as Reinhold Niebuhr kept a certain distance.[10] Reggie L. Williams claims that Bonhoeffer's "mental grid" changed during his immersion in the Black church and community experiences, as well as wider Black literature.[11] He "seemed naturally disposed to seeing society from the perspective of others."[12] In later life, Bonhoeffer reflected on the "Negro spirituals," which "sing with moving expression about the distress and liberation of the people of Israel . . . the misery and distress of the human heart . . . and love for the Redeemer and yearning for the kingdom of heaven."[13] Oppressed African Americans worshiped in a manner that was full of joy and gratitude for Christ, whilst simultaneously crying out in lament over their present suffering and injustice. This is a key factor influencing the sort of embodiment Bonhoeffer seeks to cultivate later through his christological interpretation of the Psalms in *Prayerbook of the Bible*.

BONHOEFFER AND THE PSALMS

Brad Pribbenow distills Bonhoeffer's unique approach to the psalms into what he calls a "two-pillar" hermeneutic.[14] First for Bonhoeffer, the psalms are *prayers*. Second, they are *prayed by Jesus Christ* during his earthly incarnation as well as in eternity, both for and with the church. Bonhoeffer links the psalms inseparably to prayer, arguing that the psalms are about forming disciples in "finding the way to and speaking with God" and "for that one needs Jesus Christ."[15] There are many people

---

9. De Gruchy, "Editor's Introduction," in Bonhoeffer, *DBWE* 8:22.
10. Cone, *Cross and the Lynching Tree*, 41–42.
11. Williams, *Bonhoeffer's Black Jesus*, 79.
12. Williams, *Bonhoeffer's Black Jesus*, 79.
13. Bonhoeffer, *DBWE* 16:457–58.
14. Pribbenow, *Prayerbook of Christ*, 93.
15. Bonhoeffer, *DBWE* 5:155.

in contemporary Christian circles who express that certain language or particular psalms are not really their thing because they "cannot relate" to them. Bonhoeffer would argue that such a perspective is a theologically individualistic, self-focused way of regarding prayer, and the Psalter as a whole for that matter. Citing Luke 11:1, he notes how the disciples ask Jesus, "Lord, teach us to pray," and highlights that this is the only thing the disciples ask Jesus to teach them. He critiques the common assumption that prayer is constituted by the overflow of one's soul. Christian prayer requires guidance and mediation, and God's word offers the content for learning what to pray. But critically, these human words given within the Psalter are also God's word because Christ "has brought before God every need, every joy, every thanksgiving, and every hope of humankind."[16] Prayer is only possible in Jesus Christ, who prays with and also includes humanity in his prayers.

Bonhoeffer is not disregarding personal expression or the reality of particular experiences in prayer. Rather, it is of the utmost concern to him that those who base prayer primarily in their own sentiments, or reason, risk funneling the scope and effectiveness of prayer through the fallible and fallen sensibilities of the self. To do so dislodges Christ from being the central origin, mediator, and goal of prayer, and seeks to pray not according to God's word. For Bonhoeffer, therefore, Christians are called to participate in the prayers of Christ, who has borne the entirety of human nature on himself before God through his own prayer, and invites others to pray like him, with him and through him, as per the Psalter.[17]

What may sound constrictive actually broadens the scope of prayer beyond one's own gaze to include content that is guided by God's word and not according to the *cor curvum in se* (the heart turned in on itself). In other words, Bonhoeffer believes that one does not pray through the horizon of a White German, but in step with the Jewish Jesus, who has borne all of human nature in himself before God in prayer and has done so faithfully. This means that the Psalter "can become our prayer only because it was his prayer."[18] And because believers pray Christ's prayers, the primary focus is on Christ praying in and through us as his body on earth. He goes on to claim that "the prayer of the Psalms teaches us to pray as a community. The body of Christ is praying, and I as an individual recognize that my prayer is only a tiny fraction of the whole

---

16. Bonhoeffer, *DBWE* 5:157.
17. Bonhoeffer, *DBWE* 5:158–59.
18. Bonhoeffer, *DBWE* 5:160.

prayer of the church."[19] Bonhoeffer cites the antiphony and repetition in many psalms as reminders that Christians do not pray alone. Whether gathered or scattered, individuals pray as part of the community, making it truly prayer. In a Finkenwalde lecture entitled "Christ in the Psalms," he even claims, "Those who have never yet prayed the Psalms within the church-community itself but rather alone, by themselves, do not yet know them."[20] He is not dissolving the individual into community. Bonhoeffer understands the christological "structure" of human personhood as an *individual* in *relation to others*.[21]

Before distilling Bonhoeffer's approach to the psalms of penitence, it is worth briefly presenting how he classifies all the different psalms. To an extent, he envisions penitence as a posture within each classification, though some are more explicit than others. He offers ten categories of psalms: (1) creation; (2) law; (3) history of salvation; (4) messiah; (5) church; (6) life; (7) suffering; (8) guilt; (9) enemies; and (10) the end. He makes explicit reference to the Penitential Psalms in his discussion of psalms of guilt (*Die Schuld*),[22] though he does reference Ps 102 in the section on psalms of suffering (*Die Leiden*).[23] This indicates that he places the Penitential Psalms broadly within the guilt category, though he sees them spilling over into others as well, and indeed, he does not reduce the psalms of guilt to penitence alone, as well shall see.

PENITENCE: GUILT AND INNOCENCE IN CHRIST

Bonhoeffer caveats his exploration of the psalms of guilt by claiming that "there are fewer prayers for the forgiveness of sins in the Psalter than we expect."[24] Indeed, most psalms depend upon the implicit knowledge of forgiveness. He argues: "Christian prayer is diminished and endangered

---

19. Bonhoeffer, *DBWE* 5:57.
20. Bonhoeffer, *DBWE* 14:387.
21. Bonhoeffer, *DBWE* 1:127, 158, 227–28. See also Muers, "Anthropology," 196–209.
22. Bonhoeffer, *DBWE* 5:171–73.
23. "The Psalter has rich instruction for us about how to come before God in a proper way in the various sufferings that the world brings upon us. The Psalms know it all: serious illness, deep isolation from God and humanity, threats, persecution, imprisonment, and whatever conceivable peril there is on earth (13, 31, 35, 41, 44, 54, 55, 56, 61, 74, 79, 86, 88, 102, 105, and others)." Bonhoeffer, *DBWE* 5:169.
24. Bonhoeffer, *DBWE* 5:171.

when it revolves exclusively around the forgiveness of sins. There is such a thing as confidently leaving sin behind for the sake of Jesus Christ."[25] Pribbenow explains that Bonhoeffer "brings to light a misguided tendency in the church to remain uncertain of our forgiveness in Jesus Christ, thus leading us to wallow in guilt and to doubt God's ability to forgive and cleanse from sin."[26] Rather than perpetually wallowing in sorrow over one's corruption, which can often be nothing more than a *lupē tou kosmou* (worldly sorrow; see 2 Cor 7:8–11) that evades repentance, a genuine *lupē tou theou* (godly sorrow) is a penitent mode of human existence through which God draws people to obedience in faith. True disciples of Christ do not confess their sin in a way that seeks an alibi for disobedience under the veneer of pious exhibitionism. Rather, disciples of Christ are "those who from their hearts daily reject sin, who every day reject everything that hinders them from following Jesus and who are still unconsoled about their daily unfaithfullness and sin."[27] Christians contend daily for obedience to Christ's call amidst the alluring temptation for their hearts to turn inwards (the *cor curvum in se*). The ultimate focus is Christ, not sin *per se*. Focusing on "sorrow over a lack of faith repeatedly comes from disobedience . . . such sorrow all too often corresponds to the comfort of cheap grace."[28] Penitence, repentance, sorrow over sin and guilt; these postures are penultimate ways of being in the world which orient believers in light of God's word revealed in Christ, the first and the last word concerning sin and guilt. As such, penitence must be wary of its pious counterfeits.

That said, Bonhoeffer notes that "in no way is the prayer of repentance [*das Bußgebet*] absent in the Psalter."[29] He then couches the significance of the Penitential Psalms explicitly:

> The seven so-called penitential psalms (6, 32, 38, 51, 102, 130, 143), yet not these alone (Pss 14, 15, 25, 31, 39, 40, 41, etc.), lead us into the very depth of the recognition of sin before God. They help us in the confession of guilt. They turn our entire trust to the forgiving grace of God, so that Luther has quite rightly called them the "Pauline Psalms." Usually a particular occasion leads to such a prayer. It may be heavy guilt (Pss 32, 51); it may

---

25. Bonhoeffer, *DBWE* 5:171.
26. Pribbenow, *Prayerbook of Christ*, 86.
27. Bonhoeffer, *DBWE* 4:52.
28. Bonhoeffer, *DBWE* 4:67.
29. Bonhoeffer, *DBWE* 5:171.

be unexpected suffering that drives us to repentance (Pss 38, 102). In every case all hope is fixed on free forgiveness, as God has offered and promised it to us for all time in God's word about Jesus Christ.[30]

One of the more obvious dimensions to praying these psalms is immediately apparent. Psalms of guilt clearly offer a language for disciples to confess personal or corporate sins that need to be acknowledged. Whether he is correct or not, Bonhoeffer opines that "the Christian will find scarcely any difficulty in praying these psalms."[31] On another level though, if we follow Bonhoeffer's thinking from earlier in this chapter, psalms of guilt should arguably be prayed regardless of whether one "feels" or "thinks" we need to do so. Believers pray as reconciled sinners, and therefore confess their sins and repent in response to faith in Christ, not solely according to their own self-judgment of this or that sin.[32] Whether disciples discern sin in themselves or not is perhaps not of primary importance and could even be misleading at times. Michael Mawson notes that the psalms of guilt, as well as the other two lament categories (suffering and enemies), "witness to the fact that Scripture directs us away from ourselves and towards God in Christ . . . allowing them to challenge and unravel our assumptions and ideas."[33] One of the problems of sin for Bonhoeffer is the very reality that human beings tend to judge from within themselves what is good or evil, and therefore, what requires their repentance and what does not. In other words, to only confess the sins I perceive in myself could ignore one's humanity as a sinner as revealed in Christ.[34]

There is another dimension to praying the psalms of guilt which takes the "pray-er" even deeper. Because Bonhoeffer interprets the psalms christologically, and moreover, "Christo-somatically" (i.e., Christ once prayed and still prays them in both his eschatological and earthly body), this results in a somewhat idiosyncratic approach to this category. To explain this, consider first how he approaches the psalms of suffering:

> We can and we should pray the psalms of suffering, not to become completely caught up in something our heart does

---

30. Bonhoeffer, *DBWE* 5:171–72.
31. Bonhoeffer, *DBWE* 5:172.
32. See Bonhoeffer, *DBWE* 2:124.
33. Mawson, "Scripture," 132–33.
34. See Bonhoeffer, *DBWE* 4:157.

not know from its own experience, nor to make our own complaints, but because all this suffering was genuine and real in Jesus Christ; because the human being Jesus Christ suffered sickness, pain, shame, and death, and because in his suffering and dying all flesh suffered and died.[35]

Elsewhere, in a Bible study from Finkenwalde on "King David," Bonhoeffer claims Jesus is the descendent of David according to both the flesh and promise, that Christ is prefigured in him, and that David witnesses to Christ.[36] The psalms are therefore genuinely David's in a penultimate sense, whilst ultimately being Christ's prayers. This is what Bonhoeffer means when he explains how Christ prays psalms of guilt: "Certainly David spoke here of his own guilt. But Christ is speaking of the guilt of all people . . . which he has taken upon himself and borne."[37] As the one who took upon himself the sins of the world, whose freedom for the world was untarnished by the *cor curvum in se*, Jesus alone prays for the forgiveness of the sin which he has made fully his own and which subsequently causes his suffering and sorrow. Having entered into solidarity with sinful, suffering humanity, "Jesus prays even the most human of all prayers with us and, precisely in this, shows himself to be the true Son of God."[38] This is far more than a display of abstract, theological acrobatics. If Christ himself has borne the guilt of the world upon himself, this means that his body genuinely bears the guilt of the world upon itself, that is, in the church. In an *Ethics* essay entitled "Guilt, Justification, Renewal," he articulates the urgency of this posture of penitence within space and time, challenging the church to renounce its anxious and self-righteous obsession over its self-preservation, and instead, bear with those who suffer at the hands of a godless, sinful world. The church vicariously bears and confesses the world's guilt as its own. "With this confession the whole guilt of the world falls on the church, on Christians, and because here it is confessed and not denied, the possibility of forgiveness is opened."[39] The church is not heroic or altruistic; believers are "simply overwhelmed by their very own guilt toward Christ" as they

---

35. Bonhoeffer, *DBWE* 5:56–57.
36. Bonhoeffer, *DBWE* 14:871–74.
37. Bonhoeffer, *DBWE* 5:166.
38. Bonhoeffer, *DBWE* 5:172.
39. Bonhoeffer, *DBWE* 6:136.

witness anew the reality of the world in light of Christ.[40] Bonhoeffer then gets more pointed:

> The church confesses that it has looked on silently as the poor were exploited and robbed, while the strong were enriched and corrupted. . . . By falling silent the church became guilty for the loss of responsible action in society, courageous intervention, and the readiness to suffer for what is acknowledged as right. It is guilty of the government's falling away from Christ.[41]

This is not a postulation on Bonhoeffer's part, but a genuine bearing of the guilt of the world in Christ's "vicarious representative action" wrought through the cross.[42] The church confesses the world's guilt, which it bears as its own because (in Christ) it is responsible and implicated in the world's evil. Only when it confesses its sin vicariously for and with the world can it be "awakened to new righteousness and new life."[43] This is why the church never ceases to operate within a posture of penitence by praying the psalms of guilt, which includes the psalms of penitence. Christ calls the church to participate in the world's guilt which, in him, it bears *for* and *with* the world as its own, because it has become Christ's.

Bonhoeffer's classification of "guilt psalms" could be somewhat misleading, given that Bonhoeffer appears to dedicate equal space towards the psalmist's penitential appeal to their innocence, not just their guilt. He notes, "It is certain that one can speak of one's own innocence in a self-righteous manner, but do we not realize that one can also pray the most humble confession of sin very self-righteously?"[44] As before, he rejects prayer which reverts to the self as an evasion of Christ's call to discipleship. The innocence that the psalms appeal to is none other than Christ's perfect innocence.

The penitent cry for God's justice in the midst of innocent suffering is profoundly concrete and relevant for Bonhoeffer. This can be witnessed in his response to the *Kristallnacht* event on November 9, 1938, where the Nazis destroyed many Jewish synagogues and shops. After this

---

40. Bonhoeffer, *DBWE* 6:136.

41. Bonhoeffer, *DBWE* 6:140–41.

42. "Vicarious representative action" (*Stellvertretung*) is a key motif in Bonhoeffer's oeuvre. See Bonhoeffer, *DBWE* 1:119–20, 146; Bonhoeffer, *DBWE* 2:87, 120; Bonhoeffer, *DBWE* 4:90, 222; Bonhoeffer, *DBWE* 14:970; Bonhoeffer, *DBWE* 15:409; Bonhoeffer, *DBWE* 16:378.

43. Bonhoeffer, *DBWE* 6:142.

44. Bonhoeffer, *DBWE* 5:172.

devastating incident, Bonhoeffer made a note in his Bible for meditation and private prayer next to Ps 74:8b, "They burned all the meeting places of God in the land." By the verse, he wrote "9.11.38."[45] In addition, he wrote to his seminarians encouraging them to pray and reflect on Ps 74.[46] Pribbenow explains that Bonhoeffer's insistence on a prayer life informed by God's word would broaden the horizons and attentiveness of disciples to the needs of the world around them. Whilst this takes us beyond the seven psalms specifically designated as "penitential," it indicates how Bonhoeffer considered them in relation to the Psalter as a whole, and how many psalms evoke something of the penitential posture in the Seven. He references these seven psalms, as well as his understanding of penitence (*Buße*) throughout the rest of his writings.

BONHOEFFER AND THE PENITENTIAL PSALMS: A SURVEY

There are over forty instances where Bonhoeffer references the Penitential Psalms, either individually or as a group. Furthermore, he discusses penitence, in some way, on numerous occasions. Therefore, a selection will be presented here to add a fuller texture regarding his thinking. Because of limited space our focus is on four Penitential Psalms: Pss 38, 51, 102, and 130. These four were selected on the basis of their apparent importance to Bonhoeffer in terms of both the number of citations he made to them and the richness of his reflections on them.

Psalm 38

The Penitential Psalms appear to cultivate a faithful theological imagination regarding the philosophical subject of theodicy. Bonhoeffer, however, had limited interest in this field, as he regards it as fundamentally anti-Christian. This was partly due to the way people uncritically and un-christologically interpreted events in Nazi Germany with abstract metaphysical explanations. Instead, he would argue, "Not everything that happens is simply 'God's will.' But in the end nothing happens 'apart from God's will' (Matt. 10:39), that is, in every event, even the most ungodly,

---

45. Bethge, *Bonhoeffer*, 607.
46. Bonhoeffer, *DBWE* 15:84.

there is a way through to God."⁴⁷ In light of this, penitence assumes a posture whereby Christians may be guilty and/or innocent and seek to be faithful as those who do not fully know or understand what is going on in the world, much as Christ himself does in his earthly life (note the reference to Ps 38):

> If I am guilty, why does God not forgive me? If I am not guilty, why does God not end my torment and demonstrate my innocence to my enemies (Pss 38, 79, 44)? There is no theoretical answer to all these questions in the Psalms any more than in the New Testament. The only real answer is Jesus Christ.⁴⁸

In many ways, Bonhoeffer perceives that the power of temptation is its tantalizing lure towards abstract answers and religious explanations for the *how* and *why* of human existence. The "twilight" of the fall of humanity denotes the inclination to offer pious answers to the serpent's godless questions.⁴⁹ This is far more insidious than a mere distinction between good and evil, right or wrong. Indeed, Bonhoeffer contends that the very enterprise of trying to distinguish these things—whether morally, ethically, or whatever—enacts and perpetuates humanity's falling away from God through seeking to be *sicut Deus* (like God).⁵⁰ In his profound Bible study on temptation, he highlights the helplessness and folly of resisting temptation from within humanity's self, even through faith in and of itself, and he gestures to the power of penitently appealing to God alone for strength:

> But even before I can test my strength, I am already robbed of my strength. "My heart throbs, my strength fails me; as for the light of my eyes—it also has gone from me" Ps 38:11 [sic]. This is the decisive fact in the temptation of a Christian, namely, that one is being forsaken, forsaken by all his strengths, indeed attacked by them, forsaken by all human beings, forsaken by God himself.⁵¹

Bonhoeffer continues to argue that when humanity experiences genuine temptation, it realizes that it previously had no power over its

---

47. Bonhoeffer, *DBWE* 8:226–27.
48. Bonhoeffer, *DBWE* 5:170.
49. See Bonhoeffer's theological exposition of Gen 3 in Bonhoeffer, *DBWE* 3:103 onwards.
50. Bonhoeffer, *DBWE* 3:115–16.
51. Bonhoeffer, *DBWE* 15:404.

ability to resist temptation before. He qualifies this in a written meditation, suggesting that there is a difference between sighing for what we think we need, and a sigh of penitence for what God has taught us to need, over and against the temptation to ask for deliverance on our own terms: "The right sighing, however, does not remain hidden to God (Ps 38:9)."[52]

Psalm 51

Bonhoeffer references Ps 51 more than any of the other Penitential Psalms. A notable early example is in a note on Luther's lectures on Romans. Bonhoeffer simply notes the imperative to "*Believe* in sin" [emphasis original] and references "Rom. 11. p. 6."[53] In this volume of Luther's works, a number of passages are cited.[54] The editors of the *Dietrich Bonhoeffer Works* note that one of the following corollaries says, "*Etsi nos nullum peccatum in nobis agnoscamus, credere tamen oportet, quod sumus peccatores* [Even if we know no sin in us, we must still believe that we are sinners]," and the editors suggest that "the last two lines of Bonhoeffer's note refer to this."[55] This would add support to my suggestion above that one confesses guilt as part of the psalms of penitence whether one is mindful of any sin or not. The revelation of God constitutes confession, not solely one's own sin-consciousness. Later in life, a Finkenwalde lecture on confirmation instruction offers the following question and answer, referring to Ps 51:1: "Do you deserve for God to help you? No, I have no claim to any help; I cannot even comprehend that God wants to help me. I can only pray: God, be merciful to me, a sinner."[56]

In *Sanctorum Communio* (Bonhoeffer's first doctorate and first published work), he cites Ps 51:7 in relation to original or inherited sin. Space is not afforded here to unpack how he understands this, but one thing worth mentioning is how he does not consider original sin to be a fatalistic, biologically hereditary phenomenon. Rather, he argues that "all humanity falls with each sin, and not one of us is in principle different from Adam; that is, every person is the 'first' sinner."[57] Original sin is the

---

52. Bonhoeffer, *DBWE* 15:506.
53. Bonhoeffer, *DBWE* 9:300.
54. Rom 11:34; 1 Cor 3:18; Luke 1:51; Ps 51:5; Ps 32:5; 1 John 1:8.
55. Bonhoeffer, *DBWE* 9:300.
56. Bonhoeffer, *DBWE* 14:795
57. Bonhoeffer, *DBWE* 1:115.

dynamic propensity by which human beings should not but nevertheless do elect their "ontic inversion into the self, the *cor curvum in se*."[58] For Bonhoeffer, the "fall" should not happen, and thus, "the doctrine of original sin is one of the most difficult logical problems of all theology"[59] which has caused endless problems regarding human self-understanding thanks to its historical construal as a cosmically determined inevitability. He offers a summary which appeals to Ps 51:1 and Rom 3:12–13:

> What does the church call this compulsion? Original sin. By calling it such, the church is saying that all human beings are sinners from their birth onward. They must sin and yet nonetheless know that they are themselves guilty. It is a mystery.[60]

There are some instances where postures of penitence, contrition, and repentance are framed by Bonhoeffer as the heart of the gospel reality in disciples.[61] To be pure is to recognize that one cannot achieve purity of heart in and of themselves and are drawn by grace and merciful judgment through to new life. In a sermon on Matt 5:8,[62] Bonhoeffer proclaims:

> The most distressing realization in the life of every Christian is that we cannot remain pure, that day by day we fall down anew and night by night must cry out to God anew: Lord, I cannot do it alone; if you make me pure, then I am pure. May God create in me a pure heart.[63]

Again, Bonhoeffer suggests that the "heart" of being pure in heart entails the penitent orientation towards God regarding one's need as a reconciled sinner, confessing repentance in relation to others as well by the power of the Holy Spirit.[64]

Psalm 102

I have mentioned above that Bonhoeffer lists Ps 102 amongst the psalms of suffering, as well as recognizing its classification as one of the seven

---

58. Bonhoeffer, *DBWE* 2:46.
59. Bonhoeffer, *DBWE* 1:109.
60. Bonhoeffer, *DBWE* 14:793.
61. See Bonhoeffer, *DBWE* 4:12, 107.
62. "Blessed are the pure in heart, for they will see God."
63. Bonhoeffer, *DBWE* 10:515.
64. See other references relating Ps 51 to this theme in Bonhoeffer, *DBWE* 4:45; Bonhoeffer, *DBWE* 14:14, 477, 810, 813.

Penitential Psalms.[65] He also cites it in reference to psalms about the end. He suggests that the Psalter (and Old Testament) does not express the New Testament belief in an eschatological future in the same way. This is because the "long line of events of salvation history moving toward the end of all things, is from the viewpoint of the Old Testament still a single undivided whole."[66] For Bonhoeffer, therefore, "life in community with God is certainly always directed beyond death. Death is indeed the irreversible bitter end for body and soul. It is the wages of sin, and this must not be forgotten (Pss 39, 90). But on the other side of death is the eternal God (Pss 90, 102)."[67] The psalmist's longing for physical recovery has an eschatological dimension for Bonhoeffer in that they declare amidst earthly despondence "the children of your servants shall live secure; their offspring shall be established *in your presence*."[68]

In some notes on the concept of gratitude, Bonhoeffer opines that the gifts of God are "*transformed* into *thanksgiving*!" [emphasis original].[69] He explains, "In thanksgiving we give back to God what he gave us. In this sense we desire help so that gratitude to God may be increased."[70] As well as other Bible references, he notes Ps 102:18–19, 22: "Let this be recorded for a generation to come, so that a people yet unborn may praise the LORD: that he looked down from his holy height, from heaven the LORD looked at the earth . . . when peoples gather together, and kingdoms, to serve the LORD (NRSV)." There is a sense that eschatological hope entails a penitent's struggle to be sustained by the promise of God's presence in the here and now, not out of entitlement, but through God's faithfulness and mercy precisely to those who are penitent, and to those who come after them.

Psalm 130

In *Discipleship*, Bonhoeffer shares a line from Luther's hymn, "Out of the Depths I Have Cried to You," in reference to his concept of costly grace: "When Luther said that our deeds are in vain, even in the best of lives,

---

65. *DBWE* 5, 169.
66. *DBWE* 5, 176.
67. *DBWE* 5, 176.
68. Ps 102:28; emphasis added.
69. Bonhoeffer, *DBWE* 15:380.
70. Bonhoeffer, *DBWE* 15:380–81.

and that, therefore, nothing is valid before God 'except grace and favor to forgive sins,' he said it as someone who knew himself called to follow Jesus, called to leave everything he had up until this moment, and in the same moment called anew to do it again."[71]

In a London sermon from 1933, Bonhoeffer preaches on a verse from 2 Cor 5:10: "For all of us must appear before the judgment seat of Christ, so that each may receive due recompense for actions done in the body, whether good or evil."

Alluding to Ps 130:3, his script reads:

> And here it says in the Bible, against everything we think of as fair play, that one day at the end we will have to stand revealed before Christ, with all that we are and have been, and not only before Christ but also before all the other people standing there with us. And all of us know that we may be able to stand trial in many a human court, but not in that of Christ. "Lord, who could stand?" . . . Christ will judge. His spirit will distinguish between the spirits.[72]

Over and against all ethical sensibilities, moral convictions and pious motives, Christ will have the last word concerning the hearts, minds, and actions of human beings. Penitence recognizes that no one can stand before the Lord, and that the seemingly holiest of believers dare not try to justify themselves before him.

CONCLUSION

We have seen some emphases Bonhoeffer offers regarding how we approach the Penitential Psalms today. First, as a Lutheran, Bonhoeffer foregrounds penitence as a fundamental postural dimension of the gospel. For him, "Only the penitent finds forgiveness . . . and only the one who has forgiveness finds penitence."[73] Penitence is both a command and a gift of grace proclaimed in and for the body of Christ.[74] Secondly, penitence in and of itself can be deceptive without Christ as its source, mediator, and goal. In a 1938 homily on Mic 4:9,[75] Bonhoeffer exclaims

---

71. Bonhoeffer, *DBWE* 4:50.
72. Bonhoeffer, *DBWE* 13:329.
73. Bonhoeffer, *DBWE* 15:314.
74. Bonhoeffer, *DBWE* 14:828.
75. "Why are you now crying so loudly? Is the king not with you?" This follows the

that one's own piety, self-loathing, worldly sorrow, or one's lack of faith in God can perpetuate one's enclosure in the familiar allure of the *cor curvum in se*. This is a last bastion of seeking to retain dominion over the self under the guise of religious zeal, and it is anti-Christ. "You repent without Jesus. Yet this penitence can only push you deeper into sin and misery. The new beginning will be followed by new failure, and your cries will become louder and even more godless. Therefore, beware of penitence without Jesus!"[76] This claim illuminates the difference between praying the Penitential Psalms as a pious or religious person on the one hand, and praying them christologically.

This links to the third point of this conclusion, regarding the posture of the church in relation to others, and indeed to the world. The irony is that those who depend so heavily on the grace of God can be susceptible to justifying themselves over and against others. Bonhoeffer makes the point throughout his corpus concerning the christological solidarity entailed in being the church for and with the world:

> The church-community of Jesus Christ is the place in which Christ is believed in and obeyed as the salvation of the whole world. Thus, from its beginning and by virtue of its very nature, the church-community stands in a place of responsibility for the world that God in Christ has loved. *Wherever the church community does not perceive this responsibility, it ceases to be a church community of Christ.*[77]

With such a recognition, praying the Penitential Psalms is authenticated through disciples' participation in the precariousness and complexity of the joys and sorrows of the world. Participation in Christ requires sharing in the sin and suffering of the world precisely because Christ has done this, as one who was not preoccupied or held back by his own "holiness" but, profoundly, as the one who reveals what it really means to be holy. Bonhoeffer's thinking, as well as his example, demonstrates that praying the Penitential Psalms is about liberating the individual and collective from their sin, as well as the obsession with their goodness, so that they might live for and with Christ, which means living for and with others in the world that God loves. A penitent faith is, therefore, not primarily a matter of one's *own* disposition, whether cognitive or emotional.

---

translation in Bonhoeffer, *DBWE* 14:482.

76. Bonhoeffer, *DBWE* 14:483.

77. Bonhoeffer, *DBWE* 16:543; emphasis added.

On the contrary, Christian faith entails "not thinking first of one's own needs, questions, sins, and fears but allowing oneself to be pulled into walking the path that Jesus walks."[78] This is the path of penitence.

BIBLIOGRAPHY

Barker, H. Gaylon. *The Cross of Reality: Luther's Theologia Crucis and Bonhoeffer's Christology*. Minneapolis: Fortress, 2015.

Bethge, Eberhard. *Dietrich Bonhoeffer: A Biography*. Edited by Edwin Robertson. Translated by Eric Mosbacher et al. Minneapolis: Fortress, 2000.

Bonhoeffer, Dietrich. *Act and Being: Transcendental Philosophy and Ontology in Systematic Theology*. Edited by Wayne Whitson Floyd Jr. Translated by Martin Rumscheidt. Vol. 2 of *Dietrich Bonhoeffer Works*. Minneapolis: Fortress, 1996.

———. *Barcelona, Berlin and New York: 1928–1931*. Edited by Clifford J. Green. Translated by Douglas W. Stott. Vol. 10 of *Dietrich Bonhoeffer Works*. Minneapolis: Fortress, 2008.

———. *Conspiracy and Imprisonment 1940–1945*. Edited by Mark S. Brocker. Translated by Lisa E. Dahill. Supplementary material translated by Douglas W. Scott. Vol. 16 of *Dietrich Bonhoeffer Works*. Minneapolis: Fortress, 2006.

———. *Creation and Fall: A Theological Exposition of Genesis 1–3*. Edited by John W. de Gruchy. Translated by Douglas Stephen Bax. Vol. 3 of *Dietrich Bonhoeffer Works*. Minneapolis: Fortress, 1997.

———. *Discipleship*. Edited by Geffrey B. Kelly and John D. Godsey. Translated by Barbara Green and Reinhard Krauss. Vol. 4 of *Dietrich Bonhoeffer Works*. Minneapolis: Fortress, 2001.

———. *Ethics*. Edited by Clifford J. Green. Translated by Reinhard Krauss and Charles C. West. Vol. 6 of *Dietrich Bonhoeffer Works*. Minneapolis: Fortress, 2005.

———. *Letters and Paper from Prison*. Edited by John W. de Gruchy. Translated by Lisa E. Dahill et al. Vol. 8 of *Dietrich Bonhoeffer Works*. Minneapolis: Fortress, 2010.

———. *Life Together and Prayerbook of the Bible*. Edited by Gerhard Müller et al. Translated by Daniel W. Bloesch and James H. Burtness. Vol. 5 of *Dietrich Bonhoeffer Works*. Minneapolis: Fortress, 1996.

———. *London: 1933–1935*. Edited by Keith Clements. Translated by Isabel Best. Supplementary materials translated by Douglas W. Stott. Vol. 13 of *Dietrich Bonhoeffer Works*. Minneapolis: Fortress, 2013.

———. *Sanctorum Communio: A Theological Study of the Sociology of the Church*. Edited by Clifford J. Green. Translated by Reinhard Krauss and Nancy Lukens. Vol. 1 of *Dietrich Bonhoeffer Works*. Minneapolis: Fortress, 1998.

———. *Theological Education at Finkenwalde: 1935–1937*. Edited by H. Gaylon Barker and Mark S. Brocker. Translated by Douglas W. Stott. Vol. 14 of *Dietrich Bonhoeffer Works*. Minneapolis: Fortress, 2013.

———. *Theological Educational Underground: 1937–1940*. Edited by Victoria Barnett. Translated by Claudia D. Bergmann et al. Supplementary materials translated by Douglas W. Stott. Vol. 15 of *Dietrich Bonhoeffer Works*. Minneapolis: Fortress, 2011.

---

78. Bonhoeffer, *DBWE* 8:480.

———. *The Young Bonhoeffer 1918–1927*. Edited by Paul Duane Matheny et al. Translated by Marcy C. Nebelsich, with assistance of Douglas W. Stott. Vol. 9 of *Dietrich Bonhoeffer Works*. Minneapolis: Fortress, 2002.

Brock, Brian. *Singing the Ethos of God: On the Place of Christian Ethics in Scripture*. Grand Rapids: Eerdmans, 2007.

Cone, James H. *The Cross and the Lynching Tree*. Maryknoll, NY: Orbis, 2011.

DeJonge, Michael P. *Bonhoeffer's Reception of Luther*. Oxford: Oxford University Press, 2017.

Goebel, Johannes. "When He Sat Down at the Piano." In *I Knew Dietrich Bonhoeffer: Reminiscences by His Friends*, edited by Wolf-Dieter Zimmerman and Ronald Gregor Smith, 124–25. London: Collins, 1966.

Greggs, Tom. *Theology Against Religion: Constructive Dialogues with Bonhoeffer and Barth*. London: Bloomsbury, 2011.

Hopkins, Theodore J. *Christ, Church, and World: Bonhoeffer and Lutheran Ecclesiology After Christendom*. Lanham, MD: Lexington, 2021.

Krötke, Wolf. *Karl Barth and Dietrich Bonhoeffer: Theologians for a Post-Christian World*. Translated by John P. Burgess. Grand Rapids: Baker Academic, 2019.

Mawson, Michael. "Scripture." In *The Oxford Handbook of Dietrich Bonhoeffer*, edited by Michael Mawson and Philip G. Ziegler, 123–36. Oxford: Oxford University Press, 2019.

Muers, Rachel. "Anthropology." In *The Oxford Handbook of Dietrich Bonhoeffer*, edited by Michael Mawson and Philip G. Ziegler, 196–209. Oxford: Oxford University Press, 2019.

Oliveri, Vincent Thomas. "The Word for the Church and the World: Dietrich Bonhoeffer's Pastoral Theology of the Word of God." PhD diss., University of Aberdeen, 2023.

Pangritz, Andreas. *Karl Barth in der Theologie Dietrich Bonhoeffers—eine notwendige Klarstellung*. Berlin: Alektor Verlag, 1989.

Pribbenow, Brad. *Prayerbook of Christ: Dietrich Bonhoeffer's Christological Interpretation of the Psalms*. Lanham, MD: Lexington, 2018.

Schlingensiepen, Ferdinand. *Dietrich Bonhoeffer, 1906–1945: Martyr, Thinker, Man of Resistance*. Translated by Isabel Best. New York: T. & T. Clark, 2010.

Williams, Reggie L. *Bonhoeffer's Black Jesus: Harlem Renaissance Theology and an Ethic of Resistance*. Waco, TX: Baylor University Press, 2014.

Part 3

The Penitential Psalms Today

10

The Musical Legacy of the Seven Psalms

Jonathan Arnold

INTRODUCTION: MUSIC AND THE PSALMS

The connection between psalms, worship, music, and spirituality is ancient and enduring. All human emotion and experience are contained within the psalms, and they would have been musically expressed from the earliest times. They are, after all, primarily songs. The story of God's people, through triumph and tragedy, is mapped out in heartfelt expression of exaltation to desolation, and musicians have used the words of the psalms in music to demonstrate their devotion to God and to express their own life experience.

The psalms were written to be sung with instruments[1] and were an important part of Jewish worship in the temple throughout the religious year for major festivals as well as to accompany sacrifices, and they continue to be an essential feature of synagogue liturgy to this day. The psalms were part of the liturgy of the early church.[2] According to Tertullian they were either sung by a solo voice or responsorially (solo followed by a choral or congregational response).[3] From the seventh century onwards the solo role was reduced and more choral and antiphonal versions emerged. Psalms were also at the heart of medieval Christian life and thought.[4]

---

1. Smith, "Psalm I," 449.
2. See Eph 5:18–19 and Col 3:16.
3. Bailey, "Psalm II," 451.
4. See, for example, chapters 4 and 5 of this volume.

Monks chanted them to plainsong daily in the Divine Office; lay people recited them in the offices of the Virgin Mary and of the Dead; children learned them as the basis of their ABCs; exegetes meditated upon them in commentaries; artists illuminated them in manuscripts; and composers drew upon them for their polyphony. More than any other book of the Bible, the Psalms provided the language and imagery for speaking about God and his relationship to the human soul. The Psalms were sung not only as praise, prayer, and confession, but also in the light of the New Testament as a way of connecting raw human experience to the salvation story of incarnation, passion, resurrection, and ascension.

Cassiodorus (c. 485–585) promoted the medicinal properties of the Penitential Psalms for the soul as part of liturgy, which secured their place in church worship throughout the Middle Ages.[5] They were to be sung at Lauds on Fridays in Lent and on Ash Wednesday—the first three at Mattins, Ps 51 at Communion, and the last three at Vespers. They were sung at English coronation services until the reforms of 1603.[6]

The principal method of singing the psalms in medieval Europe was, of course, plainchant. Gregorian chant emerged in the ninth and tenth centuries and was a synthesis of even older Roman and Gallican chants. It is structured around a series of eight "modes" or "tones" rather than modern Western musical keys. In English cathedrals, both monastic and secular, they were sung by the clerks of the choir, or Vicars Choral.[7] At York, for instance, the precentor was chief cantor, or singer, whilst the chancellor instructed choristers and Vicars Choral on divinity and church history and examined the Vicars Choral in psalms and histories at the end of their first year.[8]

In all the turbulence of the religious conflicts of early-modern England, music became both an expression of true religious sentiment and a source of devotional solace, as well as a way of reaching out to believers of similar allegiance. Psalm settings were a powerful way of asserting religious practice, especially in the communal and "common prayer" singing of metrical psalms in the vernacular, whereby believers were taught the Scriptures in their own language and conformed to a unified liturgical

---

5. For a fuller exploration of Cassiodorus and the Penitential Psalms see chapter 3 of this volume.

6. Cross and Livingstone, *Dictionary of the Christian Church*, 1489.

7. Lehmberg, "Reformation of Choirs," 47.

8. Harrison, *Life in a Medieval College*, 24.

practice.⁹ But psalm settings could also be used in both private and public devotional ways to express rebellion against such Reformation conformity, whether in Latin or English. Composers, performers, and listeners always found a way to express their true feelings, whatever the religious authorities dictated. In music, and the psalms in particular, Christians found an outlet to express their innermost beliefs. During the Reformation the music of the psalms became a useful tool, even weapon, for expressing theological conviction and identity. The words of the psalms were employed polemically in the turmoil between Catholic and Protestant believers. In the sacred choral music of the early-modern period, psalm settings could denote secretive, or not-so-secretive, allegiances, and the manner of psalm word setting became an important factor in how religious fervor was expressed. An example of Protestant fervor, as expressed in musical paraphrases of the Penitential Psalms, can be found in William Hunnis' *Seven Sobs for a Sorrowfull Soule* of 1583, which was largely for domestic private devotion.¹⁰

The psalms and their musical settings were also a key feature in European Reforms. For Martin Luther (1483–1546), music was the greatest of God's gifts, next to theology, and was one that could work on both disclosive and affective levels.¹¹ On the disclosive plane, earthly music was a poor reflection but gave a glimpse of the beauty and perfection of celestial music. In Augustinian terms, we must hear *through* the inferior music of this world to hear the perfect music of the world beyond. However, Luther also found that, according to the Orphic tradition, music was affective to the human emotions and spirit. Combined with the word of God in Scripture, it could enable a powerful transformation: "Music combines the emotional power of sound with the spiritual power of God's Word in such a way as to affect the soul."¹²

The most influential Reformer of psalm-singing was, however, John Calvin (1509–64). Calvin did not attribute to music the elevated status that Luther did, nor did he banish it like Zwingli, but rather subdued it to the word, especially in his use of metrical tunes to set the psalms, which became popular through the Genevan Psalter and spread throughout the Reformed world. The advantage of the musical setting, for Calvin and generations of followers, was that the music could enable the participant

---

9. See chapter 4 of this volume.
10. King'oo, "William Hunnis," 615–31.
11. Brown and Hopps, *Extravagance of Music*, 10–11.
12. Irwin, "So Faith," 69.

to learn, digest, and meditate upon the word of the psalms. This was its primary purpose.

At the heart of Calvin's thought on music is a sense of inner piety. Vernacular psalm-singing, as part of prayer, was to be as similar as possible to the liturgy and theology as practiced by the primitive church.[13] So, in Calvin's view, the "Psalms can incite us to lift up our hearts to God and move us to an ardor in invoking and exalting with praises the glory of His name."[14] The Genevan Psalter sold tens of thousands of copies in Calvin's lifetime and helped define the Reformed tradition thereafter.[15] For Calvin, worship should be simple and language verbal, for "the voice of man . . . assuredly excels all inanimate instruments of music."[16] Thus, Calvin's emphasis upon monophonic, syllabic, metrical psalm-singing was based upon a desire for a logocentric simplicity and comprehensibility in worship that finds its origins in a Platonic ideal of text over music, where the music closely matches the words and carries their meaning to the listener.[17] Such ideas were transmitted by the sixteenth-century humanists, by whom Calvin was clearly influenced.[18] With the different musical modes employed, Calvin's kind of music does not simply conform to the text, it creates a mood of its own, just as the psalms in his psalter are poetic paraphrases of Scripture itself. Thus, music was not there merely to embellish the words but to be a distinctive force which led the worshiper to greater inner piety and a heartfelt response to God.[19] Genevan tunes are still sung throughout the world, remaining popular in Hungary and the Netherlands since the Reformation, in American hymns, and a new edition and translation of the Genevan Psalter has emerged in the Reformed Church in Japan.[20]

Psalms were sung in English country parish churches by "West Gallery" singers and instrumentalists in the late 1700s and early 1800s, as well as in urban churches. Independent and Presbyterian churches remained

---

13. Garside, "Calvin's Theology of Music," 10–14; van 't Spijker, "Bucer's Influence on Calvin," 32–44; Begbie, *Modernity*, 13–14n12.

14. Calvin, "Organization of the Church," 53, quoted in Begbie, *Modernity*, 14.

15. Begbie, *Modernity*, 12; Witvliet, "Psalter in Calvin's Geneva," 203–29; Trocmé-Latter, "Psalm-Singing in Geneva," 145–63.

16. Calvin, *Book of Psalms* 1:404.

17. Hárran, *Word-Tone Relations*, cited in Begbie, *Modernity*, 21.

18. For example, Lanfranco, Vincentino, Zarlino, and Stoquerus.

19. Begbie, *Modernity*, 25–27.

20. Brink, "Reformed Approach to Psalmody," para 34.

musically conservative, with metrical psalms but with the exclusion of organs. However, the psalms remained a popular source of texts for composers throughout the Baroque, classical, and Romantic eras. Allesandro Scarlatti (1660–1725) wrote forty motets, with thirty-seven of them being psalm settings. With the rise of sacred music's performance in public concerts, Psalms remained a favorite text for composers such as Mendelssohn, Schumann, Dvorak, Liszt, Bruckner, and Elgar, and in the twentieth century, for Kodaly, Stravinsky, Bernstein, Schnittke, Rubbra, and many others.[21] The psalms continue to inspire composers today, such as Sir James MacMillan with his excellent setting of the *Miserere* (Ps 51).

In today's church psalm-singing comes in many forms. In the Roman Catholic Church psalms may be sung to traditional Gregorian chant. In Westminster Cathedral in London, for instance, psalms are sung daily by the choir to the Latin chant of the *Gradualia* and Missal, whereas at more informal worship in other Catholic churches, psalms may be heard set to a variety of musical styles. In the Anglican church, one may still hear plainchant psalms sung, or in a responsorial, with a soloist or choir singing the text of the psalm whilst the congregation responds with a refrain. But very often the psalms are sung to Anglican chant, which grew out of the plainchant tradition during the English Reformation. It allows for four or more parts to sing the psalm in harmony, following simple chordal chants. The choir recites the words of the psalm to these chords, with "pointing" to show where the chord and word changes should occur. Miles Coverdale's translation of the Psalms, found in the *Book of Common Prayer*, is usually used (first published as *Goostly Psalmes and Spirituall Songs*, which were initially banned by Henry VIII in 1535). Anglican chant was well established by the eighteenth century. The earliest known chants are by John Blow, Henry Purcell, and their contemporaries. Psalms are used as part of the liturgy throughout the year and are often sung daily in Anglican cathedrals. The Penitential Psalms are particularly suited to liturgical seasons of repentance, such as Advent, Lent, and especially Ash Wednesday and Holy Week. Psalms are also sometimes paraphrased into poetry so that they may be sung as hymns; they are sung to the popular simple refrains of Taizé chant and those composed by musicians such as Margaret Rizza (b. 1929) and, in more evangelical,

---

21. Boyd, "Psalm IV," 468–69.

charismatic, or Pentecostal churches, the Penitential Psalms have been paraphrased into lyrics for songs, sung by worship bands.[22]

THE PENITENTIAL PSALMS

The Penitential Psalms have a special place in musical liturgical history, as of all the psalms, they have inspired composers through the ages. The intensity of the texts offers a huge range of opportunities for artistic expression, where music may act like a gloss, to carry and intensify the deep meaning of the text, almost homiletically, to the heart of the repentant listener.[23] In the following summary, I will be concentrating on the Western classical tradition of sacred music.

The range of liturgical occasions on which musical settings of the Penitential Psalms can be used throughout the year is another reason why the Seven hold a preeminent place in church music history, partly evidenced by the complete polyphonic settings that are still in use today. In the Renaissance, William Byrd (c. 1540–1623) published an English set in his *Songs of Sundrie Natures* of 1589; the Flemish composer Orlandus Lassus (1532–94) set them in Latin in his *Psalmi Davidis Poenitentiales* of 1584; and the Venetian musician Giovanni Croce (1557–1609) composed an unusual set as they use Italian sonnet-form translations of the Penitential Psalms by Francesco Bembo. These were widely distributed, translated into English, and published in London as *Musica Sacra* and into Latin as *Septem Psalmi Poenitentiales*. The seven psalms have also been set by Thomas Tomkins (1572–1656), John Dowland (1563–1626), and Giovanni Gabrieli (1533–85). This latter set is noteworthy as they make explicit use of instruments, with Gabrieli attempting faithfully to portray the emotions of the psalmist, which he believed had not been achieved up to that time. The early Baroque German composer, Heinrich Schütz (1585–1672), was also a prolific setter of the Penitential Psalms. Mozart's *David Penitente* for two soloists, chorus and orchestra, based on the *Kyrie* and *Gloria* of his Mass in C Minor, is a paraphrase of the Seven in Italian.[24]

---

22. Such as "He Will Keep You" by Sovereign Grace based on verses from Ps 130; "Devouring Fire" by Jason Silver based on Ps 50; "But Thou O Lord Shall Ensure For Ever" by Steve Kuban based on Ps 102: "Dark Was the Night" by The War Within based on Ps 102.

23. I am grateful to Dr. David Allison for these insights on this and on Josquin's *Infelix Ego*.

24. Gillingham, *Psalms Through the Centuries* 2:67.

PSALM 6

This psalm has been seen as a corresponding lament to that of Jeremiah and its artists and musical expressions have largely been Christian, with an emphasis on the discontinuity between suffering and sin, and Christ sharing the first with humanity but not the second.[25]

The lament for those suffering from illness and oppression, and the plea for deliverance in Ps 6, was set to music by Schütz in two hymns, *Ach, Herr, straf mich nicht* (1619) and *Ach Herr mein Gott, straf mich doch nicht* (1628). The paraphrase of Ps 6, *Herr, straf mich nicht in deinem Zorn*, was set by Johann Crüger in 1640, which inspired the chorale by Johann Sebastian Bach (BWV 338). Orlando Gibbons' "O Lord in Thy Wrath" is based on Ps 6:1–4.[26] In France, Henry Desmarets set the psalm in his "Grands Motets Lorrains" (1713), and another Baroque composer, Georg Philipp Telemann (1681–1757), composed a version, *Ach Herr, strafe mich nicht*, for violins, viola, organ, soloists, and choir. There is also a beautiful English verse anthem for two soprano soloists, chorus, and continuo by Henry Purcell (d. 1695). More recently, Max Reger composed a chorale fantasia for organ, one of his two *Zwei Choralphantasien* (1899). In the twentieth century there are settings by Jules Van Nuffel (1935) and Norma Wendelburg (1973). More recently, Cheryl Frances-Hoad (b. 1980) has set Ps 6 in English for choir, which was commissioned for the 2014 Festival of Saint Cecilia and first performed by the combined choirs of Westminster Cathedral, Westminster Abbey, and St. Paul's Cathedral.

PSALM 32

In some Jewish traditions, Ps 32 is recited as the "song of the day" on Yom Kippur, the Day of Atonement, due to its solemn themes of forgiveness and repentance. Verse 8 ("Thou art a place to hide me in"), with its sense of safety and deliverance, is part of the "Foundation of Repentance" recited on the eve of Rosh Hashanah, the Jewish New Year. In the Middle Ages the psalm was recited in Christian monasteries at Mattins on Sundays and is sung today at Vespers on the Thursday of the first week of the four-week cycle of liturgical prayers. In the *Book of Common Prayer*,

---

25. Gillingham, *Psalms Through the Centuries* 2:61–63.
26. Gillingham, *Psalms Through the Centuries* 2:67.

this psalm is appointed to be read on the evening of the sixth day of the month, as well as at Mattins on Ash Wednesday.

There are fewer settings of Ps 32 than the other Penitential Psalms, but notable pieces are Schütz's paraphrase *Der Mensch vor Gott wohl selig ist* (1628) and Purcell's "Blessed is He" setting of verses 1–7, 10, and 11, used during Lent. A fine setting of verses 1–6 by Samuel Sebastian Wesley, for alto, tenor, and bass, was published in *The European Psalmist* as "Blessed Is the Man," and his "Thou Art My Hiding Place" sets verses 7–12.

PSALM 38

Verse 22 of Ps 38 is part of the long Tachanun recited on Mondays and Thursdays in Jewish liturgy. From around AD 530, Ps 38 was sung in Benedictine monasteries during Mattins on Mondays. Since the reforms of the Second Vatican Council in the Catholic Church (1962–65) the psalm is sung at the liturgy of the hours on Friday in the second week of the four-week cycle. In Anglican liturgy the psalm can be sung at Mattins on Ash Wednesday. We have inherited a fine setting, *Domine ne in furore* (c. 1450–1521), by Josquin des Prez, and J. S. Bach set the fourth verse in the opening chorus of his cantata *Es ist nichts Gesundes an meinem Leibe*. Igor Stravinsky set Ps 38:13–14 in the first movement of his *Symphony of Psalms* (1930), bringing the text alive in a full orchestral and large choir version for the concert-going public. Howard Blake's *Benedictus* (1986) intersperses excerpts from the *Rule of Saint Benedict* and opens with an "anguished, relentless and intense" setting of Ps 38 to the accompaniment of woodwind.[27] John Tavener's mammoth *Veil of the Temple* (2003) places Ps 38 at the end of the second long cycle of music.

PSALM 51

This is by far the most well-known Penitential Psalm and most widely set to music. It is the central (fourth) psalm of seven and its pureness of penitent tone, as well as its heading—"To the leader. A Psalm of David, when the prophet Nathan came to him, after he had gone in to Bathsheba" (NRSV)—suggest that it has a central role if the seven are read as David's prayers.

27. Gillingham, *Psalms Through the Centuries* 2:236.

It has had a huge influence on liturgy and culture. In Judaism, verses from the psalm are used in *Selichot*, others in *Tefillat Zakkah* prior to the *Kol Nidrei* service on Yom Kippur eve. Verse 17, "O Lord, open my lips," is recited as a preface to the Amidah in all prayer services. The psalm is recited on Yom Kippur night in Sephardi Judaism. In the *Siddur Avodas Yisroel*, it is sung for *Shabbat Parah* and *Shabbat Ki Tavo*, and sung on Wednesday nights after the recital of *Aleinu* in *Maariv*. In the Eastern Orthodox Church, the psalm is read or sung several times every day: at Compline, the Midnight Office, Mattins, the Third Hour, and for many, at private morning and evening prayer. In the Coptic Church's book of hours, the *Agpeya*, it is recited at every office throughout the day as a prayer of confession and repentance. In Western Christianity, a priest can instruct someone to pray it as penance after Confession. Verse 7 ("Thou shalt purge me with hyssop, and I shall be clean") is traditionally sung as the priest sprinkles holy water over the congregation (known as *Asperges me*). It is prayed during Lauds (Morning Prayer) every Friday in the liturgy of the hours. Parts of Ps 51 are used as a responsorial psalm on Ash Wednesday.

The *Miserere* (so named for its opening *Miserere mei, Deus* or "Lord, have mercy on me") was a frequently used text in Catholic liturgical music before the Second Vatican Council. Most of the settings, which are often used at Tenebrae (meaning "darkness," a service in Holy Week), are in a simple *falsobordone* style (plainchant alternating with harmony). During the Renaissance many composers wrote settings. The earliest known polyphonic setting, probably dating from the 1480s, is by the Ferrara-based Italian Johannes Martini (c. 1440–98). The long polyphonic setting by Josquin des Prez (1503/1504) was inspired by the prison meditation *Infelix ego* by Girolamo Savonarola (1452–98) before his execution for preaching against the Medici family. Incarcerated in his Florentine cell on May 8, 1498, and awaiting death, Savonarola penned the words of his penitential and visionary *Infelix ego* as a meditation on Ps 51 [50]. The text became extremely popular after Savonarola's death and was translated, along with an incomplete meditation on Ps 30, *In te, Domine, speravi*, into several different languages. Josquin's setting, which was unusual for its time in repeating the words *Miserere mei, Deus* as a homophonic refrain at the end of each verse, was hugely influential on Renaissance composers, such as Lassus and Jean Lhéritier (c. 1480–c. 1552), who also set Savonarola's text.[28] Even though printing the text became prohibited after 1559 in Italy, there were more English editions printed than any other European language, especially between 1534 and 1578. It is no surprise, therefore, that composers chose to set the text to music. The glorious setting for six voices, for instance, composed nearly a hundred years after Savonarola's death by the English Catholic composer William Byrd (1543?–1623), is the crowning glory of the tradition of setting Savonarola's meditation especially in its intensity and expression.[29]

The middle phase of Byrd's career (1575–91) is characterized by seriousness, gravity, and despondency. The 1580s were the most difficult time for recusants (Catholics living in Protestant England), with the execution of missionary priests, beginning with Edmund Campion (1540–81), the execution of Mary Queen of Scots (1542–87), and the sending of the Armada (1588). In this time, he issued *Songs of Sadness & Pietie*, *Seven Penitential Psalms*, and two volumes of *Cantiones sacrae*, many of whose texts speak of suffering, exile, the destruction of Jerusalem, and the burden of captivity. These texts were code for Byrd's, and his Catholic friends', captivity under the Protestantism and anti-Catholicism of Elizabethan England. The composition of these doleful pieces coincided with the suffering and persecution of the Byrd family: namely, their residence at Harlington in Middlesex between c. 1577 and c. 1595.

Despite the suspicions, censoring, and even silencing of music in the religious turmoil of what we now call the Reformation, Byrd's setting of *Infelix ego* is not only a supreme example of an enduring musical language of the high Renaissance, but perhaps his greatest legacy, written during the height of Elizabethan reforms. The music beautifully reflects the words, alluding to a sense of exile—both Byrd's own as a Catholic in a Protestant land, and Savonarola's ostracism in his own city of Florence. The relation between polyphony and homophony, redolent of Thomas Tallis' (1505–85) *Suscipe quaeso Domine* in the musical texture, emphasizes the rhetorical questioning of the text, with rising melodies that seem to plead for mercy, finally leading to a coda which suggests, perhaps, that redemption and pardon have been granted at last. The piece presented a public witness to a personal faith and a message of hope to a persecuted Catholic audience.

28. P. Macey: sleeve notes to *Scattered Ashes: Josquin's Miserere and the Savonarolan Legacy*, a recording by the vocal ensemble Magnificat, directed by Philip Cave (Linn Records, London, 2016).

29. Published in 1591 in Byrd's *Cantiones Sacrae*; see Brown, *Cantiones Sacrae*, xxiv-xxvi.

Later in the sixteenth century Lassus wrote an elaborate setting as part of his *Penitential Psalms*, and Palestrina, Andrea Gabrieli, Giovanni Gabrieli, and Carlo Gesualdo also wrote settings. However, surely the best-known setting is the seventeenth-century version by Roman School composer Gregorio Allegri. Until 1870 the piece was sung by the papal choir during the Tenebrae offices in Holy Week. The original setting by Allegri is rather simple—a nine-part chant for two choirs, alternating plainchant and homophonic polyphony, known as *falsobordoni*. It was the custom to elaborate the simple structure of the music with embellishments, including very high-pitched notes.[30] These are now the famous recurring top Cs of the piece, sung by a soprano or a treble. The piece has been recorded hundreds of times by many cathedral choirs and professional consorts, and it is often performed in concert. It is performed liturgically as part of Ash Wednesday and during Lent. A now-legendary recording of the *Miserere*, along with Palestrina's *Missa Papae Marcellae* (Palestrina being another Roman School composer), was largely responsible for launching The Tallis Scholars' international success.

According to a letter written by Leopold Mozart to his wife, Wolfgang Amadeus Mozart visited the Vatican in 1770 and heard the *Miserere*, committing it to manuscript after just one hearing. Whatever the truth is, it was also admired by Goethe and Mendelssohn and other Romantics. It was first published by Burney in 1771, but the version commonly heard today was reconstructed and is based on an incorrect version published by William Smyth Rockstro (1823-95) as an illustration in an article in the first edition of *Grove's Dictionary of Music and Musicians* (1880) and an edition with embellishments by Robert Haas in 1932. An English version was then made by Sir Ivor Atkins in the 1950s, which was made popular by a recording of the choir of King's College Cambridge. Thus, the version we hear today bears little resemblance to anything that might have been heard in the Sistine Chapel in Allegri's day.[31]

In addition to the above, there are four settings by Marc-Antoine Charpentier (1643-1704) and a fine version, *Tilge, Höchster, meine Sünden* by J. S. Bach, which was a version of the music from the opening of Pergolesi's *Stabat Mater* of 1736, for two voices and orchestra. G. F. Handel (1685-1759) set the psalm as one of his "Chandos Anthems," large multi-movement choral and orchestral works for concert

30. Roche, "Allegri," para. 2.
31. Roche, "Allegri," para. 2.

performance, dedicated to the duke of Chandos. In the English choral tradition, S. S. Wesley's *Wash Me Throughly* [sic] is a perennially popular setting of verses from Ps 51 and often performed as part of cathedral and church liturgy. Modern composers who have written notable settings of the *Miserere* include Michael Nyman (b. 1940), Arvo Pärt (b. 1935), and Sir James MacMillan (b. 1959).

PSALM 102

In Judaism Ps 102 is one of the additional hymns sung at Yom Kippur, and the first verse is recited by the sheaves of barley in Perek Shirah. Sephardi Jews recite verse 14 after the prayer of Ein Keloheinu in the morning service. This verse is also used as a popular Jewish song called "*Atah takum*," with the refrain "ki va moed" (the time has come). Verse 1 has a prominent place in Catholic and Anglican liturgies, where it is split as an antiphon, as a call ("Hear my prayer, O Lord") and the response ("and let my cry come unto Thee").

Perhaps the most famous setting of the opening verse is by Henry Purcell, which is often sung by cathedral and church choirs. A more modern setting is by Howard Goodall (b. 1958).

PSALM 130

This psalm is recited responsorially before the open Torah ark during the morning service from Rosh Hashanah until Yom Kippur, a custom revived in the twentieth century. It is also one of the fifteen Songs of Ascents recited after the Shabbat afternoon prayer in the period between Sukkot and Shabbat HaGadol (the Shabbat prior to Passover). From the early church onwards, it was appointed to be sung at the beginning of the Vespers service on Tuesday. In the current liturgy of the hours, the psalm is recited or sung at Vespers on the Saturday of the fourth week of the four-week cycle of liturgical prayers, and on Wednesday evenings. It is also used in the Requiem Mass and the prayer for the dead, as well as the "Bell Prayer." The *De Profundis* (out of the depths) bell is a slow, solemn, and measured toll of the bell that marks the end of the day.

This psalm has frequently been set to music. It was sometimes used for funeral services, especially under its Latin incipit *De profundis*. Martin Luther paraphrased Ps 130 as the hymn "*Aus tiefer Not schrei ich zu dir*" (Out of deep distress I cry to you), which has inspired several composers, including Bach cantatas *Aus der Tiefen rufe ich, Herr, zu dir* and *Aus tiefer Not schrei ich zu dir*, and works by Mendelssohn and Reger. From the twentieth century there exists a fine choral setting of *De Profundis* by Arvo Pärt and one by Jean-Jacques Grunenwald (1911–82). The *De Profundis* is not often used as a movement in a musical setting of the Requiem Mass, but *Out of the Deep*, based on Ps 130, is included in John Rutter's English setting of 1985.

PSALM 143

In Judaism Ps 143 is used during Rosh Hashanah. In the Orthodox Church this psalm is recited at every Orthros, Paraklesis, salutations to the Virgin Mary, and Holy Unction service. Heinrich Schütz composed a metered paraphrase of Ps 143 in German, *Herr, mein Gebet erhör in Gnad*, SWV 248, for the Becker Psalter, published first in 1628. Henry Purcell set Psalm 143 as a verse anthem. Alan Hovhaness set verses 1 and 5 in his 1936 work "Hear My Prayer, O Lord."

CONCLUSION

The Penitential Psalms have a special place in the Psalter and a very significant influence in the musical tradition, inspiring composers to write for the liturgy in almost all Christian denominations, and for the religious life of Jews throughout the world. Musical settings can be heard through the various liturgical religious calendars in many countries and in many styles. The themes of penitence, despair, repentance, forgiveness, healing, and hope are just a few of the characteristics that continue to attract composers to set these evocative and emotional texts. We are heirs to a rich musical and devotional heritage that stretches from pre-Christian times to the present. Whether we hear these works in a church or cathedral service, a synagogue or concert hall, or in recorded versions in the privacy of our own homes, the Penitential Psalms in music will be a source of inspiration, an aid to prayer, a medicine for healing and reconciliation, and a means through which we can, as humans, reach into the depths of our being and wrestle with the complexities and confusions of existence, and our need for divine salvation. Out of the deep we will continue to cry to the Lord, "Have mercy on me," for centuries to come.

BIBLIOGRAPHY

Bailey, Terence. "Psalm II. Latin Monophonic Psalmody." In *New Grove Dictionary of Music and Musicians*, edited by Stanley Sadie, 20:451–63. Oxford: Oxford University Press, 2001.

Begbie, Jeremy. *Music, Modernity and God: Essays in Listening*. Oxford: Oxford University Press, 2013.

Boyd, Malcolm, and Alejandro E. Planchart. "Psalm IV. Polyphonic Psalms." In *New Grove Dictionary of Music and Musicians*, edited by Stanley Sadie, 20:467–71. Oxford: Oxford University Press, 2001.

Brink, Emily R. "A Reformed Approach to Psalmody: The Legacy of the Genevan Psalter." Calvin Institute of Christian Worship, June 10, 2005. https://worship.calvin.edu/resources/articles/reformed-approach-psalmody-legacy-genevan-psalter.

Brown, Alan. *The Byrd Edition Volume 3: Cantiones Sacrae 1591*. London: Stainer and Bell, 1979.

Brown, David, and Gavin Hopps. *The Extravagance of Music*. London: Palgrave Macmillan, 2018.

Calvin, John. "Articles Concerning the Organization of the Church and of Worship at Geneva." In *Calvin: Theological Treatises*, edited and translated by J. K. S. Reid, 47–55. London: SCM, 1954.

———. *Commentary on the Book of Psalms: Volume I*. Translated by James Anderson. Edinburgh: Calvin Translation Society, 1845.

Cross, F. L., and E. A. Livingstone, eds. *Dictionary of the Christian Church*. Oxford: Oxford University Press, 1997.

Garside, Charles. "The Origins of Calvin's Theology of Music, 1536–1543." *Transactions of the American Philosophical Society* 69 (1979) 1–36.

Gillingham, Susan. *Psalms Through the Centuries, Volume 2: A Reception History Commentary on Psalms 1–72*. Wiley Blackwell Bible Commentaries. Hoboken: Wiley-Blackwell, 2018.

Hárran, Don. *Word-Tone Relations in Musical Thought: From Antiquity to the Seventeenth Century*. Neuhausen-Stuttgart: American Institute of Musicology, 1986.

Harrison Frederick. *Life in a Medieval College: The Story of the vicars choral of York Minster*. London: John Murray, 1952.

Irwin, Joyce. "'So Faith Comes from What Is Heard': The Relationship Between Music and God's Word in the First Two Centuries of German Lutheranism." In *Resonant Witness: Conversations Between Music and Theology*, edited by Jeremy S. Begbie and Steven R. Guthrie, 65–82. Grand Rapids: Eerdmans, 2011.

King'oo, Clare Costley. "William Hunnis and the Success of the Seven Sobs." *Renaissance Studies* 29 (2015) 615–31.

Lehmberg, Stanford E. "The Reformation of Choirs: Cathedral Musical Establishments in Tudor England." In *Tudor Rule and Revolution: Essays for G. R. Elton from His American Friends*, edited by DeLloyd J. Guth and John W. McKenna, 45–67. Cambridge: Cambridge University Press, 1982.

Roche, Jerome (revised by N. O'Regan). "Allegri, Gregorio." *Grove Music Online* (2001). http://doi.org/10.1093/gmo/9781561592630.article.00602.

Smith, John Arthur. "Psalm I. Biblical and Early Christianity." In *New Grove Dictionary of Music and Musicians*, edited by Stanley Sadie, 20:449–51. Oxford: Oxford University Press, 2001.

Trocmé-Latter, Daniel. "The Psalms as a Mark of Protestantism: The Introduction of Liturgical Psalm-Singing in Geneva." *Plainsong and Medieval Music* 20 (2011) 145–63.

Van 't Spijker, Willem. "Bucer's Influence on Calvin: Church and Community." In *Martin Bucer: Reforming Church and Community*, edited by David F. Wright, 32–44. Cambridge: Cambridge University Press, 1994.

Witvliet, John D. "The Spirituality of the Psalter in Calvin's Geneva." In *Worship Seeking Understanding: Windows into Christian Practice*, edited by John D. Witvliet, 203–29. Grand Rapids: Baker, 2003.

11

Preaching the Penitential Psalms

STEPHEN I. WRIGHT

INTRODUCTION

"PREACHING" A BIBLICAL TEXT is distinct from giving a lecture or writing a commentary on it. Christian preaching entails deploying the text in the service of announcing the word of God as supremely revealed in Jesus Christ. In this process the preacher seeks to allow the text to speak on its own terms while also letting it point to that supreme revelation. In doing so preachers will have in mind the needs of a particular group of hearers on a particular occasion.

Each part of the Bible therefore presents its own possibilities and challenges for preaching. Allowing the text to speak involves taking seriously its historical setting and literary genre, and in light of these not only elucidating its meaning but also seeking to echo its rhetorical force.[1] Letting the text point to Christ involves locating its theological import within the sweep of God's revelation. Maintaining a healthy tension between the specific text and the trajectory of biblical theology can raise special challenges when preaching from the Old Testament.[2]

The purpose of this chapter is to discuss opportunities and questions for preaching presented by the Penitential Psalms and their place

---

1. In this I follow the trend of much modern homiletics, notably the so-called "New Homiletic" associated with the names of Fred B. Craddock, Thomas G. Long, and Eugene L. Lowry. See for instance Long, *Preaching and Literary Forms*.

2. For a helpful articulation of this task in relation to the Psalms, see Mays, *Preaching and Teaching*, 444–90.

within God's revelation. First, I will make some observations on preaching the psalms in general. Second, I will highlight aspects of the rhetoric and theology of the Seven Psalms as they relate to the task of preaching. Third, I will discuss a recent sermon on one of these psalms to illustrate the matters previously raised.

PREACHING THE PSALMS

The uniqueness of the book of Psalms within Scripture is summed up in the title of a book by Howard Neil Wallace: *Words to God, Word from God*. On the one hand, the Psalms are human creations—poems addressed variously to God, his creation, and his people, including outpourings of frustration towards the wicked or enemies as well as more general testimonies of faith and wisdom.[3] On the other hand, they have been collected for instructional, as well as liturgical or devotional, purposes,[4] and are received by the church as part of God's word to humanity. So how are preachers to do justice to them?

The original situations that gave rise to specific psalms are largely lost to us. Apart from a few titles appended later, and some references to the circumstances of the exile, there are few clues as to what may have lain behind their composition. As we find them, they are the hymnbook of a community, expressing its faith in language all can share. Therefore, although reference to putative historical background may sometimes help to bring them to life, it is the psalms' internal poetic dynamics which offer a preacher the most fruitful avenues of insight into their meaning and force.

These dynamics include structural patterns such as parallelism and a rich variety of imagery. The preacher needs to consider how to capture not only the meaning but also the emotive force thus generated. For example, we might echo the way in which they build emphasis by using closely equivalent terms in succeeding lines.[5] Their imagery can spark creative use of figures of speech in preaching and even become a sermon's organizing principle. The texts evoke moods such as anger, sadness, quiet

---

3. Some psalms do include passages more akin to prophetic speech in which God addresses people, but these constitute only a small proportion of the book.
4. On this see McCann and Howell, *Preaching the Psalms*, 16–17, 37–38.
5. For instance, the various terms for sin in Ps 32:1–2 and Ps 51:1–5.

reflectiveness, exultation, or thanksgiving. Preachers can aim to evoke a similar mood, or series of moods, through the sermon.[6]

As a component of God's revelation, the Psalms attest to his character of faithful love. But they can also be seen as God's authorization of a range of human expressions of emotion, from jubilation and triumph through quiet contentment to sorrow, anger, and fear. This is liberating. It entails recognizing that the psalmists' desires are not necessarily exemplary, nor their theology perfect. Rather, it gives permission for honesty before God, and thus paves the way for genuine relationship with him. In Walter Brueggemann's words, the Psalms are "both models and permits. We stand under their discipline, and we are authorized by their freedom."[7]

The Psalms have stimulated rich christological reflection. The God of whom and to whom they speak, the God of creation, redemption, protection, and guidance, of ultimate triumph and sovereignty, is recognizably the one fully revealed in Christ. But there is also a tradition associated particularly with Augustine, Luther, and Bonhoeffer[8] of reading psalms as prayers of the Christ who identified himself totally with the human condition. For Augustine, a key text in support of this was Ps 22, used by Jesus on the cross (Matt 27:46/Mark 15:34); modern historical scholarship on the Gospels points in the same direction.[9] As we are joined to Christ, the limitations of the psalmists' prayers and ours are transcended; we can pray them in and through him, confident that his Father hears us, and will vindicate us as he did his Son.

The continued use of the Psalms in Christian worship means that they can be spoken and heard with these christological overtones, which can be brought out from time to time through preaching, not least in the context of the Eucharist. In the Revised Common Lectionary,[10] a psalm is normally set for the principal Sunday service as a response to the Old Testament reading, but links can often also be drawn to the readings from the New Testament and the Gospels. The psalms are fertile texts for

---

6. On the significance of the form of the psalms for preachers see Wallace, *Words to God*, 146–48; McCann and Howell, *Preaching the Psalms*, 51–85.

7. Brueggemann, *Psalms*, 34.

8. See the chapters by Jason Byassee, Channing Crisler, and Tim Judson elsewhere in this volume.

9. Bauckham, *Jesus*, 255–62.

10. Or lectionaries based upon it, such as the Common Worship lectionary of the Church of England.

stimulating the dialogue between divine revelation and human response at worship's heart.

As Wallace argues, the psalms thus offer a unique vehicle for the preacher to foster the spiritual growth of a congregation and shape its praying.[11] He points out that a psalm's anonymity allows the preacher to point to a range of situations in which the congregation might identify with their words.[12] The "conversation" between the psalmist and God which is overheard in the psalms can be dramatized in the double use of psalm verses in a service, both as elements of proclamation and at different points in the liturgy, for example as calls to worship, words of confession, or refrains in intercession.[13] While some parts of psalms are always applicable—such as summons to praise God, and petitions for him to make his ways known—others reflect individual circumstances of deep trouble or answered prayer which will not find an immediate echo in the experience of all worshipers. But in such cases the preacher can help their hearers to see how praying the psalm can enable them to empathize with what others are going through and intercede for them: to "rejoice with those who rejoice, weep with those who weep" (Rom 12:15 NRSV). Thoroughly personal psalms can thus be a gateway into a deeper sense of community.[14]

We turn now to a more detailed examination of how preaching can help congregations inhabit the spirit of the seven Penitential Psalms within the larger perspective of biblical revelation.

THE PENITENTIAL PSALMS: POETRY AND THEOLOGY FOR PREACHING

Six of these psalms are framed as a direct address to God, though with internal variations as noted below. The one exception is the more reflective Ps 32, though vv. 5–7 do address God as "you." They express sorrow for sin, but much more than that: indeed, Pss 6 and 102 contain no explicit reference to sin or forgiveness. When penitence is articulated, it is within the context of lament for suffering of various kinds, personal and

---

11. Wallace, *Words to God*, 142–45.
12. Wallace, *Words to God*, 145–46.
13. See the ideas in Wallace, *Words to God*, 127–29, 153–55.
14. On this see McCann and Howell, *Preaching the Psalms*, 57–60, 78–79.

national.[15] Preachers can show how these psalms encourage us to bring prayers not only of repentance but of longing for deliverance of all kinds to God, without hesitation or shame. But we can also echo their dramatic elements and vivid language.

We may note three dramatic features which a preacher might echo. First, a sermon might use the first-person form, expanding on the psalmist's cries and longings—a sermonic prayer. This could bring the humanity of the psalmist close to the hearers through the humanity of the preacher. Second, the preacher might vary their rhetoric through echoing the psalmist's exhortations directed to other humans—the "workers of evil" (Ps 6:8), the "righteous" (Ps 32:11), "Israel" (Ps 130:7), or any who might record for posterity God's answer to prayers (Ps 102:18–22). Third, sermon structure and tone can reflect the twists and turns in the sequence of the psalmists' thought: for example, the pleading and lament of Ps 6:1–7 followed by a sudden sense of renewed confidence in v. 8.[16] Another structural feature, chiasm, cannot be imitated directly in preaching, being a literary pattern more apparent to the eye than the ear—though it contributes importantly to meaning, as we will see below.

These psalms are also replete with vivid imagery which cries out to be heard, and seen, in preaching. The preacher needs to weigh up the resonance of images in their original context and today's to assess whether they need to be translated somehow for their impact to be felt.[17]

Sin itself is something from which one needs to be *cleansed*, as the use of various washing-related words in Ps 51 testifies (vv. 2, 7, 9, 10). Although rooted in ancient rituals of purity, this arguably remains a psychologically suggestive metaphor today. But most striking in these psalms is the language used for the physical and mental agonies in which the psalmist finds himself.

Sometimes this seems to represent the psalmist's symptoms literally. Consider his descriptions of his bones: shaking (6:2), crushed (51:8), burning like a furnace (102:3), clinging to his skin (102:5).[18] This might not be modern medical language, but it surely denotes real physical sensations. Such is the case too with festering wounds (38:5), burning loins (38:7), and a throbbing heart (38:10). There may be an element of

---

15. Snaith, *Seven Psalms*, 11–12, suggests that these psalms are to be regarded more as songs of the humbled ('*anniyim*) than the humble ('*annawim*).

16. Compare the more subtle shifts in Ps 102.

17. On this task see Szumorek, *Seeing and Showing*.

18. See also the imagery in 6:6, 7; 32:3; 38:5, 7, 10; 143:3.

hyperbole in the pictures of a bed flooded with tears (6:6), eyes or body wasting away (6:7; 32:3), sight gone (38:10), and life crushed (143:3), but it is surely rooted in physical reality. Spiritualizing such imagery so that it speaks only of inward agonies seems a travesty.[19] When the psalmist does speak of what we would call his psychological condition, he (like us) uses simile, as in 102:11 ("I wither away like grass"),[20] and metaphor, as in 130:1 ("Out of the depths I cry to you, O LORD").[21]

The psalmist's language about God is boldly metaphorical. Positively, God is his hiding place and refuge (32:7; 143:9). Negatively, God's "arrows" have sunk into him, and his "hand" has come down on him (38:2). The contrasting uses of a familiar anthropomorphism seem to sum up the plea at the heart of these psalms: "Hide your face from my sins" (51:9), and conversely, "Do not hide your face from me" (102:2; 143:7). Thus the vivid representation of the psalmist's suffering is matched by the portrayal of God in vivid human terms.

These psalms invite the preacher to help hearers enter this image-rich world. Although some of the imagery may be helpfully expanded and adapted for contemporary ears—there is no reason, for instance, why our depiction of contemporary suffering should be limited to the parts of the body named by the psalmist, or our metaphors for existential agony limited to his—we can seek to let the embodied nature of these prayers embolden our hearers to come before God as we are, name their experience, and connect it, perhaps through hard wrestling, to what they have discovered of his character and commitment to them.

Theologically, there is profound continuity between these psalms and the New Testament. They bear witness to God's graciousness, righteousness, and saving power. Sin is seen not only as something done (or not done) on a particular occasion, but as something deeply affecting the human condition (51:5; 130:3; 143:2), as for instance in Rom 1–8. The "righteous" (Ps 32:11) are not the morally perfect, but those in a right relationship with God, as in Rom 1:17, etc. Luther used Ps 51 in support of his doctrine of justification—understandably in view of its honest acknowledgment of sin and God's right to judge, prayer for cleansing, longing for the joy of restored relationship, and reference to God's "Holy

---

19. *Contra* Luther, who read such texts non-literally as expressing the necessary agonies of the guilty conscience: King'oo, *Miserere Mei*, 63–94.

20. See also Pss 38:4b, 13, 14; 102:6, 7; 143:6.

21. See also Ps 38:4a.

Spirit" in v. 11.[22] In the Revised Common Lectionary it is appropriately set for Ash Wednesday, the start of the penitential season of Lent. The preacher will have little difficulty in deploying these psalms as witnesses to God's good news.

In some respects, however, tensions arise. To begin with, these psalms seem to undermine the traditional conception of Christ as the speaker of the psalms. Can a sinless Christ be heard saying "For I know my transgressions, and my sin is ever before me" (Ps 51:3 NRSV), and similar things? Augustine pointed the way here by showing how we find in such words Christ's complete identification with his body, the church.[23] Thus a preacher can use these texts to draw hearers deeper into the mystery of the atonement. "'He committed no sin,'" yet "he himself bore our sins in his body on the cross" (1 Pet 2:22a, 24 NRSV). In that sense, he spoke *our* confession as he hung there (with all the attendant shame) and on that basis continues to make intercession for us (Heb 7:25).

But a wider issue is raised here. Repentance and forgiveness are minor themes in the Psalms when compared to the New Testament.[24] As noted above, even these "penitential" psalms have a much broader theological compass. Mays offers wise pointers to dealing homiletically with the tensions that arise from this difference. He comments that in Christian tradition, "The use of the entire Psalter has kept a place for the range of physical and public and social experiences" (i.e., in addition to sin and forgiveness) "that constitute human neediness,"[25] and "use of the prayer-psalms argues against a reduction of salvation to the forgiveness of sin."[26] The Penitential Psalms illustrate his point through two features which compel us to a deeper wrestling with their theology.

First, they force us to confront the experience of God's anger in the identical opening words of Pss 6 and 38. In 6:1 this seems imminent, if not already present; in 38:1–8 the psalmist is already feeling the full force of it in severe physical pain and weakness.[27] Such sentiments present a problem for the Christian preacher. The notion that disaster or disability is automatically to be regarded as a punishment from God is directly contradicted by Jesus (Luke 13:1–5; John 9:1–3). On the basis of such

---

22. Wallace, *Words to God*, 97.
23. See chapter 3 by Jason Byassee in this volume.
24. As noted in Mays, *Preaching and Teaching*, 479–90.
25. Mays, *Preaching and Teaching*, 485.
26. Mays, *Preaching and Teaching*, 490.
27. See also Ps 51:8; 102:9–10.

texts pastors frequently challenge the folk-religious idea that when "bad things happen" it is because one has offended God in some way. Yet these psalms (and other biblical texts) stubbornly ascribe all kinds of affliction directly to God and often specifically to his anger at human sin. How are we to interpret such texts as elements of divine revelation and models for prayer?

Perhaps it is most helpful to present these statements about God's anger as truthful, but not the whole truth. We should not seek to evade the psalmists' witness that suffering *can* be caused by God's anger against us for our sin: "There is no health in my bones because of my sin" (38:3b). Although they do not yet see how God will absorb his own anger on the cross and thus draw the sting from our experience of it, their very pleas show confidence that God's mercy will prevent him displaying his anger to its full and justified extent. Nor, as we will see shortly, do they imply that *all* suffering can be ascribed to God's anger on account of specific sin(s) of the sufferer. Preachers can encourage their hearers to recognize the occasions when suffering is a consequence of sin, but also to realize that in Christ, suffering never indicates the withdrawal of God's love (Rom 8:18–39).

To ignore the language of God's anger or imply that it is somehow to be left behind in the Christian era does not do justice either to Scripture or to the pastoral opportunity these psalms open up. It is precisely because they show how one can express one's sense of this anger along with faith that his mercy will restrain it that they have value. But it is also true that Scripture presents God's wrath as directed against whole nations, not just individuals (e.g., Isa 9:12, 17, 21; 10:4; Lam 2:1–3). In Rom 1:18–32 Paul recognizes the manifestation of the wrath of God in the widespread breakdown of human society resulting from suppression of the truth about God. A sense of being caught up in a whole environment that is estranged from God is perhaps hinted at in those psalms in our group (Pss 6 and 102) in which God's anger is mentioned, but personal sin is not. Indeed Ps 102 seems to come from an exilic context in which the anger of God has been discerned behind the destruction of Zion, now "dust" (v. 14), and in which the personal desolation of the psalmist (vv. 3–11) is set in the wider context of the people's captivity (v. 20). Correspondingly, the expressions of hope are not just for the speaker, but for Zion itself (vv. 12–22; noting also Ps 130:8).

The second challenging theological feature of these psalms, closely related to the first, is the psalmists' awareness of and attitude towards their "enemies." The writer of Ps 38 is very aware of his own sin and its consequences, but equally protests about the sin of others, who are his foes "without cause" and who "hate him wrongfully" (v. 19), indeed oppose him because he follows the good (v. 20). So his confession of sin is not tantamount to admitting that all his troubles arise from God's just anger.[28] On the contrary, he speaks as one who waits on Yahweh (v. 15), i.e., is "righteous," for whom sin is an aberrance; and it is precisely when his foot slips—when he sins and experiences the consequences—that his enemies seize their chance to gloat over him and gratuitously add to his justified woes (v. 16).[29] The writer of Ps 143 knows the rigors of God's holiness (v. 2), but when he says, "The enemy has pursued me, crushing my life to the ground, making me sit in darkness like those long dead" (v. 3), he does not simply accept this as God's punishment. Rather, he calls on God to save him from his enemies (vv. 9, 12).

Such petitions set the awareness of sin in the wider context of a constant battle with enemies who have no cause for their enmity. They will resonate especially with those bearing the brunt of persecution for their faith in Christ. But they raise wider, much-discussed questions for preaching the Psalms.[30] It is one thing to be sure that one's enemies will be ashamed and terror-struck (Ps 6:10), but quite another to ask God to destroy them (Ps 143:12), in the light of Jesus' command, "Love your enemies" (Matt 5:44). The long-standing Christian interpretation of such petitions to refer to the spiritual, rather than human, forces ranged against us (Eph 6:12) enables a positive appropriation of the texts. But the immediate, physical dimension of the rescue the psalmists cry out for should not be underplayed. Unjustified opposition comes to us regularly in human form. In these psalms (particularly Pss 6, 38, and 143) we see how an awareness of having sinned against God can coexist with a raw sense of being sinned against oneself. Even while loving human enemies, it is possible to pray for deliverance from them. The Penitential Psalms thus set the dynamics of sin on a wide canvas, and may rescue the oversensitive soul from being so overwhelmed by a sense of their own inadequacy before God that they fail to recognize that worldwide web of sin in which we are indeed sinned against as well as sinners.

---

28. *Contra* Augustinian "penitential hermeneutics" which interpreted the Penitential Psalms pervasively through the lens of God's eschatological judgement: King'oo, *Miserere Mei*, 1–24.

29. See also Ps 69:4–5.

30. See for instance the helpful treatment in Creach, *Violence*, 153–240.

REFLECTION ON A SERMON

To earth the above reflections, I offer some comments on a sermon I preached in a UK Baptist church where I have been an occasional visiting preacher for many years.[31] I had freedom to choose my text, so I decided to preach on a Penitential Psalm. As the service was to include Communion, the celebration of the new covenant "for the forgiveness of sins," I chose the most celebratory, Ps 32.

To set the tone for the service and emphasize the Psalms' function of guiding our praying as well as our believing and living, I used the opening declaration (v. 1) and closing exhortation (v. 11) of Ps 32 as the call to worship, and vv. 3–5 to introduce the act of confession. The whole psalm was the first reading, and 1 John 1:1—2:2 the second. John here echoes the psalmist's testimony to the importance of confession (1:7–9a). These elements prepared for the exploration of the psalm in the sermon, which in turn paved the way for the celebration of God's forgiveness in the Lord's Supper.

In preparation I was struck by the psalm's joyful mood and its witness to the double-sided relationship of God with his people—his readiness to forgive and deliver them, and their need to be honest about their sin and open to his leading. Theologically there was no difficulty in employing it as testimony to God's character and ways as supremely revealed in Jesus. Paul quotes vv. 1 and 2a to link the forgiveness enjoyed by the psalmist to the "righteousness" of God revealed in Christ (Rom 4:6–8), thus echoing the psalmist's call to the "righteous" to be glad in Yahweh (v. 11). Mindful of some Christians' tendency to exaggerate the distinction between the covenants, I emphasized that the psalm "shows that the wonder of God's forgiveness was experienced by people many centuries before Jesus."

Given the universality of sin, my relative ignorance of the congregation was no bar to applying the psalm's message, including its pastorally helpful insight into the exhausting experience of being "in denial" about it (vv. 3–4).[32] In preparation I also pondered current news items, since resonance between the text and current events can allow God's word to

---

31. The full text of the sermon can be found at https://www.PsalterMark.com.

32. I take these verses as describing the consequences of *not acknowledging sin*, rather than the consequences of sin itself (though inevitably, the two are closely related): *contra* Greidanus, *Preaching Christ*, 278, 280–81, who describes this experience as God's "punishment" of the psalmist.

be heard more sharply. Situations in the general consciousness included the UK general election campaign, the scandal of the historic transfusions of infected blood, injustices meted out on Post Office employees falsely accused of fraud, and the wars in Gaza, Ukraine, and Sudan. I noted especially the connection between the psalmist's recognition of the need for honesty about sin (vv. 3–5) and the patterns of cover-up in public life which display a general reluctance to be transparent and self-critical.

I regularly write a "focus" and "function" statement to help keep a sermon on track.[33] On the basis of the above reflections, my "focus" statement was, "It is a joyful state to be transparent before God, honest about our sin, assured of his forgiveness and open to his guidance." The intended "function" was "to foster a sense of celebration of God's readiness to forgive and guide, and reflection on the consequences of denying the reality of sin."

I sought to develop a "form" for the sermon which embodied the focus and might—under God—fulfill the function,[34] drawing on rhetorical features of the psalm itself.[35] I could have adopted a narrative structure for all or part of the sermon. Personal confession would not have been appropriate, but a real-life or fictional story, or imaginative expansion of a biblical one, could have brought the psalmist's testimony in vv. 3–5 to life.[36] But I wanted to capture other elements too, particularly the celebratory mood as well as the divine instruction (vv. 9–10). Another possibility would have been to follow the text verse by verse, helping hearers to engage on an intellectual and emotional level with its sequence of thought. One could note, for instance, the rhythm of threefold repetition highlighted by Sidney Greidanus: three ways of speaking of forgiveness (1–2), sin (1–2a, 5), suffering (3–4), confession (5), God's protection (7), and God's guidance (8), culminating in three exhortations to rejoice (11).[37]

However, in my study of the psalm, I had been struck particularly by its chiastic structure. As Greidanus points out, "An ancient chiastic

---

33. As recommended by Long, *Witness*, 127–35.

34. Long, *Witness*, 135.

35. For another discussion on preaching Ps 32 with attention to its rhetoric, see Smith, "Preaching the Psalms," 19–28.

36. Brueggemann, "Preaching the Psalms," 15, discusses how the plotlines in the Psalter may be connected to the recurring plotlines in our lives.

37. Greidanus, *Preaching Christ*, 277.

structure does not make for a good modern sermon outline," but is nevertheless a significant clue to interpretation.[38] I therefore decided on a third option for the sermon structure, in which I would capture the psalm's mood by echoing its opening celebration of the happiness of being forgiven at the start of the sermon ("We've come here this morning to celebrate," outlining the reasons why), and relating this to the celebration of Communion at the end. In the center I would use a PowerPoint presentation of the chiastic structure to elucidate the dynamics of the two-sided relationship which the psalm explores. I judged that this congregation would find this interesting and helpful, which some comments received afterwards proved correct. I presented the chiasm in a simplified and color-coded form as follows:

    1–2   How happy it makes us when we know that the LORD has forgiven us!
        3–4   When I covered up my sin, how painful it was.
            5   I confessed my sin—and you forgave me!
        6–7   May others enjoy the openness and security this has brought me.
    8–9   God says "I will guide you if you don't resist me."
10–11   Those who trust in the LORD enjoy his steadfast love—so celebrate![39]

I commented in turn on the outer, central, and intervening verses. I pointed out that the framing verses 1–2 and 10–11 remind us that God himself and his attitude towards us are our objective reason to celebrate. (I did not comment on the one line in the psalm about the wicked [v. 10a]: one has to be selective, but perhaps I took too easy a route here.) I then drew attention to v. 5, noting that the central position of the psalmist's account of his experience of God's forgiveness following confession suggests its pivotal importance in the psalm and in life. I went on to show how in vv. 6–7 the psalmist revels in the security of his restored relationship with God, urging others also to realize its benefits. Finally I commented on the intervening sections. Verses 3–4 speak of the negative consequences of suppressing the truth about one's own sin; vv. 8–9 give

---

38. Greidanus, *Preaching Christ*, 279. See also Tornfelt, "Preaching the Psalms."

39. This analysis differs slightly from those of Greidanus, *Preaching Christ*, 279, and VanGemeren, *Psalms*, 311 (cited in Greidanus, *Preaching Christ*, 295). This illustrates the inevitable element of subjectivity in such analyses—which by no means invalidates the insights to be gained through the exercise.

their positive counterpart, God's promise of his ongoing guidance and command to be receptive.[40]

I summarized the truth that emerges from this pattern by saying that "the psalm helps us to celebrate God's forgiveness, but also reflect on the attitude we need to have if we are to go on enjoying it." But I also wanted to warn people against oversensitivity. From my own experience, and from Jer 17:9, I remarked on how difficult it was to understand ourselves, and discern what is more or less pleasing to God, but returned to Ps 32:8 to encourage the congregation with God's promise of guidance: "Embraced in his steadfast love, we can allow ourselves to grow gently in self-awareness, not beating ourselves up for every wrong move or step that seemed in retrospect foolish."[41]

This led to the sermon's conclusion, where I reminded people that Communion was a shared celebration of God's gift of forgiveness to us all through Christ, and that if we are to enjoy a relationship with God, we need also to be in a right relationship with others. Here I turned attention briefly outwards to the world in which the pain of denying sin is so evident, pointing ahead to the time of intercession to follow. Finally, I encouraged the congregation to come to the Communion not in a smug, "I'm-all-right" spirit, but thankful for God's love, open to his searchlight, and longing for others too to enjoy his blessing.

As I reflect self-critically on the sermon, I am aware that I could have used more creative language to echo the psalm's use of imagery, such as the body wasting away (v. 3), the rush of mighty waters (v. 6), and God as a hiding place (v. 7). The example of the "horse or mule" in v. 9 seemed to need little adjustment: "It's no good being stubborn as a mule." But I did try to inject some freshness and realism into the central concepts of sin and forgiveness. "Sin" has become a tired piece of theological jargon in parts of the church (and little understood outside it). So in my opening celebration of God's forgiveness at the start, instead of speaking of "sin" explicitly I said, "Our lives go all over the place, missing the right path, failing to follow instructions, getting caught up in unimportant things at the expense of important ones, sometimes deliberately blocking out God's voice." I also wanted to cut through any misunderstanding of God's forgiveness as a mere impersonal transaction (of the "passport-to-heaven" variety). Perhaps more vividly than any other biblical passage,

---

40. A striking feature of the chiasm I omitted to note is the appearance of the name of Yahweh at the beginning (v. 2), middle (v. 5), and end (v. 11) of the psalm.

41. Whiting, "PsalterMark."

this psalm presents it as deeply personal. So I invited people to think of a falling-out with another human, the pain that causes to both, and the relief of reconciliation as a reflection of the dynamics of our relationship with God.

CONCLUSION

The Penitential Psalms offer a rich scriptural resource for preaching. Like other psalms, they allow us to eavesdrop on the prayers and meditations of forebears in faith, inviting us into their thought world, revealing insights into the character of God and giving us language for our own praying. While modeling honesty about human sinfulness and trust in God's forgiveness, they seek God's salvation in a fuller sense, encompassing rescue from sin's consequences and the afflictions meted out undeservedly by enemies. They can thus act as powerful pointers to the gospel of Christ, who both bore those consequences and afflictions and mediates that salvation for all. Their poetic form and vivid language offer many possibilities for creative preaching which seeks to capture their mood, echo their tone, and let their power as "Words to God, Word from God" be felt.[42]

BIBLIOGRAPHY

Bauckham, Richard J. *Jesus and the God of Israel: "God Crucified" and Other Studies on the New Testament's Christology of Divine Identity*. Milton Keynes, UK: Paternoster, 2008.
Brueggemann, Walter. "Preaching the Psalms." *Journal for Preachers* 37.2 (2014) 11–20.
———. *The Psalms and the Life of Faith*. Edited by Patrick D. Miller. Minneapolis: Fortress, 1995.
Creach, Jerome F. D. *Violence in Scripture*. Interpretation: Resources for the Use of the Bible in the Church. Louisville: Westminster John Knox, 2013.
Greidanus, Sidney P. *Preaching Christ from Psalms: Foundations for Expository Sermons in the Christian Year*. Grand Rapids: Eerdmans, 2016.
King'oo, Clare Costley. *Miserere Mei: The Penitential Psalms in Late Medieval and Early Modern England*. Notre Dame, IN: University of Notre Dame Press, 2012.
Long, Thomas G. *Preaching and the Literary Forms of the Bible*. Minneapolis: Fortress, 1989.
———. *The Witness of Preaching*. 3rd ed. Louisville: Westminster John Knox, 2016.
Mays, James L. *Preaching and Teaching the Psalms*. Edited by Patrick G. Miller and Gene M. Tucker. Louisville: Westminster John Knox, 2006.

---

42. I am grateful to Debra Reid for her comments on a draft of this chapter.

McCann, J. Clinton Jr., and James C. Howell. *Preaching the Psalms*. Nashville: Abingdon, 2001.

Smith, Kenneth W. "Preaching the Psalms with Respect for their Inspired Design." *Journal of the Evangelical Homiletics Society* 3.2 (2003) 4–31.

Snaith, Norman. *The Seven Psalms*. London: Epworth, 1964.

Szumorek, Adam. *Seeing and Showing the Unseen: Using Cognitive Linguistics in Preaching Images and Metaphors*. Carlisle, UK: Langham Monographs, 2023.

Tornfelt, John V. "Preaching the Psalms: Understanding Chiastic Structures for Greater Clarity." *Journal of the Evangelical Homiletics Society* 2.2 (December 2002) 4–31.

VanGemeren, Willem A. *Psalms*. Edited by Tremper Longman III and David E. Garland. Vol. 5 of *The Expositor's Bible Commentary*. Rev. ed. Grand Rapids: Zondervan, 2008.

Wallace, Howard Neil. *Words to God, Word from God: The Psalms in the Prayer and Preaching of the Church*. Aldershot, UK: Ashgate, 2005.

Whiting, Mark J. "PsalterMark." PsalterMark. https://www.PsalterMark.com.

12

The Beauty of Penitence

Karen Case-Green

"I am struck with the truth, that far more of our deepest thoughts and feelings pass to us through perplexed combinations of concrete objects... in compound experiences incapable of being disentangled, than ever reach us directly and in their own abstract shape."

—Thomas De Quincy[1]

INTRODUCTION

The poet Emily Dickinson underlined this sentence in her copy of Thomas De Quincey's *Autobiographical Sketches*. Sadly, Amherst First Congregational Church viewed "concrete objects" as something of a distraction from Scripture, and Dickinson was left to explore them through her poetry. Such disregard for materiality is still shared by many churches today, and penitence can become quite an abstract, disembodied affair.

The suspicion is understandable. After all, the second commandment is: "You shall not make for yourself an image in the form of anything in heaven above or on the earth beneath or in the waters below. You shall not bow down to them or worship them" (Exod 20:4–5 NIV). The human heart has a tendency to worship things instead of the Creator. The Reformation added to a suspicion of materiality, particularly regarding

---

1. As appearing in De Quincey, *Sketches*, 39.

penitence. It was, after all, in response to Tetzel's preaching on indulgences that Luther published his *Ninety-five Theses*, a central step in the chain of events that led to the Reformation. For the so-called Magisterial Reformers the idea that one could receive remission of divine punishment by giving alms, touching a relic, or visiting a shrine was an anathema.

The iconoclasm which followed the Reformation led to growing nervousness around the literal way in which penitence was depicted by artists. Again, this suspicion was not without foundations. For example, in the fifteenth-century private devotional book of hours commissioned by the Duke of Berry, God appears in a ring of seraphim above, while King David is pinned to the ground below by arrows. The artists were attempting to depict the penitential Ps 38:2, "Your arrows have pierced me." The effect is farcical.

The Reformation, combined with the Enlightenment, has therefore left a residue of suspicion regarding materiality. This may explain why many nonconformist churches are so visually "beige," and why penitence is engaged at a very abstract level rather than in any concrete way. Yet it is impossible to read the Bible without encountering visual imagery. In the Old Testament, one of the energies of the Hebrew language is its figurative, concrete nature.[2] This is clearly seen in the Penitential Psalms, with their rich array of metaphors. Images and visualization are vital aspects of the Psalms; indeed, some metaphors have become so well known that they are clichés. "The depths" image is one:

> Out of the depths I cry to you, Lord;
> Lord, hear my voice.
> Let your ears be attentive
> to my cry for mercy.
> (Ps 130:1–2 NIV)

The "broken heart" image is another:

> My sacrifice, O God, is a broken spirit;
> a broken and contrite heart
> you, God, will not despise.
> (Ps 51:17 NIV)

Given that clichés are well-worn truths, the fact that these images are such a part of our common vocabulary are proof of their power. They

---

2. Soskice, *Metaphor*, 10–11; 20–21.

should not be discarded. Rather, creative engagement can serve to make these images "new" again through the process of defamiliarization.

The first part of this chapter explores the cycle of penitence in Ps 32 and reflects on what, if anything, can be considered "beautiful" about penitence. The second half explores how the creative arts might be used to help us engage afresh with the Penitential Psalms, both individually and corporately.

WHY IS PENITENCE BEAUTIFUL?

Penitence is beautiful because it is our first step on the road to restoration. God the Father, Son, and Holy Spirit are community, and God's desire for relationship with us is writ large in the revelation of Scripture. The beauty of penitence is that it acknowledges the pain of our broken relationship with God which prepares the way for God's grace. Nowhere is this seen better than in the Penitential Psalm, Ps 32. The psalmist remembers his state before he admitted his guilt.

> When I kept silent,
> my bones wasted away
> through my groaning all day long.
> For day and night
> your hand was heavy on me;
> my strength was sapped
> as in the heat of summer.
> (Ps 32:3–4 NIV)

The imagery is very physical, even visceral. We sense the dry groans of the psalmist; it is as if he were experiencing his sin as a physical disease. Indeed, the church fathers saw sin as deforming, a disease of the soul.[3] Part of the beauty of penitence is its honest engagement with the very real crisis at the heart of humanity. To visually "name" this dis-ease will be for some people their entry point into the salvation drama. It was for Peter Hitchens, brother of the famous atheist Christopher Hitchens. Peter recalls seeing Rogier van der Weyden's painting, *The Last Judgment*:

> Another religious painting. Couldn't these people think of anything else to depict? Still scoffing, I peered at the naked figures fleeing towards the pit of Hell, out of my usual faintly morbid interest in the alleged terrors of damnation. But this time I gasped,

---

3. Allender, *Sabbath*, 7.

my mouth actually hanging open. These people did not appear remote or from the ancient past; they were my own generation. Because they were naked, they were not imprisoned in their own age by time-bound fashions. . . . They were me, and the people I knew. . . . I had a sudden strong sense of religion being a thing of the present day, not imprisoned under thick layers of time. A large catalogue of misdeeds, ranging from the embarrassing to the appalling, replayed themselves rapidly in my head. I had absolutely no doubt that I was among the damned, if there were any damned. And what if there were? How did I know there were not? I did not know.[4]

This painting played a key role in Hitchens' restoration to faith.

Naming our guilt before God is vital. The psalmist acknowledged his sin to God and sought to cover nothing up:

> Then I acknowledged my sin to you
> and did not cover up my iniquity.
> I said, "I will confess
> my transgressions to the Lord."
> And you forgave
> the guilt of my sin.
> (Ps 32:5 NIV)

This act of bringing things into the light is a significant step towards restoration. God forgave the psalmist and intimacy was restored: the psalmist experienced God as his "hiding place" once again, where God surrounds him with "songs of deliverance" (v. 7). Heavy silence gives way to joy.

Penitence (our part) and forgiveness (God's part) lead to restoration of relationships. This is the beauty of penitence. However, bringing our sin into the open may be ugly and painful. T. S. Eliot compared it to undergoing an operation in the opening of Part IV of "East Coker."[5] Jesus bled on the cross so that we might be healed of sin's "distemper," but we need first to come under the knife in order to address what Satterthwaite calls "the deep taproot of sin."[6] Psalm 32 teaches us that, until we open our wound to God, we cannot be saved from it. Keep sin hidden and it festers; bring it into the light and we bring it before a surgeon who heals and forgives. We are not responsible for the act of healing. Our job is simply to confess our sin.

4. Hitchens, as cited in Case-Green and Sakakini, *Imaging*, 19–20.
5. Eliot, *Four Quartets*, 18.
6. Satterthwaite, *Spiritual Detox*, 53.

This happens in the Twelve Step program. Addictions from drugs, alcohol, emotional dependency, and sexual addiction are all brought into the open in these tailor-made programs. The first step is naming one's addiction before the group: "Hi, my name is _____, and I'm an alcoholic." You acknowledge that you are powerless over your problems and that your life has become unmanageable.[7] It is a step of humility. In Step Four, a moral inventory is made of all the people you have hurt, along with any resentments you carry towards those who have damaged you.[8] Satterthwaite compares confession to the act of being sick, of vomiting up the toxins of sin that are poisoning your soul.[9] This is not about self-flagellation but rather *health*.

The church can learn much from the Twelve Step program about confession and restoration. John Mark Comer suggests that any working model of spiritual formation will mirror the tripart elements of (1) radical self-awareness, honesty, and confession; (2) total surrender to God's power; and (3) a loving, tight-knit community to both love you and keep you accountable.[10] Rarely is such candor found in our churches today. Yet unless we allow Jesus to "question the distempered part," we are left with stunted growth and an inability to move toward restoration.

TO WHOM IS PENITENCE BEAUTIFUL?

That restoration is the goal should not be forgotten in any act of penitence. Take the story of the feast in the house of Simon the Pharisee (Luke 7:36–50). It has been a popular one through which artists have explored the theme of penitence. We are told that a "sinful woman"[11] comes to anoint Jesus at the Pharisee's house. Weeping, she brings an alabaster flask of ointment, wets Jesus' feet with her tears, wipes them with the hair of her head, kisses his feet, and anoints them with the ointment. While his host judges Jesus for allowing a woman to do this to him, Jesus praises her.

It is a visually rich story and has been the subject of much art. However, Jesus' point, that this woman showed him true hospitality (while Simon the Pharisee did not), is often lost on artists. Mary Magdalene is

7. Arterburn and Stoop, *Recovery Workbook*, 4.
8. For example, Arterburn and Stoop, *Recovery Workbook*.
9. Satterthwaite, *Spiritual Detox*, 39.
10. Comer, *Practicing the Way*, 95.
11. The "sinful woman" has been assumed, since the time of Pope Gregory I, to be Mary Magdalene.

usually depicted in a way that underlines her vulnerability. For example, in the seventeenth-century work by Peter Paul Rubens, *Feast in the House of Simon the Pharisee*, Mary crawls along the floor in a state of undress, accentuating her sexuality and vulnerability. Other examples include: *Mary Magdalene Washing Christ's Feet at the House of Simon the Pharisee* (Studio of Guillaume Courtois), Juan de Valdes Lealor's *Christ in the House of Simon the Pharisee*, and the thirteenth-century work from Burgundy, *Mary Magdalene Washes Jesus Feet with Her Hair*, to name a few. Ruben's *Christ and the Penitent Sinners* also contains a kneeling, semi-clad Mary Magdalene, covering her breasts as she bends over, while the male "penitents" stand upright, including King David, who wears a crown on his head.

We must be careful when we talk about "the beauty of penitence." To whom is penitence beautiful, after all? Art historian Maryanne Saunders points out that, while women may be depicted in a salacious way, men are usually depicted with nobility, suggesting that their penitence is different.[12] Such art has often fed on voyeurism rather than penitence. Mary Magdalen becomes a spectacle; we revel in her "fallen" state rather than her restored state.

Here we must return to that Penitential Psalm *par excellence*, Ps 51. Clearly, David had wronged other people when he committed adultery with Bathsheba and had her husband killed. Yet he confesses to God:

> Against you, you only, have I sinned
> and done what is evil in your sight.
> (Ps 51:4a NIV)

How can David say this? In chapter 2 Briggs considered a key contextual factor that softens the jarring of our modern sensibilities when we hear no mention of Uriah and Bathsheba in David's confession. As he considers the language of sin in the Old Testament, he concludes that: "There is no need to deny that broken human relationships were culpably caused, but the language of sin tended to be reserved mainly for the offense against God, i.e., even when the offense against God was the interpersonal transgression."[13] For the purposes of this chapter, we can ask: if God is the main party who is offended when we sin, then surely penitence should primarily be beautiful to him? Only he can judge. Only he can truly absolve.

---

12. Saunders, "Politics of Penitence."
13. See Briggs, chapter 2, p. 28 of the present volume.

A more accurate visual response to the story of Simon the Pharisee, therefore, might show the woman restored to dignity. After all, Jesus finishes by telling her: "Your faith has saved you; go in peace" (Luke 7:50). The Pre-Raphaelite artist, Dante Gabriel Rossetti, captured this in his painting, *Mary Magdalene Leaving the House of Feasting*. Here we see a very different Mary. She leaves the house with purpose and dignity, her head up, her feet swift.[14] As Ps 32 teaches us, confession leads ultimately to restoration. In confession you are not only confessing the sin but also confessing what is *true* about who you are in Christ.[15] Saunders writes of Rossetti's painting:

> The overwhelming impression given by this work is one of redemption, forgiveness, and moving on. Mary moves swiftly from her old life and devotedly into the new one she has chosen with Christ. Although depicting a story of contrition, Rossetti appears to celebrate the vulnerability and bravery it takes to repent rather than relishing the spectacle.[16]

Mary Magdalene goes in peace. This is surely the beauty of penitence.

PENITENCE AS PART OF EMBODIED PRAYER

The activities below are designed to help us enter into meaningful penitence before God, using body as well as mind. Matter matters, and what we *do* can, in turn, do things to us. Some activities can be done individually; others can be used corporately. These activities are not "acts of penance" to amend for our sinful actions, but rather prepare our hearts for repentance and restoration. As the psalmist says:

> You do not delight in sacrifice, or I would bring it;
> you do not take pleasure in burnt offerings.
> My sacrifice, O God, is a broken spirit;
> a broken and contrite heart
> you, God, will not despise.
> (Ps 51:16–17 NIV)

Embodied acts can break up our hard hearts where they are hardened and prepare a riverbed for God's grace to flood through. The rest of this chapter is a series of suggestions for exploring embodied penitence.

---

14. Saunders, "Politics of Penitence."
15. Comer, *Practicing the Way*, 95.
16. Saunders, "Politics of Penitence."

The Daily Examen

The Ignatian practice of Daily Examen provides opportunity for daily self-examination to discern God's presence in each day:[17]

1. Ask God for light and become aware of his presence.
2. Give thanks for the day that is past. It was a gift from God. What are you grateful for?
3. Review the day and ask the Holy Spirit to help you as you look back on it. Pay attention to where God was present.
4. Face up to any dis-ease—in your life and in you.
5. Look toward tomorrow and ask God's help for it.

Psalm 139:23–24 is a helpful prayer to use with the Examen:

> Search me, God, and know my heart;
> test me and know my anxious thoughts.
> See if there is any offensive way in me,
> and lead me in the way everlasting.

To engage with this in a more embodied way, you could spread out a cloth before God and write or use symbols of the things that represent your day. Include those things where you sensed God's Spirit had gone missing, including your resentments. Spreading something concrete before God's loving gaze is a sign of vulnerability and transparency, as well as supplication. The psalmist writes:

> I spread out my hands to you;
> I thirst for you like a parched land.
> (Ps 143:6 NIV)

Here the Twelve Step's "inventory" may be useful. Ask the Lord to show you where you offended him, in thought or word or deed; where you fell short of his likeness. Then cover those things, trusting that the blood of Jesus covers you.

Holy Ground Project

"Holy Ground" is a mobile art installation by the artist Paul Hobbs. At the center of a circular, sandy installation stands a red stainless steel tree,

---

17. Manney, "Examen Prayer Card," para. 1.

reminiscent of the burning bush. Colored lights are trained on it to create a fiery effect. Empty shoes are laid on the edge of the circle, facing the center, calling to mind God's words to Moses: "Take off your sandals, for the place you are standing is holy ground" (Exod 3:5).

Among those represented by the empty shoes are: a thief, a refugee, the despised, the rejected. Hobbs writes: "All have encountered the living God, arriving at a place of holy ground; where they must, metaphorically at least, remove their shoes in acknowledgment of God's holiness."[18] The installation can be hired for your church or community space. It works particularly well during Lent.

Communion

There is a danger of overfamiliarity with Communion. While in some denominations communicants come forward and kneel to receive bread and a shared cup (thus inviting an embodied, communal response), in most nonconformist churches worshipers remain sat in their seats, passing around individual cups and pieces of bread. Penitence can become a very cerebral, private affair.

The visual activities below are designed to aid defamiliarization, with the hope of leading to more meaningful penitence in Communion.

Seeing Yourself

Before coming to Communion use this prayer of confession by Holly Satterthwaite:

> Merciful Father, I feel worn down and heavy.
> I'm sorry for the hypocrite I can be.
> I'm sorry for hiding my darkness from you. I avoid you, even though I know opening up to you is what's best for me.
> I'm sorry for tailoring a false image of myself to other people rather than embracing your process of transformation.
> Forgive me for how judgmental my heart can be to others.
> Forgive me for the anger I can feel in my mind towards them.
> Forgive me for believing my identity is in my own hands rather than created and shaped by you.
> Thank you for speaking forgiveness and grace over all my sins.
> Thank you for never giving up on me.

18. Hobbs, "Holy Ground."

Thank you for loving me with a steadfast love.
Amen[19]

Place a full-size mirror in front of the elements of bread and wine. Invite the congregation to come forward, one at a time. As they hear the words "The body of Christ broken for you. . . . The blood of Christ shed for you," they see the reflection of themselves in the mirror.

Cross and Communion Table

Artist and craftsman in wood Stephen Owen created a lectern and communion table for Millmead's (Guildford Baptist Church, UK) chapel.[20] Carved in oak, the lectern is pierced by an iron nail at the base, a stark reminder of the price Jesus paid for our redemption. Cracks have developed at the wooden base, where the congregation can tuck prayers of confession. The communion table has a gaping hole in its base, a reminder of the empty tomb. Images of the pieces can be projected as you come to Communion.

Hard Stones

Read the story of the woman caught in adultery who was about to be stoned to death (John 8:1–12) or show a clip from one of the Gospel films. Jesus said, "Let the one who has never sinned throw the first stone!" Before Communion, give each person a stone. Invite them to think about a time when they have judged someone or wanted to hurt them. Tell them to feel the stone in their hands. As people come to Communion, they lay their stones down on the communion table before taking the bread and wine, a sign of surrendering judgment to God.

Clean Stone

Find some muddy stones and wash them clean in a bowl of water. Alternatively, place a bowl of water next to some pens (the washable ink variety). Invite people to write on the stones where they have sinned against God and their fellow human beings.

19. Sattherwaite, *Spiritual Detox*, 116.

20. Owen, "Designs in Wood." These pieces won the 2019 Art and Christianity design award for art in a religious context.

Place a card with the prayer below next to the water bowl. As the stones are washed clean, say the words of the Prayer of Preparation from the Church of England:

> Almighty God,
> to whom all hearts are open,
> all desires known,
> and from whom no secrets are hidden:
> cleanse the thoughts of our hearts
> by the inspiration of your Holy Spirit,
> that we may perfectly love you,
> and worthily magnify your holy name;
> through Christ our Lord.
> Amen.[21]

You could write your sins on the stones and then throw them into a pond or the sea, allowing them to sink. Avoid doing this if you have a dog who is wired to retrieve things. I once invited someone to let go of something and, when they threw it into a pond, my labrador promptly retrieved it!

Walking a Labyrinth

Stand at the entrance of a labyrinth. Say a prayer asking Jesus to walk with you. As you begin walking, tell Jesus what you have done that may have grieved him. Offer those things to him as you walk together. You might want to say "the Jesus Prayer" as you walk: "Lord Jesus Christ, Son of God, have mercy on me, a sinner." When you reach the center of the labyrinth, stand still or kneel and offer thanks for God's mercy. Ask the Lord to show you how he sees you now. Walk out of the labyrinth saying a "breath" prayer of one word which you repeat (for example: "Forgiven," "Child of God," "Set free").[22] If you do not have access to a large labyrinth then you can use a finger labyrinth.

---

21. The Church of England, "Prayer of Preparation."
22. You could walk the labyrinth barefoot. Feeling the ground beneath us can remind us that we come from dust and to dust we will return.

Broken Tiles

In the course book *Imaging the Story*, the biblical story of salvation is put in conversation with visual art. Participants read Gen 1–2 and paint a tile with something they want to celebrate in creation (e.g., an animal or plant). Next, participants read Gen 3 and beyond to see how sin fractures human relationships with God, with each other, and with the natural world. Later, in Gen 6, they read of God's regret at human wickedness, which led to the flood.

In response, participants take someone else's tile, go outside, and smash it into pieces. Holding the broken fragments, they name the damage they have done or have had done to them through sin. In silence, they place the tile pieces before God, ideally on a communion table, meditating on a Penitential Psalm like:

> My sacrifice, O God, is a broken spirit;
> a broken and contrite heart
> you, God, will not despise.
> (Ps 51:17 NIV)

A participant from the *Imaging the Story* course run in Haslemere (UK) wrote:

> It felt awful smashing someone else's tile, breaking all the creativity, love and pleasure they had put into painting it. It ... brought home how our sin and broken world breaks God's heart. It felt so wrong destroying someone else's creation. Holding the tile piece reinforced that we had destroyed something which was beautiful and was now broken, with rough edges. Inwardly I wept with God. I had to look away as I smashed the tiles. It felt like wanton destruction of something beautiful.

When we come to Christ's death and resurrection, participants take part in a communal art project, gluing tile fragments onto strips of Perspex. Slowly the form of a cross takes shape and is hung in the sanctuary. As we share in Christ's brokenness and suffering, so too we share in his resurrection, along with the whole of creation.

Ash Wednesday

Lent has traditionally provided a time for penitence for the Christian community. It begins on Ash Wednesday. Coming from a nonconformist tradition, I still remember being "ashed" at my first Ash Wednesday service. It was a humbling experience. Ash and oil are mixed together and these words said:

> Let us receive these ashes as a sign of the spirit of penitence with which we shall keep this season of Lent. God our Father, you create us from the dust of the earth: grant that these ashes may be for us a sign of our penitence and a symbol of our mortality; for it is by your grace alone that we receive eternal life in Jesus Christ our Saviour. Amen.[23]

Psalm 102 can also be used to prepare for the ashing, particularly verses 3–4 and 9 (NIV):

> For my days vanish like smoke;
> my bones burn like glowing embers.
> My heart is blighted and withered like grass;
> I forget to eat my food. . . .
> For I eat ashes as my food
> and mingle my drink with tears.

The congregation approaches the celebrant and a sign of the cross is marked on each forehead in ash, with the words: "Remember that you are dust, and to dust you shall return. Turn away from sin and be faithful to Christ."

Tears of St. Peter

In the art installation *Tears of Saint Peter*, Brazilian artist Vinicius Silva de Almeida reveals the healing power of tears. The hung installation consists of 6,000 light bulbs filled with water.[24] The effect is one of raindrops, or tears, a reminder of the tears that Peter shed when he betrayed Jesus (Luke 22:56–62). Yet tears formed part of Peter's journey to restoration. Peter was privileged to be the first male disciple to see the risen Christ, and he later became the "rock" upon which Christ built the church. Unlike Judas, who closed himself off from divine mercy, Peter stayed open and was thus able to avail himself of God's grace. His tears of penitence

---

23. The Church of England, "Imposition of Ashes at Home."
24. Antonova, "Repentance (Transforming Tears)."

brought healing. The installation reminds us that this journey to restoration passes through repentance.[25]

Almeida's art installation could be displayed on a screen with, for example:

> I am worn out from my groaning.
> All night long I flood my bed with weeping
> and drench my couch with tears.
> My eyes grow weak with sorrow;
> they fail because of all my foes.
> Away from me, all you who do evil,
> for the Lord has heard my weeping.
> (Ps 6:6–8 NIV)

Rarely is there room for such lachrymal response in Protestant worship. Yet tears are cleansing as well as releasing. After crying, people often speak of feeling more at peace, resolved, and even cleaner. Tears can carry the toxins away, like confession.[26]

A Book of Hours

The Penitential Psalms are regularly incorporated into the text of a standard book of hours. Making a book of hours or a breviary during Lent can be a good way to meditate on these psalms. A book of hours can be made by painting over a hardcover baby book in gesso and then devoting each double page to an "office," with the corresponding psalm and related image. For example:

- The depths/*De profundis* (Ps 130)
- Couch drenched with tears (Ps 6)
- Piercing arrows (Ps 38)
- Crushed bones (Ps 51)
- Broken spirit . . . contrite heart (Ps 51)
- Waiting for the Lord/watchmen (Ps 130)

Below is a table of the offices with times and suggested readings.[27]

---

25. Antonova, "Repentance (Transforming Tears)."

26. Satterthwaite, *Spiritual Detox*, 75.

27. These suggestions are adapted from Case-Green and Sakakini, *Imaging the Story*, 118–19.

Name of Office	Time	Readings
Vigils	2:00 a.m.	Ps 6; Ps 95:1
Lauds	6:00 a.m.	Ps 32; Ps 67
Terce	9:00 a.m.	Ps 38; Ps 121
Sext	12 noon	Ps 51; Ps 123
None	3:00 p.m.	Ps 102: Ps 126
Vespers	6:00 p.m.	Ps 130; Luke 1:46–55
Compline	9:00 p.m.	Ps 143; Ps 91

A breviary is a smaller object and can be carried in one's pocket. It can be made as follows:

1. Cut eight pieces of rectangular card to pocket-size.
2. Punch a hole at the end of each piece.
3. Write, paint, or print your name or initials on the first piece of card.
4. Using the table above, write the title and time of day of each office on each separate card beginning with Vigils.
5. Create a design for the theme of each particular "hour" and select a verse from a Penitential Psalm.[28]

Kyrie Confession

A *Kyrie*[29] confession can be led by two people standing with their backs to each other, each offering a bidding in turn, such as:

> Christ the light of the world has come to dispel
> the darkness of our hearts.
> In his light let us examine ourselves and confess our sins.[30]

CONCLUSION

The Penitential Psalms contain a rich array of visual images that help us engage in repentance with the whole of our being. The prayer activities outlined above not only defamiliarize familiar images in order that we see

---

28. Case-Green and Sakakini, *Imaging the Story*, 118.
29. "*Kyrie*" is Greek for Lord.
30. The Church of England, "B Penitence."

them afresh, they also break up the hard ground of our hearts and prepare us, by God's grace, for restoration. Such activities are never ends in themselves: they are only ever windows. A decade before the iconoclasm of Oliver Cromwell destroyed much of England's Christian art, the poet-priest George Herbert wrote:

> Doctrine and life, colors and light, in one
> When they combine and mingle, bring
> A strong regard and awe; but speech alone
> Doth vanish like a flaring thing,
> And in the ear, not conscience, ring.[31]

BIBLIOGRAPHY

Allender, Dan. *Sabbath: The Ancient Practices*. Nashville: Thomas Nelson, 2009.

Antonova, Clemena. "Repentance (Transforming Tears)." The Visual Commentary on Scripture. https://thevcs.org/peters-denial-christ#repentance-transforming-tears.

Arterburn, Stephen, and David Stoop. *The Life Recovery Workbook for Sexual Integrity*. Colorado Springs: Tyndale, 2020.

Case-Green, Karen, and Gill Sakakini. *Imaging the Story*. Eugene, OR: Cascade, 2017.

The Church of England. "B Penitence." https://www.churchofengland.org/prayer-and-worship/worship-texts-and-resources/common-worship/common-material/new-patterns-12.

———. "Morning Prayer, Order One: Prayer of Preparation." https://www.churchofengland.org/prayer-and-worship/worship-texts-and-resources/common-worship/holy-communion-service.

———. "The Imposition of Ashes at Home." https://www.churchofengland.org/sites/default/files/2021-02/the-imposition-of-ashes-210201-final_0.pdf.

Comer, John Mark. *Practicing the Way: Be with Jesus. Become Like Him. Do as He Did.* London: SPCK, 2024.

De Quincey, Thomas. *Autobiographical Sketches*. Boston: Ticknor, Reed, and Fields, 1853.

Eliot, T. S. *Four Quartets*. London: Faber and Faber, 1944.

Herbert, George. *The Complete English Poems*. Edited by J. Tobin. London: Penguin, 1991.

Hobbs, Paul. "Holy Ground Project." https://www.arthobbs.com.

Manney, Jim. "Examen Prayer Card." https://www.ignatianspirituality.com/examen-prayer-card.

Owen, Stephen. "Designs in Wood." Stephen Owen. https://www.stephenowen.com.

Satterthwaite, Howard. *Spiritual Detox*. London: SPCK, 2021.

Saunders, Maryanne. "The (Gender) Politics of Penitence." The Visual Commentary on Scripture. https://thevcs.org/redeeming-sinful-woman.

Soskice, Janet. *Metaphor and Religious Language*. Oxford: Clarendon, 1985.

---

31. Herbert, *Poems*, 61–62.

13

The Seven

A Prosimetrum

EDWARD CLARKE

IT TOOK ME TWO Lents to write my Penitential Psalms, poems which now form part of my collection, *A Book of Psalms*, published by Paraclete Press in 2020. These poems are not usually translations or versifications: they are conversations with, and hesitations about, the ancient texts. You may see them as slightly unruly imitations or transplantations of their originals, although they are intended to be poems in their own right.[1] The making of my book felt like an initiation, and I began to see the book of Psalms as the two-doored cave of the Bible, with the seven I shall discuss here stationed along its dark and brightening passages. Since my engagement with the Penitential Psalms is also a record of my deepening relationship with the book of Psalms as a whole, I will describe my journey through it.

Although my book must have been conceived when I made a version of Ps 1 in heroic couplets in the autumn of 2015, I did not then proceed in a straightforward way from 1 to 150. Instead, I made a version of Ps 2 in heterometric stanzas, and then fled the Psalms altogether for a year, only to find, the following autumn while taking stock of my work, that I had, in fact, been making poems out of different psalms without really knowing it. From then on, until the autumn of 2018, I wrote nothing but Psalm poems, selecting my source text for each poem initially by way of a sortes, but soon taking the pseudepigraphic superscriptions of the

---

1. See Clarke, *Book of Psalms*, 7.

Psalms as a guide, and beginning with the Sons of Korah sequence before moving on to those related to Asaph.

It was Lent 2017 by the time I had finished the Asaph Psalms, and so I turned to the Penitential Psalms, or "Lent's string of prayers,"[2] only managing 6, 32, 38, and 51, before Easter. Then I returned to Ps 3 to engage with those traditionally attributed to David in the order in which they are presented. I would have been a good way through the David Psalms by the time it was Lent again, and I made versions of 130 and 143 in the spring of 2018. (I had already written my version of 102 in the summer of 2016 before I knew really that I was making Psalm poems.) Finally, I continued to the end of David's Psalms, and then turned slightly on my tracks to tackle the Songs of Ascent and doxologies of book 5, revisiting 130 in the process.

When I encountered Ps 6 then, I was still at quite an early stage of my journey through the book, and yet to deal with most of the other David Psalms. My poem stays quite close to the structure of the original text as I tried to work out a new idiom of complaint and invented a new stanza to serve my purposes. Some of the synonymous repetition of cola of the Hebrew poetry is present in my poem, even as I try to exploit the distinctive resources of English poetry:

> O God, don't bollock me in anger,
> Don't rebuke me hotly,
> Stoop, God, over my sunken state,
> Splint, God, my bones that shake:
>   My soul shakes greatly,
>   And you, God, how much longer?
>
> Return to me, airlift my soul,
> Save me for sake of kindness,
> Or just because in death there's no
> Memento that I know:
>   Inside the blindness
>   Of earth just earth to hold.
>
> I flood my couch with heavy tears
> And make my bed high seas:
> I swim to gasping point by night,
> My eyes without eyesight,
>   Like enemies
>   That rain archaic spears.

2. Clarke, *Book of Psalms*, 49.

> Stop making trouble, and God receives
>   The cry of my tears, and God
> Receives my prayer, and God has heard
>   His song: let all I feared
>   Shake as a wood
>   That turns against seared leaves.[3]

Now, as I reread the poem in Lent 2024, its intensification of clasp rhyme brings to mind enfolding wings in stanza 1, the suffocation of the grave in stanza 2, and the all-encompassing darkness of night in stanza 3. The heterometric form of each stanza of the poem, with lines indented according to their metrical length, is made to be in a kind of counterpoint to that pattern. There is discordance between rhyme and metrical shape, since my tetrameters, trimeters, and dimeters form a pattern—434323—which does not quite match the rhyme scheme of abccba: ababcb would be a better fit, if rhymes were meant to correspond with metrical lengths of lines, as they almost do in George Herbert's "The Flower," whose stanzas mine recall in their diminished form. But then the speaker of my poem is in a dire and discordant state, shipwrecked on the cares of this world, drowning in the sea of time and space, and praying for a rescue helicopter.

I must have intended the wood at the end of my poem to be another symbol of life on earth, thinking of the beginning of Dante's *Divine Comedy* or Uccello's painting *The Hunt* in the Ashmolean. This wood is not in the original psalm, but its vexed state comes out of me pondering the old Hebrew text. I would have been struggling with the KJV—"Let all mine enemies be ashamed and sore vexed" (Ps 6:10)[4]—and trying to draw out literal senses at the heart of the original words, finding palpitation and shaking in "sore vexed" and paleness in "ashamed." The enemies are internalized into my fears in my poem and compared with a wood in the process of turning on itself and shedding its "yellow, and black, and pale, and hectic red"[5] leaves in an autumn storm. This wood could also stand for me writing this new kind of poem and turning against a secular idiom or last season's pages of nature poetry. The figure on my couch in this poem, and I should add that I do write on my couch in the early hours of the morning, is juxtaposed in the living room of my mind with

---

3. Clarke, *Book of Psalms*, 14–15.

4. All quotations from the Holy Bible, in this chapter, are from the King James Version, 1611 Edition.

5. From "Ode to the West Wind"; see Shelley, *Major Works*, 412.

the figure on Wordsworth's couch "in vacant or in pensive mood" whose heart "dances with the Daffodils."[6]

By the time I was ready for 32, there must have been daffodils sprouting, and perhaps that accounts for the bulbs in my version of it, although I thought I was meditating on Henry Vaughan's rumination of Herbert's "The Flower," "I Walk'd the Other Day." The opening formulation, "When first," also calls into play Herbert's second Jordan poem in *The Temple*, to signify that my poem is written in imitation of it:

> When first I tried to make your songs my own,
> Without much knowledge, how your language works,
> Or even how it sounds, spoken or sung,
> Quickly I paged throughout concordances
> And let mine eyes run under splendid entries
> In massive dictionaries, down passages
> Compiled so many centuries ago.
> I thought your verses fructifying soil,
> The passages at last a garden's paths,
> And so I dug for primary roots of words,
> But found my ignorant, literal style only covered
> My sins in so much soil, and not at all
> As God would, had I worked to lever them
> Clean from out the cluttered ground. How hard
> For a man to be righteous without his work. How hard
> For me to say at last: "Blessed is he
> Whose transgression is forgiven, whose sin is covered."[7]

By the end of the poem, I seem to have taken the whispered advice of Herbert's "friend" in the second Jordan poem, as I *"copie out"*[8] the opening line from the psalm in the KJV, as if I am about to begin again. The complex of allusions here and the slightly archaic register reveal my trepidation at undertaking this book and finding the voice I need to rise to the Psalms. I seem to need all the support I can get, and there is a self-consciousness to this piece of blank verse: the poem is no doubt about my remaking of Ps 6 only a week or so before. A few months later, I will be rereading the whole of Herbert's *The Temple* and Vaughan's *Silex Scintillans*, two major models for me in this work, and taking classes to learn Biblical Hebrew to make the most out of Brown-Driver-Briggs and

---

6. From "I Wandered Lonely as a Cloud"; see Wordsworth, *Major Works*, 304.
7. Clarke, *Book of Psalms*, 44.
8. Herbert, *English Poems*, 367.

Strong's *Exhaustive Concordance*. I must have felt, in contemplating this Psalm in early 2017, "as the horse, *or* as the mule *which* have no understanding: whose mouth must be held in with bit and bridle, least they come neere unto thee" (Ps 32:9), but praying for instruction and to be taught which way to go.

When I thought of the physical sickness of the psalmist in 38 in terms of the wretched lovesickness of Bernard de Ventadorn in "Can vei la lauzeta mover," I was still looking for guidance in the European tradition of poetry, this time going back to its very origins to find my way through these even older songs:

> Did he cry, Ai, las,
> The man that praised the lark
> Against the light, because
> He felt in love a dark
>   Discrepancy
> Like that between Lent's string of prayers
>   And the infancy
> Of spring for which the winter cares.
>
> His lady's stealthy absence
> Is God asleep in man,
> Each dawn of ours the fragments
> Of light before the sun
>   In Genesis.
> Believe him when he says he'll die:
>   Such sicknesses
> Manifest the oldest lie.
>
> And do not flatter yourself
> He led a life like yours
> Of lazy affairs: your health
> Disguises sinful sores
>   That man looks on;
> He found himself a remedy
>   Of infinite song
> And freed his wounds' old melody.[9]

I would have been immersing myself in commentaries on the Psalms at this stage of writing, and turning back to those books now, it seems that I can retrace the steps of my making of this poem as I attempted to

---

9. Clarke, *Book of Psalms*, 49–50.

diagnose de Ventadorn's lovesickness and David's ailments. Henry Wansbrough showed me that "such a rich cornucopia of horrors simultaneously cannot be meant literally,"[10] and I can see that I underlined just one sentence in the entry on this psalm in my copy of the *New International Commentary* on the Psalms: explicating verses 3–8, the authors say, "This section speaks not of a physical ailment, but of how sin and guilt feel."[11] But it would have been Ambrose who captured my imagination:

> Now look at some lascivious youth openly displaying his debauchery; his life is spent in love affairs; he lounges around like that rich man who was clothed in fine linen and purple; daily he enjoys the most sumptuous dinners. . . . He is perfectly delighted with himself and flatters himself that he smells sweetly. . . . He does not know that his soul is bleeding and festering, and he will not accept that his wounds are foul-smelling. . . . But the holy prophet David found for himself a remedy of everlasting salvation. For he freely spoke of his own wounds and confessed that his sores were foul and festering because of his foolishness.[12]

That lascivious youth is addressed in my poem, but I must confess here that it is really me or my younger self, caught up in the manifold pleasures of this world, whom I admonish. The manifold things of this world can be explained as coming from a pure unity in terms of an "irradiation from a luminary,"[13] and so "each dawn of ours" is really "the fragments / Of light before the sun / In Genesis": that "light of mine eies," that "is gone from me" (Ps 38:10), or which I cannot perceive when I am buried in materialism and sick to death of empirical analysis and debauchery. Like Coleridge and William Blake, I see that each of us has a responsibility to complete "the eternal act of creation in the infinite I AM"[14] in our own radiant art: "A Poet a Painter a Musician an Architect: the Man / Or Woman who is not one of these is not a Christian."[15] At the end of the decaying kind of time, the poet in my poem "found himself a remedy / Of infinite song / And freed his wounds' old melody," and so, as one song calls another, "I wil powre upon the house of David, and upon

10. Wansbrough, *Psalms*, 60.
11. deClaissé-Walford et al., *Book of Psalms*, 358.
12. Ambrose, *Commentary on Twelve Psalms*, 123–24.
13. Plotinus, *Enneads* 5.3.15, 454.
14. Coleridge, *Biographia Literaria* 1:304.
15. From *Annotations to the Laocoön*; see Blake, *Complete Poetry and Prose*, 274.

the inhabitants of Jerusalem the spirit of grace and of supplications, and they shall looke upon me whom they have pearced."[16]

If the crucifixion can be discerned in the background of my conversation with 38, then the first stanza of the next poem I made, 51, turns that image around to contemplate March blossom appearing, just as Herbert's poem, "The Flower," appears after or at the foot of his poem, "The Cross," in *The Temple*. Like Andrew Marvell who asks to be turned into an "inverted Tree,"[17] I take guidance from Plato:

> Now we ought to think of the most sovereign part of our soul as god's gift to us, given to be our guiding spirit. This, of course, is the type of soul that, as we maintain, resides in the top part of our bodies. It raises us up away from the earth and toward what is akin to us in heaven, as though we are plants grown not from the earth but from heaven.[18]

The lascivious youth addressed in 38, who is "absorbed in his appetites," now devotes himself in 51 to "the love of learning and to true wisdom"[19] through re-creation of the Psalms and the making of a new song. In the first two stanzas the poet prays for help in making his poem, a prayer made out of words that ask to be cleansed of mundane use and commerce; and then a voice is imagined as speaking out of the incipient poem from its future in eternity:

> The flower forgives the branch its falling short
> Of March and would identify itself
> With its ideal, the fruit it must have caught
> Of air, another season's massive wealth:
> Blot out those lines of mine that miss their mark
> With flowers of loving kindness, flowers of March.
>
> A multitude of words went out to me
> And would be washed of business back in town.
> Cleanse us, they said, of our iniquity,
> Unloose us from desire as you stoop down.
> Next day, as I was coming up for air,
> A voice reminded me, I am your prayer.

---

16. Zech 12:10 KJV; see also John 19:37.
17. From "Upon Appleton House"; see Marvell, *Poems* 1:80.
18. From *Timaeus* 90a; see Plato, *Complete Works*, 1288–89.
19. From *Timaeus* 90b; see Plato, *Complete Works*, 1289.

> Against you only have I sinned, you might
> Be justified in saying (when you shall speak):
> I was conceived in play and shaped in doubt,
> But do you see I am the truth you seek,
> The Russian doll that has no other in it,
> The harsh note in the music of the linnet.
>
> Cleanse me with hyssop: I shall find your voice.
> Wash me and I am whiter than flowers of snow.
> Play me back: my broken bones rejoice.
> Blot out the iniquity of all I know.
> Create in me a clean hospitable heart,
> My lines shall sing as windows do in March.[20]

I recall the old pear tree in our back garden in Oxford when I read these lines, now sadly pollarded, and the blackbirds amongst its snowy blossom, whose song resonated through our back windows, then open at the end of winter. The psalmist asks to be washed so he can be even whiter than that snow. My poem imagines the poet as John baptizing words in the wilderness and time stopping as a voice suddenly appears in his poem. Herbert piously wished, in a letter to his mother, "that my poor Abilities in *Poetry* shall be all, and ever consecrated to Gods glory" [emphasis original],[21] eventually baptizing his art in his two Jordan poems. In this poem, the poet would, like Vaughan, make "a wise exchange of *vain* and *vitious subjects*, for *divine Themes* and *Celestial praise*" [emphasis original],[22] and so the seven Penitential Psalms become a kind of soul-making ladder or kabbalistic tree for the poet to climb in his work.

As I have outlined above, the next poem in this sequence, 102, or "The Sparrow," was made in July 2016, about a year before the four that come before it in this submerged sequence in my *Book of Psalms*, but it takes on a new resonance as part of the upbuilding Seven: I did after all decide to subtitle it "A Penitential Psalm," as I did the others, when I put it in the book. In the original Psalm it is hoped that the Lord "shall build up Zion" (Ps 102:25) as "of old hast thou laid the foundation of the earth: and the heavens *are* the work of thy hands" (Ps 102:16). In my poem, all the sixteenth- and seventeenth-century translators of the Bible, epitomized by Tyndale and the makers of the Douay-Rheims and Geneva

---

20. Clarke, *Book of Psalms*, 61–62.
21. Walton, *Lives*, 268.
22. Vaughn, *Works*, 558.

Bibles, are imagined as builders, "all collectively labouring to embody a vision whose realization will be only when all is done 'on earth as it is in heaven,' according to the archetype of the human Imagination."[23] There is also an allusion to Ps 118 in the opening: "The stone *which* the builders refused: is become the head *stone* of the corner" (Ps 118:22). Christ liked to quote those words, but when Peter heard them, he projected his new name and saw Christ as a "living Stone" (1 Pet 2:4), and that we too, "as lively stones, are built up a spiritual house, an holy Priesthood, to offer up spiritual sacrifice, acceptable to God by Jesus Christ" (1 Pet 2:5):

> Rebuilders of the book of John and Moses
>   Refused no stone, thank God,
> To make a voice for us, in wildernesses
>   Of Antwerp, Rheims, Geneva,
>   In prison mumbling,
>   In fear and trembling,
>   The time it takes the weaver
>   To wake up in the wood,
> The space of no career or priesthood.
>
> Madly they hoped the ploughboy and the housewife,
>   The maid among the kine
> And even the glowing traveller, the south side
>   Of the Downs, would hum
>   Unto the farms
>   New tunes for Psalms
>   As at the beam of the loom,
>   And souls would be refined
> Threaded phrase by threaded line.
>
> But did you let their cry come unto thee,
>   O Lord, and hear their prayer?
> Incline an ear unto eternity
>   To ease a troubled heart:
>   Hide not thy face
>   These fragile days
>   That fall upon the hearth.
>   For I am lit with care
> That winds itself out everywhere.
>
> And I have watched, and am become as a sparrow

---

23. Raine, *Golgonooza*, 107.

> Alone upon the lead.
> O Lord, how amiable is this house, my narrow
> Perch, thine holy book,
> This sacred space
> That owes its use
> To nothing much: the nook
> The swallow recoats for her bed,
> The door through which thou shalt raise the dead.[24]

The weaver in the first stanza is Bottom in Shakespeare's *A Midsummer Night's Dream*, but, "if it be the ploughman guiding his plough, let him chant in his own language the mystic psalms. If it be the weaver sitting at his loom, let him ease his labour by citing in rhythm something from a gospel."[25] Translators of the Bible, from Jerome to Erasmus to Tyndale, have hoped such men and women might sing "alleluia" and rouse themselves with David. Unfortunately, Tyndale did not live to translate the Psalms, and most English poets have drawn on Miles Coverdale's translation of them, which was included unrevised in the *Book of Common Prayer* for centuries, and so familiar from church services. The liturgical reformations of the twentieth century—"a fad of a few crazy priests"[26]—meant that Coverdale's translations were rewritten by W. H. Auden and others, and my preferred translation is the 1611 text of the KJV, made by scholars who went back to the original Hebrew to refine Coverdale's use of the Latin Vulgate and Luther. In my poem I imagine myself as "a sparrowe alone upon the house top" (Ps 102:7), a building which I see as emblematic of that great edifice of the Bible in English. By the end of the poem, though, I was also thinking, more hopefully, of words of Ps 84: "The sparrowe hath found an house, and the swallow a nest for her selfe, where she may lay her young" (Ps 84:3). Can it be true, I must be asking myself, that the book of Psalms provides a space or "Coigne of Vantage" for me to make my pendent poem and "procreant Cradle?"[27] The birds at the end of this poem I now equate with the blossom in my remaking of 51.

---

24. Clarke, *Book of Psalms*, 108–9.

25. Erasmus, *Collected Work* 45:18.

26. Auden, 1971 letter to Johnson, quoted in Johnson, *Auden, the Psalms, and Me* 15.

27. Shakespeare, *Macbeth* 1.6.7 and 8, as quoted in Shakespeare, *Complete Works* 3:502.

The first part of my version of 130 was written in July 2018, so two years after my version of 102, as I made my way cheerfully through the Psalms of Ascents to complete my engagement with the book of Psalms as a whole. I would have been teaching in a summer school in Oxford and looking forward to a few weeks in Italy. In my poem, I imagine this leg of the journey of my book as a walk through the Cinque Terre in Liguria, and that I have met my earlier rendering of 130, alone, drunk, and despairing, in one of the fishing villages: Vernazza, as I recall. That earlier version, made in Lent a few months before, constitutes the final two stanzas of the poem, in short measure:

> Working my way
> Through the Songs of Ascents,
> My head and heart already on holiday,
> Upon a path that runs through terraces,
>   Spilling themselves, like shelves of scent
>   Of herbs and citruses
>   A hand has swept across and smashed,
> I found I reached the penitential calm
>   Of Lent's penultimate Psalm,
> My version of it against a wall, trashed.

>   Trashed and crying
>   Out of the depths
> It must have taken most of the night trying
> To reach, alone, out in the bars about
>   The town, I guess, its vows unkept
>   Because Lent's gone, no doubt.
>   I'll wait with it the rest of the night.
> It is a voice, which lacks salt, that I must stir,
>   To which I add salt, a year
> And a day, tasting to get it just right, or upright.

>   Out of the depths I cried to you:
>   Hear my voice and lend an ear.
> If you should watch and mark iniquity
>   Who stands? Forgive and then you're feared.

>   I wait and wait and hope for word,
>   "More than they that watch for the morning":
> Let us hope in loving kindness, "*I say,*

More than they that watch for the morning" [emphasis original].[28]

Those final two poor little stanzas of mine have had to bear the attention of another grander and altogether more exuberant poem that would take care of them, and now these two poems, shackled together, have been brought into this prosimetrum. What do they have to say for themselves? Each might plead that he represents an extreme of engagement with a psalm. The stanzas in short measure are really just a versification of the psalm in the KJV, made with some consultation of the original Hebrew and written in the tradition of Sternhold and Hopkins, in a form that could be sung to any number of tunes in church. In this way they can be related to Herbert's "The 23 Psalm," Vaughan's "Psalm 121," and John Milton's translations of Pss 80–88. The form of the first two extravagant stanzas of my poem is in the tradition of the serious playfulness of the Sidneys' quite literary and heterometric versions of the Psalms, although I am not at all translating in this part of the poem. The closest early modern precedent for the kind of engagement you find with the text here might be Herbert's calling of Ps 38 into "The Quip," which was perhaps inspired by Ambrose too.

Like Herbert I open my Bible and wish "that I knew how all thy lights combine, / And the configurations of their glorie! / Seeing not onely how each verse doth shine, / But all the constellations of the storie."[29] When I open my 1611 text of the KJV to read Ps 143, conveniently, I see a star in the margin showing how verse 2 "marks" Exod 34:7 and that "both do make a motion / Unto"[30] Gal 2:16. David implores the Lord: "Enter not into judgment with thy servant: for in thy sight shall no man living be justified" (Ps 130:2). The Lord proclaims his name to Moses, descending in a cloud to Sinai, "keeping mercie for thousands, forgiving iniquitie and transgression and sinne, and that will by no meanes cleere *the guiltie*, visiting the iniquitie of the fathers upon the children, and upon the childrens children, unto the third and to the fourth generation."[31] But we know with Paul "that a man is not justified by the works of the Law, but by the faith of Jesus Christ, even we have beleeved in Jesus Christ, that we might be justified by the faith of Christ, and not by the workes of the

---

28. Clarke, *Book of Psalms*, 137–38.
29. From "H. Scriptures II"; see Herbert, *English Poems*, 210.
30. From "H. Scriptures II"; see Herbert, *English Poems*, 210.
31. Exod 34:7.

Law: for by the workes of the Law shall no flesh be justified."[32] My final "Penitential Psalm" begins by wondering how these three texts "make up some Christians destinie":[33]

> Do you have faith in me? Then hear my prayer.
> Or did you take the shape of every child
> That's born, and grow up through two thousand years,
> Only to hatch a plot to have me killed?
> My eyes are overwhelmed: I see no God.
> My ears are desolate: I hear of none.
> But then the blackbird sings his infinite song:
> I see the blossoms snow on paths you trod.
> I remember the days of old and meditate
> On all your works, the work of your skilled hands,
> And stretch forth my blind hands to pray and take:
> My soul thirsts after you as a thirsty land.[34]

Paul understood, "I am crucified with Christ. Nevertheless, I live, yet not I, but Christ liveth in me."[35] Jung perceived that "God, in the shape of the Holy Ghost, puts up his tent in man, for he is obviously minded to realize himself continually not only in Adam's descendants, but in an indefinitely large number of believers, and possibly in mankind as a whole."[36] The desolate speaker of the first part of my engagement with 143, emblematic of late modern mankind, puts himself into "that conflict into which Christianity inevitably leads," that burden under which we still groan: "*God wanted to become man, and still wants to*" [emphasis original].[37] He also remembers, "Even the enlightened person remains what he is, and is never more than his own limited ego before the One who dwells in him, whose form has no knowable boundaries, who encompasses him on all sides, fathomless as the abysms of the earth and vast as the sky."[38]

The words of David "do finde me out, & parallels bring, / And in another make me understood."[39] My poem has another twelve-line terza

---

32. Gal 2:16.
33. From "H. Scriptures II"; see Herbert, *English Poems*, 210.
34. Clarke, *Book of Psalms*, 148–49.
35. Gal 2:20.
36. Jung, *Answer to Job*, 84.
37. Jung, *Answer to Job*, 153.
38. Jung, *Answer to Job*, 180.
39. From "H. Scriptures II"; see Herbert, *English Poems*, 210.

rima stanza, which stays quite close to the end of the original psalm as it prays to "the One who dwells in him," or "the infinite I am" at the limit of the poem: this quite autonomous living subject that the quickening mind, in the act of making the poem, perceives and half creates:

> Hear quickly the headlong fall of my poor words,
> Hide not your face from them lest they assume
> The haggard face of office-going herds
> That hurry on down as if to be exhumed.
> Cause me to hear your loving kindness this morning:
> I trust that I will lift myself in such talk.
> Pull me from plots of those without your learning:
> Cause me to know the way to take my walk.
> Teach me to act with your imagination.
> Lead me into the land of prophecy.
> Quicken me with honest indignation.
> I am that man that I might write and see.[40]

The medium of my poem is the same medium as the conversation of commuters, that deathly crowd that keeps on flowing over London Bridge, but it prays that its words might be heard so that they may be cleansed of business back in town. In it I ask for guidance as I make my *Book of Psalms* before my small children awake: "Cause me to hear your loving kindness this morning." Remembering the first psalm, "Cause me to know the way to take my walk," for "Prosperous is that man, or blessed with joy, / Who has not walked through streets and fields of his day / In agitated company."[41] When my poem says "Quicken me with honest indignation," you might hear the words Isaiah spoke to Blake: "I saw no God. [sic] nor heard any, in a finite organical perception; but my senses discover'd the infinite in every thing, and as I was then perswaded. & remain confirm'd; that the voice of honest indignation is the voice of God, I cared not for consequences but wrote."[42] Sometimes, like so many today, "My eyes are overwhelmed: I see no God. / My ears are desolate: I hear of none. / But then," even as I write these lines, six or so Lents later, quite literally and spiritually speaking, "the blackbird sings his infinite song: / I see the blossoms snow on paths you trod."

---

40. Clarke, *Book of Psalms*, 149.

41. Clarke, *Book of Psalms*, 9.

42. From Plate 12 of *The Marriage of Heaven and Hell* in Blake, *Complete Poetry and Prose*, 38.

BIBLIOGRAPHY

Ambrose. *Commentary on Twelve Psalms*. Translated by Íde M. Ní Rian. Dublin: Halcyon, 2000.
Blake, William. *The Complete Poetry and Prose*. Edited by David V. Erdman. Berkeley: University of California Press, 2008.
Clarke, Edward. *A Book of Psalms*. Brewster: Paraclete, 2020.
Coleridge, S. T. *Biographia Literaria*. Edited by James Engell and W. Jackson Bate. 2 vols. Princeton: Princeton University Press, 1983.
deClaissé-Walford, Nancy, et al. *The Book of Psalms*. Grand Rapids: Eerdmans, 2014.
Erasmus, Desiderius. *Collected Works of Erasmus: Paraphrase on the Gospel of Matthew, Volume 45*. Edited by Robert D. Sider. Toronto: University of Toronto Press, 2008.
Herbert, George. *The English Poems*. Edited by Helen Wilcox. Cambridge: Cambridge University Press, 2011.
Johnson, J. Chester. *Auden, the Psalms, and Me*. New York: Church Publishing Incorporated, 2017.
Jung, C. G. *Answer to Job*. London: Routledge, 1987.
Marvell, Andrew. *The Poems and Letters*. Edited by H. M. Margoliouth. Revised by Pierre Legouis. 2 vols. Oxford: Oxford University Press, 1971.
Plato. *Complete Works*. Edited by John M. Cooper. Indianapolis: Hackett, 1997.
Plotinus. *The Enneads*. Translated by Stephen MacKenna. New York: Larson, 1992.
Raine, Kathleen. *Golgonooza, City of Imagination: Last Studies in William Blake*. Ipswich: Golgonooza, 1991.
Shakespeare, William. *Complete Works*. Edited by Herbert Farjeon. 4 vols. London: Nonesuch, 1953.
Shelley, Percy Bysshe. *The Major Works*. Edited by Zachary Leader and Michael O'Neill. Oxford: Oxford University Press, 2003.
Vaughan, Henry. *The Works*. Edited by Donald R. Dickson et al. 3 vols. Oxford: Oxford University Press, 2018.
Walton, Izaak. *The Lives*. Oxford: Oxford University Press, 1927.
Wansbrough, Henry. *The Psalms: A Commentary for Prayer and Reflection*. Abingdon: Bible Reading Fellowship, 2014.
Wordsworth, William. *The Major Works*. Edited by Stephen Gill. Oxford: Oxford University Press, 2000.

Epilogue

Ian Stackhouse

I HAVE BEEN A pastor now for nearly thirty-five years. For all of that time I have been engaged in the usual practices of pastoral care: preaching the word, administering the sacraments, visiting the sick, and so on. What I haven't done so much of, which has surprised me, is receive confession. It's not that it has never happened. Just the other day, someone came to see me who was clearly troubled, and in the course of the conversation asked if they might make a confession. So it happens. But it's quite rare.

Maybe I'm not the kind of pastor someone would want to confess their sins to. The possibility has occurred to me. Or maybe I have an especially holy congregation? Maybe. What is more likely the case, and I can only speak from my own Protestant evangelical tradition, is that confession is just not important anymore (if it ever was, of course, for us non-Catholics). As Eugene Peterson so famously put it: "Instead of attributing the suffering to 'the sins of the fathers,' it has assigned them to the neuroses of the mothers."[1] The mindset that congregants come with these days is much more that of the counselee rather than the penitent; and pastors collude with it by playing the therapist rather than the confessor. Indeed, such is the triumph of the therapeutic within our communities[2] that it is likely that pastors are more conversant these days with Carl Rogers than they are Karl Barth. Speaking about my own seminary training, I recall being expected to know something about depression, which is a good thing of course. What I wasn't required to know, nor was I tutored in, was the anatomy of sin and its cure through confession and absolution.

---

1. Peterson, *Five Smooth Stones*, 138.
2. See Rieff, *Triumph of the Therapeutic*.

As Kathleen Norris points out with reference to the Presbyterian tradition she reconnected with after many years away: our prayers of confession "seem less prayer than a memo from one professional to another. At such times I picture God as a wily writing teacher who leans across the table and says, not at all gently: 'Could you possibly be troubled to say what you mean.'" [sic] To which question Norris replies: "It would be refreshing to answer, simply, 'I have sinned.'"[3]

This unfamiliarity with, or rather the disdain with which we regard the language of penitence goes right through the system, if I can use that phrase to describe our life together. We notice it in our songnody, our youth ministry, and our outreach. I think it was Tom Wright who reminded the creators of the popular Alpha course that the first word of the gospel is "repentance" and that to seek to soften repentance in the interests of relevance is to pay a theological and pastoral price later. As my old mentor used to say, with reference to the easy decisionism which is so much part of our evangelical culture, what you end up with in that scenario is the equivalent of a beautiful black stallion that no one can ride because it has never been broken in. Unfortunately, I have been around too long in this milieu to know how painfully true this can be. What you hope for are people who are teachable, humble, and open to grace; what you get, without that initial puncture of pride, is obstinance, arrogance, and self-righteousness. Add to that the psychology of victimhood which is now so deeply embedded in our culture, and you have a job on your hands.

This is why the project that Mark Whiting has embarked upon to reintroduce the Penitential Psalms is so hopeful. It doesn't sound hopeful. Any book with the word "penitential" in the title is not exactly designed to become a bestseller, certainly not in our times. And penitential psalms are surely the ones you skip over to get to the praise ones, or the ones that make you feel good. But what these psalms teach us is that feeling good can often be a result of facing the bad—of having the courage to own the dark stuff in our lives as a prelude to freedom. Again, in a culture that has made a virtue of playing the victim, taking offense, or blaming others, owning one's own sins is becoming increasingly unfashionable. Easier to highlight structural evil and social injustice than to engage in the rather trivial matter of one's own misdemeanors. But as William Kirk Kilpatrick so wryly puts it in a little-known book, *Psychological Seduction*, with reference to our judgment before God: "I am afraid, alas, the questions

---

3. Norris, *Amazing Grace*, 165.

will be much more personal than that. . . . We shall find that our private lives and our personal sins are taken with quite a bit more seriousness in heaven than our position on global issues."[4]

This being so, then the retrieval of the Penitential Psalms becomes a vital part of our spiritual journey. At some point along the way we have to be able to say with David, "Against you, you only, have I sinned and done what is evil in your sight."[5] We have to feel the terror of being cast away from his presence, otherwise all that we will engage in is what St. Paul calls "worldly sorrow" which is nothing more than regret.[6] I have seen this many times in my pastoral work: embarrassment about being found out—maybe an affair, or a fraud—but nothing close to the contrite and broken heart that elicits God's mercy. One cannot induce this of course. It is a work of the Spirit. But by recovering the language of penitence, which naturally happens if we pray the psalms, then we at least have a chance of saying with David, when confronted by the prophet Nathan, those six most critical words: "I have sinned against the Lord."[7] David could have defended himself. As king, he could have ordered the execution of the prophet for having the temerity to expose his crime. As it was, he took the opportunity to confess his wickedness. Unlike Saul, who fell into himself when he sinned, David fell into God. And although he would live with the consequences of his actions for the rest of his life, Ps 51 sits there as one of the high points of Scripture. This is David at his best. It is why, I believe, he is known as a man after God's own heart. It's not so much his exploits, so much as his ability to bring his whole heart before God.

As we survey the other Penitential Psalms or, better still, pray them, we enter a world that is completely alien to our modern sensibilities. It is a world that is uncomfortably primitive. As far as Ps 38 is concerned, the healing of the body is undoubtedly linked to confession of sin, whereas Ps 32 invokes the notion of God's anger. In Ps 6 we find ourselves bargaining with God to show mercy on the rather dubious basis that no one can praise God from the grave. Scholars get round this, sometimes by humor and sometimes by cynicism. Implicit in their commentary is that anyone with a rational mind wouldn't pray this way. But all that simply confirms to someone like me, who does their theology from below, is that they have never sat in an ordinary Christian congregation. I'm not saying

4. Kilpatrick, *Psychological Seduction*, 88.
5. Ps 51:4 NIV.
6. 2 Cor 7:10.
7. 2 Sam 12:13 NIV.

the theology is sound. I too have problems with a theology that links suffering to sin—as did Jesus of course. But then again, the psalms are not sound. They are real. They are prayers from the depths. They are prayers of a desperate soul. They are prayers of someone who fears they might be forsaken by God. That these notions offend our scholarly reason says more about scholarship than it does about prayers. These are the fears that ordinary people carry. They are more than met in the Penitential Psalms by the mercy of God: "His anger lasts only a moment, but his favor lasts a lifetime."[8] The morning does indeed "bring word of his unfailing love."[9] He will indeed respond to the prayer of the destitute.[10] But not before we have got everything out there, even our most existential fears. Otherwise, what are these psalms doing there? Like the imprecatory psalms, they are there for a reason. They may not be pretty. Real prayer hardly ever is. But they are precious in the life of faith.

How we might reinstate these psalms in a church culture that is largely in reaction to penitential piety is going to prove a challenge. At a time when so few Anglicans know, let alone cherish, the *Book of Common Prayer*; when so many Catholics sit uneasy with the confessional; and when Pentecostals simply don't know what to do in the sanctuary other than praise, then it's going to take some skill. My guess is that it might have to ride on the back of a much bigger project, which is to reintroduce the psalms as a whole. Or maybe wait for a season like Lent and see if that might allow space for the Seven Psalms as something like a prophylactic for the seven deadly sins. Whichever way we go about it, we should be intentional. In my opinion, contemporary spirituality is crying out for it; its content can be so effete as to be dishonest. As Bonhoeffer so wisely discerned, our lack of rigor when it comes to confession—not least our reluctance to confess our sins to one another—eventuates in nothing more than self-forgiveness, which of course is no forgiveness at all.[11] At a time when so much in mainstream culture is about self-actualization, it is going to take some skill to demonstrate that inward penitence, as a mark of the church and a means of grace, need not be the suppression of our individualism, which is what the church is often accused of, but rather its flourishing. In a climate of liberalism, where grace has ended up in some circles as nothing more than sentimentality, the adage of late Victorian

---

8. Ps 30:5 NIV.
9. Ps 143:8
10. Ps 102:17.
11. Bonhoeffer, *Life Together*, 91.

preacher P. T. Forsyth might be worth revisiting: "If we spoke less about God's love and more about his holiness, more about his judgment, we should say much more when we did speak about his love."[12]

Which brings us, without contrivance, to the cross of Christ, because who should be the first beneficiary of its atoning power but the penitent thief? What he was doing there alongside Jesus we don't quite know. Like Barabbas, who quite literally could say that Jesus took *my* place, maybe the man was a revolutionary. Or maybe just a thief. Either way, he knew Jesus was innocent, whereas he was not. His accomplice, the other side of Jesus, was decidedly impenitent. We call him that. Indeed, he mocked Jesus as he hung there on the cross. But this man, with a penitent heart, and believing Jesus to have kingly status, spoke like a true psalmist when he asked that he might be remembered when Jesus came into his kingdom. We tend to think this last-ditch plea is the exception, not the rule. In our tradition we tend to be a bit suspicious of deathbed conversions. But from all that has been said about the Penitential Psalms, maybe Luke is telling us that this desperate plea of the thief on the cross is not the exception but the rule. After all, how does anyone get saved but through penitence and faith? Thank you, Mark, for pulling this collection of essays together. May they prove an agent of renewal in our day.

BIBLIOGRAPHY

Bonhoeffer, Dietrich. *Life Together*. London: SCM, 2015.
Forsyth, P. T. *The Cruciality of the Cross*. Rochester: Stanhope, 1948.
Kilpatrick, William Kirk. *Psychological Seduction: The Failure of Modern Psychology*. London: Arthur James, 1983.
Norris, Kathleen Norris. *Amazing Grace: The Vocabulary of Faith*. New York: Riverhead, 1988.
Peterson, Eugene H. *Five Smooth Stones for Pastoral Work*. Grand Rapids: Eerdmans, 1980.
Rieff, Peter. *The Triumph of the Therapeutic*. New York: Harper & Row, 1966.

---

12. Forsyth, *Cruciality of the Cross*, 39.

Subject Index

Absalom, 35
absolution, 62, 219
Acts, book of, 44, 62
Adam, 51, 95–96, 97, 99, 102, 148, 215
Advent, xiv, 161
Alcuin of York, xiv
Alexander, Gavin, 114
allegory and allegorical, 17, 41–42, 45, 46, 59, 77, 109
Allegri, Gregorio, xiv, xxv, 167
de Almeida, Vinicius Silva, 199, 200
Anglican, 161, 164, 168, 174, 197, 199, 201, 222
Ambrose of Milan, 208, 214
anger. *See* wrath.
Anglican chant, *See* chant.
Anselm of Canterbury, 64–65
Aquinas, Thomas, 27
Arnold, Jonathan, ix, xvii, xxv
arrow/s, 47–48, 94–95, 102, 177, 188, 200
Asaph. *See* Psalms of Asaph.
Asaphite. *See* Psalms of Asaph.
Ash Wednesday, 158, 161, 164, 165, 167, 178, 198–99
Atkins, Sir Ivor, 167
Auden, W. H., 212
Augustine of Hippo, xiii, xiv, xxiii, xxiv, xxvi, 16–18, 41–52, 53, 55, 59, 62, 69, 71, 73, 77, 79–81, 88, 174, 178

Bach, Johann Sebastian, 163, 164, 167, 169
Baggott, L. J., xxiv
Barratt, Alexandra, 77, 78, 79

Baptist, 139, 181, 196
Barth, Karl, 138, 219
Basil of Caesarea, 110
Bathsheba, 28, 29, 49, 164, 192
Beati quorum, 16
beauty, xxv, 159, 187–202
Bede, the Venerable, xiv
Bembo, Francesco, 162
Berlin, Adele, 6, 21, 33, 34, 35
Bernstein, Leonard, 161
Bethge, Eberhard, 138, 146
Blake, Howard, 164
Blake, William, 208, 216
blessed. *See* blessing.
blessing, 14, 16, 24, 33, 44, 45, 46, 48, 132, 134, 183
Blow, John, 161
bones, 22, 25, 28, 31, 42, 43, 57, 109–12, 126, 176, 179, 189, 199, 200, 204, 210
Briggs, Richard S., ix, xvii, xxii, 192
Briggs and Briggs, Charles A. and Emilie Grace, 20, 21, 23, 25, 27, 30, 32, 34
Boethius, 54
Bonhoeffer, Dietrich, xiv, xxiii, xxiv, 137–54, 174, 222
Book of Common Prayer, 16, 104, 158, 161, 163, 212, 222
book/s of hours, xiv, 71, 165, 188, 200
Brampton, Thomas, 74
Brock, Brian, 137
Bruckner, Anton, 161
Brueggemann, Walter, 174, 182
Burroughs, Jeremiah, 131

Subject Index

Byassee, Jason, ix, xvii, xxii, xxiii, 17, 31, 41, 46, 81, 174
Byrd, William, xiv, 162, 166

Calvin, John, xiv, 159–60
Cameron, Michael, 42
Campion, Edmund, 166
Canterbury Tales. *See* Chaucer, Geoffrey.
canticles, 71
Case-Green, Karen, ix, xvii, xxv, 190, 200, 201
Cassiodorus, xiii, xiv, xvii, xxiii, xxiv, xxvi, 16, 53–59, 69, 71–72, 80, 158
chant and chanting, 62, 158, 161, 167, 212
Charpentier, Marc-Antoine, 167
Chaucer, Geoffrey, xiv, 78
chesed, 13, 22, 29, 33, 34, 35, 183, 184, 196
Christ and christological, xxiii, xxiv, xxv, 13, 30, 42, 43–45, 46, 48, 49, 51, 75, 76, 77, 78, 79, 80, 83, 84, 88–102, 111, 112, 117, 123, 127–28, 130, 131, 132, 133, 134, 135, 139–45, 146, 147, 151, 152, 163, 172, 174, 178, 179, 180, 181, 183, 184, 185, 192, 193, 196, 197, 198, 199, 201, 211, 214, 215, 223
Chronicles, Books of, 5
Chrysostom, 62
Church of England. *See* Anglican.
Clarke, Edward, x, xvii, xxv, 203–16
Coleridge, Samuel Taylor, 208
Comer, John Mark, 191, 193
commonplacing, 111, 113
Communion. *See* Eucharist.
compunctio cordis, 62
compunction, 62, 63, 73, 82, 116
concessio, 56–58
Cone, James H., 139
confessio oris, 62, 63
confession and Confession, xiii, 24, 28, 56, 61, 63, 66, 75, 83, 84, 92, 93, 94, 124, 125, 133, 142, 144, 145, 148, 158, 165, 175, 178, 180, 181, 182, 183, 191, 192, 193, 195, 196, 200, 201, 219, 220, 221, 222

Confessions, Augustine's, 41, 49, 79, 94, 95, 96,
Constantinople, 55
contrition and contrite, 28, 30, 57, 61, 65, 72, 83, 84, 149, 188, 193, 198, 200, 221
cor curvum in se, 140, 142, 144, 149, 152
Corinthians, Paul's epistles to the, 48, 49, 110, 142, 148, 151, 221
Council of Chalon-sur-Saône, 60
Coverdale, Miles, 16, 161, 212
Crisler, Channing, x, xvii, xxiii, 12, 13, 97, 174
Croce, Giovanni, 162
Crüger, Johann, 163
cry, 16, 22, 32, 34, 79, 91, 97, 98, 99, 115, 129, 130, 133, 135, 139, 145, 149, 151, 168, 169, 177, 180, 188, 200, 205, 207, 211, 213, 222

Daily Examen, 194
Dante Alighieri, 205
David, King, xxiv, 4, 7, 8, 14, 15, 17, 21, 25, 28, 29, 35, 41, 43, 47, 49, 51, 63, 72, 73, 76, 77, 78, 79, 80, 89, 107, 109, 110, 111, 113–18, 122–36, 144, 162, 164, 188, 192, 204, 208, 212, 214, 215, 221
David Psalms. *See* Psalms of David.
Davidic. *See* Psalms of David.
Davis, Ellen, 27, 28
Day of Atonement. *See* Yom Kippur.
De profundis, 16, 72, 168, 169, 200
depths, the, 34, 58, 98–100, 102, 128, 150, 168, 177, 188, 200, 213, 222
De Quincey, Thomas, 187
Desmarets, Henry, 163
Dickinson, Emily, 187
die sieben Bußpsalmen, 87
discipline, xiv, 12, 27, 57
Divine Office, the, 158
divine wrath. *See* wrath.
Dodd, C. H., 42, 44
Domine, ne in furore, 16
Domine, exaudi, 16
Donne, John, xiv, xxii, xxiii, xxiv, xxv, 104–21
Dowland, John, 162

Subject Index

Duffy, Eamon, 71, 81, 83, 84
Dvorak, Antonin, 161

Edden, Valerie, 74–76
editing (of the Psalter), 4, 5, 8
Elgar, Edward, 161
Eliot, T. S., 190
Enarrationes in Psalmos, xiii, 43–51, 55, 79
English Psalter, 70–73
Ephesians, Letter to the, 44, 157, 180
Erasmus, 212
Eucharist, 66, 83, 158, 174, 181, 183, 184, 195–96, 198
Eve, 51, 115
Exodus, Book of, 28, 112, 135, 187, 195, 214
Explanation of the Psalms. *See Expositio Psalmorum.*
Expositions on the Psalms. *See Enarrationes in Psalmos.*
Expositio Psalmorum, 55–59, 72
Ezekiel, Book and prophet, 111, 112

fear, xxiii, 34, 83, 87–102, 129, 174, 205, 211, 213, 222
Fisher, John, xxiv, 81–84
flesh, 25, 31, 42, 50, 111, 144, 215
forgiveness, xiii, 14, 21–24, 27–30, 32–36, 46, 47, 56, 59, 60, 65, 72, 77, 79, 83, 84, 92, 125, 130, 131, 132, 133, 134, 135, 141, 142, 143, 144, 147, 151, 163, 169, 175, 178, 181–85, 190, 193, 195, 197, 206, 209, 213, 214, 222
Forsyth, P. T., 223
Fourth Lateran Council, xiv, xxiii, 53, 61, 62, 63, 65–67, 69
Frances-Hoad, Cheryl, 163
Fraunce, Abraham, 113
Frederiksen, Paula, 46
Frei, Hans, 47
fury. *See* wrath of God.

Gabriel Rossetti, Dante, 193
Gabrieli, Andrea, 167
Gabrieli, Giovanni, 162, 167
Galatians, Letter to the, 214, 214
gattungen, 9

Genesis, Book of, 28, 147, 198, 207, 208
Genevan Psalter, 159, 160
Gesualdo, Carlo, 167
Gibbons, Orlando, 163
Gillingham, Susan, x, xviii, xxvi, 5, 8, 9, 23, 25, 81, 162, 163, 164
God's anger. *See* Wrath.
God's wrath. *See* Wrath.
Goethe, Johann Wolfgang von, 167
Goodall, Howard, 168
Goldingay, John, 4, 24, 26, 31, 33, 34
Gradual Psalm/s. *See* Psalms of Ascents.
Greenberg, Irvin, 51
Gregorian chant. *See* chant.
Gregory of Nyssa, 21
Greidanus, Sidney, 181, 182, 183
Grunenwald, Jacques, 169
Guebert, Arnold, 101
Gunkel, Hermann, 9–10, 20, 21, 23, 25, 27, 30, 32, 34

Haas, Robert, 167
Hallel Psalms, 8, 36
Handel, George Frideric, 167
happy. *See* blessing.
von Harnack, Adolf, 138, 139
Hays, Richard, 13, 35
heart, 20, 29–30, 31, 47, 51, 60, 61, 62, 63, 65, 77, 78, 82, 84, 91, 94–95, 99, 100, 102, 125, 126, 129, 130, 132, 133, 134, 139, 140, 142, 143, 147, 149, 151, 157, 160, 162, 175, 176, 177, 187, 188, 189, 193, 194, 195, 197, 198, 199, 200, 201, 202, 205, 206, 210, 211, 213, 221, 223
heaven, 49, 50, 64, 94, 97, 129, 132, 139, 150, 184, 187, 209, 210, 211, 216, 221
Hebrews, Letter to the, 26, 178
hell, 51, 93, 126, 132, 189, 216
Henry VIII, 81, 161
Herbert, George, 202, 205, 206, 209, 210, 214, 215
hermeneutics, xxvi, 54, 75, 76, 77, 78, 83, 84, 180
Hitchens, Christopher, 189
Hitchens, Peter, 189–90
Hobbs, Paul, 194–95

Holy Spirit, 15, 29, 30, 38, 5, 109, 110, 113, 119, 124, 126, 129, 149, 151, 178, 189, 194, 197, 209, 215, 221
Holy Week, 161, 165, 167
Hossfeld and Zenger, Frank-Lothar and Erich, 27, 28, 31, 32, 34, 35
Hovhaness, Alan, 169
Hull, Dame Eleanor, xiv, xvii, xxiv, 77–80, 115
Hull, John, 78
Hunnis, William, 159
hyssop, 7, 84, 134, 165, 210

imagery, xxiv, xxv, 27, 33, 34, 35, 43, 57, 73, 84, 93, 94, 97, 105, 108–19, 126, 158, 173, 176–77, 184, 187, 188–89, 195, 196, 200, 201, 209
indulgences, xiv, xxvi, 67, 83, 188
iniquity and iniquities, 14, 24, 26, 28, 29, 31, 33, 45, 92, 93, 94, 96, 126, 190, 209, 210, 213, 214,
inner canon, xxiii, 11, 18, 53, 66
interpretation. *See* hermeneutics.
Isaiah, Book and prophet, 29, 80, 179, 216

Jeremiah, Book and prophet, 111, 163, 184
Jerome , Saint, 51, 212
Jerusalem, 5, 6, 31, 33, 76, 77, 166, 209
Jesus, as prayer of psalms, xxvi, 43, 44, 51, 139, 140, 144, 174
Jesus Prayer, the, 197
Job, Book of, 47, 48, 111, 215
John, Gospel and Letters of, 46, 48, 95, 148, 178, 181, 196, 209, 211
John of Damascus, 115
John of Gaunt, 78
John the Baptist, 65, 210
Joseph, patriarch, 111
Jowett, Benjamin, 124
Judson, Tim, x, xvii, xxiv, 174
Justin I , 54, 55

Kilpatrick, William Kirk, 220, 221
King'oo, Clare Costley, xvii, xxi, 63, 75, 88, 105, 113, 114, 159, 177, 180
Kingship Psalms, xiii

Kodaly, 161
Korahites. *See* Psalms of Korah.
Kuczynski, Michael P. , 63, 72, 73
Kyrkby, Dame Marget (Margaret),70

Lady Bedford, 118
lament. *See* psalms of lament.
Lamentations, Book of, 26, 112, 179
Langland, William. *See* Piers Plowman.
Lassus, Orlandus, 162, 165, 167
latin chant. *See* chant.
Lawton, David , 71, 78–80
Lazarus, 91
Lent, 28, 61, 62, 64, 69, 158, 161, 164, 167, 178, 195, 198, 199, 200, 203, 204, 205, 207, 213, 216, 222
Lenten. *See* Lent.
Levison, John, 29
Levites. *See* Levitical.
Levitical, 5
Lhéritier, Jean, 165
Liszt, Franz, 161
literal sense. *See sensus literalis.*
liturgy and liturgical, xiii–xiv, xxi, xxii, xxiii, xxiv, 8, 11, 21, 28, 33, 41, 44, 53, 54, 59, 63–67, 71, 81, 137, 157, 158, 160–65, 168, 169, 173, 175, 212
Lombard, Peter, 62
Lord's Supper. *See* Eucharist.
Luke, Gospel of, 30, 91, 93, 95, 140, 148, 178, 191, 193, 199, 201, 223
Lund, Mary Ann, xvii, 106, 107
Luther, Martin, xiv, xvii, xxiii, xxiv, 14, 82–84, 87–102, 107, 138, 142, 148, 150, 159, 168, 174, 177, 188, 212
Lutheran, 151
LXX. *See* Septuagint.
Lydgate, John, 74

MacMillan, Sir James, xxv, 161, 168
Maidstone, Richard, xxiv, 74–77, 80
Malet, Sir John, 78
manuscripts, 7, 70, 74, 75, 77, 106, 158, 167
Mark, Gospel of, 174
Mary Magdalene, 192, 193
Martini, Johannes, 165

Subject Index

Marvell, Andrew, 209
Masoretic text, xix, xxvi, 3, 4, 7, 8
Mathilda of Tuscany, 64
Matthew, Gospel of, 24, 44, 92, 146, 149, 174, 180
Mattins, 158, 163, 164
Mawson, Michael, 143
Mendelssohn, 161, 167, 169
mercy and merciful, xxv, 29, 46, 49, 57, 59, 60, 65, 73, 79, 91, 99, 100, 115, 116, 125, 127, 128, 129–31, 132, 133, 145, 148, 149, 150, 165, 166, 169, 179, 188, 195, 197, 199, 214, 221, 222
metaphor. *See* imagery.
Micah, Book of, 151
Milton, John, 214
Miserere, the, xxi, xxv, 16, 79, 161, 165–68
mirror, 114, 196
Morden, Peter, x, xvii, xxiv, 123, 127, 131, 132, 134
Morrissey, Mary, 111, 112, 118
Moses, 28, 51, 111, 196, 211, 214
Mozart, Leopold, 167
Mozart, Wolfgang Amadeus, 162, 167

Nasuti, Harry, 10–14, 20, 33
Nathan, the prophet, 28, 29, 47, 76, 164, 221
Nathanael, 45, 46
Nehemiah, 27
nephesh, 22, 35
Niebuhr, Reinhold, 139
Ninety-Five Theses, xiv, 82, 87, 188
Norris, Kathleen, 220
Nyman, Michael, 168

Office of the Dead, xiv
Origen, 17, 51
original sin, 29, 98, 111, 126, 148–49
Owen, Stephen, 196
Oxford, xxiii, 70, 74, 210, 213

Palestrina, Giovanni, xiv
Parallelism, 6, 7, 12, 57, 105, 174, 215
paraphrases. *See* psalm paraphrases.
Pärt, Arvo, 168, 169

Paul, the apostle, 11–14, 35, 43, 44, 46, 48, 90, 87, 101, 107, 110, 117, 142, 179, 181, 214, 215, 221
Pauline Psalms, 14
penance and Penance, xiv, xxiii, xxiv, 17, 42, 47, 53, 56, 57, 59–64, 66, 67, 69, 72–73, 79, 82–84, 88, 165, 193
penitence, penitent and repentance, xiii, xxv, 15, 17, 20, 21, 23, 24, 27, 28, 35, 63, 73, 95, 96, 114, 118, 124, 125, 129–31, 135, 138, 141–53, 161, 163, 165, 169, 175, 178, 187–202, 220–23
Pergolesi, Giovanni Battista, 167
Peter, the apostle, 63, 116, 199, 211
Peter, Letters of, 178, 211
Peterson, Eugene, 6, 219
Piers Plowman, xiv
Pilgrim's Progress, 127
poems. *See* poetry.
poetry, xxv, 21, 23, 31, 36, 74–77, 104–19, 161, 173, 175, 187, 203–16
Pope Gregory, xiii, 191
Pope Innocent III, 66
Potter, George, 106–11, 114–19
prayerbook of the Bible, 137, 139, 142
preaching, xxv, xxvi, 104–21, 172–86
des Prez, Josquin, xiv, 164, 165
Pribbenow, Brad, 139, 142, 146
Primers, xiv, 71, 158
prosopopoeia and prosopological, xxiv, 43, 56, 105, 108, 113–15, 117, 118
prymers. *See* primers.
Psalm 1, xxi, 203
Psalm 2, xxi, 203
Psalm 3, 7
Psalm 6, xiii, xxi, 3, 10, 12, 16, 21–23, 24, 25, 27, 56, 57, 58, 75, 90–92, 102, 106, 106, 109, 127, 128, 129, 130, 163, 175, 175, 176, 178, 179, 180, 200, 201, 204, 205, 206, 221
Psalm 9, 7
Psalm 10, 7
Psalm 14, 142
Psalm 15, 142
Psalm 22, 22, 24, 44, 174
Psalm 23, 214

Subject Index

Psalm 25 xiii, 10, 142
Psalm 27, 4
Psalm 30, 165, 222
Psalm 31, 7, 81, 142
Psalm 32, xiii, xxi, 3, 10, 12, 13, 14, 16,
    23–25, 26, 27, 28, 45, 46, 57, 63,
    72, 73, 92–94, 102, 106, 107,
    109, 112, 114, 116, 126, 127,
    128, 131, 132, 134, 148, 142,
    163, 164, 173, 175, 176, 177,
    181, 182, 184, 189, 190, 193,
    201, 207, 221
Psalm 33, 7
Psalm 34, 7
Psalm 38, xiii, xxi, 3, 10, 12, 16, 25–27,
    28, 32, 42, 43, 47, 57, 94–95,
    106, 107, 129, 130, 143, 146–48,
    164, 177, 178, 180, 188, 200,
    210, 208, 214, 221
Psalm 39, 142, 150
Psalm 40, 142
Psalm 41, 7, 142
Psalm 42, 5
Psalm 44, 5, 97, 147
Psalm 45, 5
Psalm 46, 5
Psalm 47, 5
Psalm 48, 5
Psalm 49, 5
Psalm 50, 7, 162
Psalm 51, xiii, xiv, xvii, xxi, xxv, xxvi, 3,
    7, 10, 12, 15, 16, 17, 21, 27–30,
    47, 49, 51, 57, 65, 72, 73, 74, 75,
    76, 78, 88, 95–96, 102, 106, 114,
    115, 125, 131, 133, 134, 135,
    142, 148–49, 158, 161, 164, 165,
    168, 173, 176, 177 178, 188, 192,
    193, 198, 201, 221
Psalm 67, 201
Psalm 71, 4
Psalm 72, 7
Psalm 73, 7, 36
Psalm 74, 7, 146
Psalm 75, 7
Psalm 76, 7
Psalm 77, 7
Psalm 78, xiii, 7
Psalm 79, 7, 147
Psalm 80, 7, 214
Psalm 81, 7, 214
Psalm 82, 7, 214
Psalm 83, 7, 214
Psalm 84, 5, 214
Psalm 85, xiii, 5, 214
Psalm 86, 214
Psalm 87, 5, 214
Psalm 88, 5, 214
Psalm 89, 33
Psalm 90, 150
Psalm 91, 201
Psalm 95, 201
Psalm 97, 4
Psalm 102, xiii, xxi, 3, 10, 12, 16, 17,
    30–32, 50, 58, 96–98, 102, 133,
    134, 141, 143, 149–50, 162, 168,
    175, 176, 177, 179, 199, 201,
    210, 212, 222
Psalm 104, 48, 49
Psalm 113, 8
Psalm 114, 8
Psalm 115, 8
Psalm 116, 8
Psalm 117, 8
Psalm 118, 8, 211
Psalm 120, 6
Psalm 121, 6, 33, 201, 214
Psalm 122, 6, 33
Psalm 123, 6, 33, 201
Psalm 124, 6, 33
Psalm 125, 6, 33
Psalm 126, 6, 33
Psalm 127, 6, 7, 33
Psalm 128, 6, 33
Psalm 129, 6, 33
Psalm 130, xiii, xiv, xxi, 3, 6, 7, 10, 13,
    14, 16, 17, 32–34, 58, 72, 88,
    98–100, 102, 128, 150–51, 162,
    168, 169, 176, 179, 188, 200,
    201, 214
Psalm 131, 6, 33
Psalm 132, 6, 33
Psalm 133, 6, 33
Psalm 134, 6, 33
Psalm 139, 194
Psalm 143, xxi, 3, 4, 10, 13, 16, 17,
    34–36, 47, 48, 51, 79, 100–101,
    102, 125, 169, 177, 180, 194,
    201, 214, 222

Subject Index

Psalm 144, 4
Psalm 146, 8
Psalm 147, 8
Psalm 148, 8
Psalm 149, 8
Psalm 150, 8
psalm heading/s. *See* psalm title/s.
psalm/s of lament, xxvii, 9, 10, 18, 21, 25, 26, 27, 28, 31, 32, 33, 34, 91, 94, 97, 133, 139, 143, 163, 175, 176
Psalm/s of Asaph, 4, 7, 204
Psalm/s of Ascents, xiii, xiv, xxvii, 6, 7, 33, 64, 107, 168, 204, 213
Psalm/s of David, 4, 7–8, 17, 21, 25, 35, 78, 107, 111, 116, 164, 204, 215
Psalms of Korah, 4, 5, 6, 204
psalm paraphrases, 74
psalms title/s, 4–8, 10, 17, 17, 20, 21, 24, 25, 26, 27, 28, 29, 31, 33, 35, 43, 49, 76, 78–79, 164, 173, 203
public penance, 61–62
public confession. *See* public penance.
public interiorities, 79–80
purgatory, xxvi, 26, 67, 83, 84
Purcell, Henry, 161, 163, 164, 168, 169

quadriga, 77, 109

Ravenna, 55
Reger, Max, 163, 169
Regularis Concordia, 64
revelation, 148, 172, 173, 174, 175, 179, 189
Revelation, Book of, 15
Revised Common Lectionary, 174, 178
Rhatigan, Emma, xi, xvii, xxiii, 107, 108
righteous, the, 13, 14, 35, 80, 92, 93, 97, 101, 144, 145, 176, 177, 180, 181, 206
righteousness. *See* righteous.
Rizza, Margaret, 161
Rockstro, William Smyth, 167
Rogers, Carl, 219
Rolle, Richard, xiv, xxiv, 70–75, 77, 80
Romans, Book of, 11–14, 35, 36, 97, 148, 149, 175, 177, 179, 181
Rome, 12, 66
Rosh Hashanah, 163, 168, 169

Rubbra, 161
Rubens, Peter Paul, 192
Rutter, John, 169

Samuel, Books of, 15, 28, 35, 132, 221
satisfactio operis, 62, 63, 83
Satterthwaite, Howard, 190–91, 195, 200
Saul, King, 132, 221
Saunders, Maryanne, 192, 193
Savonarola, Girolamo, 165–66
Scarlatti, Allesandro, 161
Schnittke, Alfred, 161
Schumann, Robert, 161
Schütz, Heinrich, 162, 163, 164, 169
sensus literalis, 47, 76, 77, 87, 89, 109, 205, 206
Sentences, Peter Lombard's, 62
Septuagint, xix, xxvi, 3, 4, 7, 8, 12, 24, 26, 35, 47
seven, the number, 14–15, 56, 59
seven deadly sins, the, 15, 222
Shakespeare, William, 212
Shepherd of Hermas, 59–60
Sidney, Mary (see Sidneys)
Sidney, Philip (see Sidneys)
Sidneys, xiv, 104–5, 112, 113, 214
Silva de Almeida, Vinicius, 199–200
Simpson, Evelyn, 106–11, 114–19
sin, xiii, 12, 13, 14, 15, 17, 21, 23–24, 25, 26, 27, 28, 29, 30, 31, 32, 33, 34, 35, 36, 42, 43, 46, 47, 49, 56, 58, 59–67, 72, 73, 75, 76, 82–84, 91, 92–94, 95–96, 97, 98, 102, 110, 11, 114, 117, 124, 125–27, 128, 129, 130, 131, 132, 134, 138, 141–45, 148–49, 150, 151, 152, 153, 163, 173, 175, 176, 177, 179–85, 189–91, 192, 193, 195, 196, 197, 198, 199, 201, 206, 207, 208, 210, 214, 219–22
sinner/s, xxiv, 15, 27, 28, 29, 30, 32, 34, 36, 44, 5, 58, 60, 65, 67, 75–77, 79, 84, 88, 93, 94, 114, 116, 125–33, 135, 143, 148, 149, 190, 192
Snaith, Norman, xxiv
Solomon, 7, 48
Songs of Ascents. *See* Psalms of Ascents.
Song of Songs, 44, 47, 48, 49
Sons of Korah. *See* Korahites.

soteriology. *See* sin.
sparrow (and other birds from Psalm 102), 31, 97, 210, 211, 212, 216
spirit, 14, 29, 30, 35, 45, 51, 55, 92, 93, 109, 151, 159, 188, 193, 198, 199, 200, 209
spiritual and spirituality, 11, 27, 42, 64, 69, 70, 74, 107, 112, 123, 125, 127, 130, 131, 134, 157, 159, 161, 175, 180, 191, 211, 221, 222
spirituals, 137, 139
Spurgeon, Charles Haddon, xxiii, xxiv, xxv, 122–35
Stackhouse, Ian, xi, xvii, xxvi
steadfast love. *See chesed.*
Stephanus, Robertus, 111, 112
Sternhold and Hopkins, 104, 214
Stravinsky, Igor, 161, 164
Supercessionist, 43, 48
superscriptions. *See* psalm titles.

Taizé chant. *See* chant.
Tallis, Thomas, xiv
tariff penance, 61, 65
Tavener, John, 164
Taylor, Charles, 41
tears, 12, 16, 22, 23, 57, 59, 62, 65, 76–77, 82, 91, 128–29, 131, 132, 175, 177, 191, 199–200, 204, 205
Telemann, Georg Philipp, 163
Tertullian, 157
Tetzel, Johann, 188
thanksgiving, xiii, 9, 10, 23, 133, 140, 150, 174
Theodoret of Cyrus, 17
Theodoric, 54
Tomkins, Thomas, 162
totus Christus, xxiv, 43
transgression/s, 14, 24, 28, 31, 46, 49, 92, 93, 126, 132, 178, 190, 192, 206, 214
Treasury of David, 123–35
Tyndale, William, 212

Uccello, Paolo, 205
Uriah, 28, 192

de Valdes Lealor, Juan, 192
Van Nuffel, Jules, 163
Vaughan, Henry, 206, 210, 214
de Ventadorn, Bernard, 207, 208
Vicars Choral, 158
voice/s, xxiv, 25, 31, 34, 43, 44, 73, 77–81, 89, 113–19, 124, 128, 129, 130, 188, 206, 209, 210, 211, 213,
Vulgate, xxvi, 3, 12, 63, 71, 75, 76, 77, 212

Wallace, Howard Neil, 173, 174, 175, 178
Waltke, Bruce, 21, 26, 27, 35, 61
Wansbrough, Henry, 208
wash, 7, 58, 65, 82, 95, 96, 115, 168, 176, 196, 197, 209, 210
weeping. *See* tears.
Wellhausen, Julius, 124
Wendelburg, Norma, 163
Wesley, Samuel Sebastian, 164, 168
De Wette, W. M. L., 9
van der Weyden, Rogier, 189
Whiting, Mark J., xi, xiii, xiv, xxi, 184, 220
wicked 25, 57, 58, 73, 183, 198, 221
Wilken, Robert, 41, 46
Williams, Reggie L., 139
Wilson, Gerald, 4, 5, 8, 9
Witigis, 54, 55
Wordsworth, William, 206
wrath (of God), 11–14, 22, 23, 25, 32, 42, 43, 57, 90–92, 94, 95, 96, 97, 101, 102, 126, 127, 129, 130, 132, 163, 173, 174, 178, 179, 180, 195, 204, 208, 221, 222
Wright, Stephen I., xi, xvii, xxv
Wright, Tom, 220

Yahweh Malak Psalms, 8
Yom Kippur, 23, 163, 165, 168

Zion, 5, 9, 27, 30, 31, 32, 33, 76, 133, 179, 210
Zwingli, Huldrych, 159

www.ingramcontent.com/pod-product-compliance
Lightning Source LLC
Chambersburg PA
CBHW050846230426
43667CB00012B/2173

"Without discounting the scholarly challenges to treating the Penitential Psalms as a single literary unit, the authors of this book make a persuasive case for the coherence of this 'Seven Psalm' collection and, even more so, for their fitting use within the liturgical and devotional life of the church. *The Penitential Psalms* represents an important contribution to psalms scholarship as well as an inspiring resource for preachers, worship leaders, and lay persons who take seriously the holy call to confess one's sins and, after such confession, to receive the equally holy gift of forgiveness."

—**W. DAVID O. TAYLOR**, Associate Professor of
Theology and Culture, Fuller Theological Seminary

"Professor Whiting describes himself as a 'distracted materials scientist,' which makes this volume all the more impressive. Mark's commitment to the Psalms is deeply inspiring, as is his editing of such a wide array of chapters. This volume is an authoritative guide to the content and histories of the Penitential Psalms, serving both the church and the academy. Its varied approaches and meticulous scholarship deserve to be read widely and often."

—**DANIEL JOHNSON**, Programme Leader for Theology,
Music, and Worship Studies, London School of Theology

"Mark J. Whiting has gathered an array of authors to produce a fine example of reception history. One can debate the legitimacy of The Seven as a formal group—indeed, one can disagree with some of the book's content—but a volume which encourages us to take seriously the Psalms and sin, confession, forgiveness, and reconciliation should be appreciated."

—**S. D. ELLISON**, Director of Training, Irish
Baptist College, Moira, Northern Ireland

"This thoughtfully curated volume restores the Penitential Psalms to their rightful place in literary, devotional, and cultural history. Spanning centuries, from Augustine and Cassiodorus to Spurgeon and Bonhoeffer, the essays gathered here explore the reception of these seven psalms in theology, liturgy, music, and poetry. A rich and multifaceted resource for preachers, scholars, artists, and all readers drawn to the enduring poetics and spiritual resonance of penitence."

—**Clare Costley King'oo**, Associate Professor, Department of English, University of Connecticut